# Tragedy and Triumph

# Tragedy and Triumph

## Early Testimonies of Jewish Survivors of World War II

Compiled and Translated
by
Freda Hodge

Tragedy and Triumph: Early Testimonies of Jewish Survivors of World War II
Compiled and translated by Freda Hodge

© Copyright 2018
All rights reserved. Apart from any uses permitted by Australia's Copyright Act 1968, no part of this book may be reproduced by any process without prior written permission from the copyright owners. Inquiries should be directed to the publisher.

Monash University Publishing
Matheson Library and Information Services Building
40 Exhibition Walk
Monash University
Clayton, Victoria 3800, Australia
www.publishing.monash.edu

Monash University Publishing brings to the world publications which advance the best traditions of humane and enlightened thought.

Monash University Publishing titles pass through a rigorous process of independent peer review.

Second printing

ISBN: 9781925523676 (paperback)
ISBN: 9781925523980 (pdf)
ISBN: 9781925523997 (epub)

www.publishing.monash.edu/books/tt-9781925523676.html

Series: History

Design: Les Thomas

Cover image: Joseph Schleifstein, a four-year-old survivor of Buchenwald, sits on the running board of an UNRRA truck soon after the liberation of the camp. 1945. United States Holocaust Memorial Museum, Photograph 90250.

Further information about Joseph Schleifstein can be found in the Addendum.

A catalogue record for this book is available from the National Library of Australia

Printed in Australia by Griffin Press an Accredited ISO AS/NZS 14001:2004 Environmental Management System printer.

The paper this book is printed on is certified against the Forest Stewardship Council ® Standards. Griffin Press holds FSC chain of custody certification SGS-COC-005088. FSC promotes environmentally responsible, socially beneficial and economically viable management of the world's forests.

# CONTENTS

Acknowledgements . . . . . . . . . . . . . . . . . . . . . . . . . . . . . . . . . . . . . . . . . ix

Foreword . . . . . . . . . . . . . . . . . . . . . . . . . . . . . . . . . . . . . . . . . . . . . . . . .xi
    *Konrad Kwiet*

Introduction: The Early Testimonies of *She'erit Hapletah*
in the Aftermath of World War II . . . . . . . . . . . . . . . . . . . . . . . . . . . 1
    *Freda Hodge*

Why Do We Need Historical Commissions? . . . . . . . . . . . . . . . . . . . . 16
    *M.Y. Feigenbaum*

**PART ONE** . . . . . . . . . . . . . . . . . . . . . . . . . . . . . . . . . . . . . . . . . . . 19

1   Mielice Labour Camp . . . . . . . . . . . . . . . . . . . . . . . . . . . . . . . . . 21
    *Josef Kas*

2   Life and Death of the Jews in Dubno . . . . . . . . . . . . . . . . . . . . . 30
    *Moishe Weisberg*

3   The Transport from the Death Camp Balkenheim . . . . . . . . . . . . . 41
    *Eyewitness Account by Maurice Kraus*

4   The Last Road for Twelve Hundred Bialystok Children . . . . . . . . . 44
    *Shprung-Levkowitz*

5   In Radun . . . . . . . . . . . . . . . . . . . . . . . . . . . . . . . . . . . . . . . . . . 50
    *Leib Levine*

6   A Chapter about Siedlice . . . . . . . . . . . . . . . . . . . . . . . . . . . . . . 58
    *Getzl Weisberg*

7   The Slaughter at the Edge of the Sea . . . . . . . . . . . . . . . . . . . . . . 63
    *Miriam Zweig*

8   In the Braslav Region . . . . . . . . . . . . . . . . . . . . . . . . . . . . . . . . 67
    *Moshe Treister*

| 9 | Sobibor | 76 |
|---|---|---|
| | *Yekheskel (Chaskiel) Menche* | |
| 10 | Through Ghettos and Concentration Camps: Nemencine, Ozmiana, Czeczmer, Kovno, Ponevezh and Eastern Prussia | 81 |
| | *Leah Rudovshevski* | |
| 11 | Treblinka | 88 |
| | *H. Shperling* | |
| 12 | In the White Russian Forests | 100 |
| | *Moshe Meyerson* | |
| 13 | In Camp Kaldycheva | 111 |
| | *Yudel Samsonovitz* | |
| 14 | The Last Resistance Fighters in Bialystok Ghetto | 116 |
| | *Rabbi A. Burstin* | |
| 15 | Experiences of a Jewish Aryan | 119 |
| | *Anna Holtzman* | |
| 16 | The Large Factories in Kovno Ghetto | 124 |
| | *Moshe Segalson* | |
| 17 | Volozhin | 132 |
| | *Yosef Schwartzberg* | |
| 18 | Myadel and Surroundings | 137 |
| | *Henia Menkin* | |
| 19 | In a Hungarian Work Battalion | 143 |
| | *Moshe Dov Taub* | |
| 20 | Death of a Runner | 148 |
| | *Cessia Shilling* | |
| 21 | In Auschwitz with Two Small Children | 151 |
| | *Esther Weiss* | |
| 22 | Memories of the Ghetto of Stanislavov | 166 |
| | *Lusia Gerber* | |

23  The Fortress of Death (in the Ninth Fort of Kovno) ............ 170
    *Michal Gelbtrunk*

24  Resistance Movement in the Ghetto of Kovno ................ 174
    *Rochie Ben Eliezer*

**Part Two** ............................................... 183

The Children's Narratives in *Fun Letzten Khurben* ............... 185

1  My Experiences during the War ......................... 189
   *Josef Shuster*

2  My Experiences during the War ......................... 193
   *Ella Griliches*

3  My Experiences during the War ......................... 195
   *Fania Olitzki*

4  My Experiences during the War ......................... 199
   *Arieh Milch*

5  My Experiences during the War ......................... 202
   *Yaakov Levin*

6  My Experiences during the War ......................... 209
   *Genia Shurtz*

Addendum: Select Information Pertaining to the Testimonies ....... 216

Bibliography ............................................... 220

Jews perished in extermination camps, execution sites, ghettos, slave labour camps, and on the death marches. The testimony of those who survived constitutes the main record of what was done to Jews during those years. The murderers also kept records, often copious ones. But the victims, the six million who were done to death, could leave no record. A few fragments of diaries, letters and scribbled messages do survive. But in the main, others must bear witness to what was done to the millions who could never tell their own story.

Martin Gilbert, Preface, *The Holocaust: The Jewish Tragedy*, (London: HarperCollins Publishers, 1986, p. 18)

# ACKNOWLEDGEMENTS

I am deeply grateful to the Jewish Holocaust Centre, Melbourne, for affording me the opportunity to have my book published. In particular, my heartfelt thanks go to the Director of the Centre, Warren Fineberg, and to Dr Michael Cohen for the encouragement and unwavering support which they offered to me, during the whole period from my initial proposal to the actual publication of the book. Special thanks are due to Dr Michael Cohen for his meticulous proofreading of *Tragedy and Triumph*.

My sincere thanks go to the Kadimah Jewish Cultural Centre and National Library in Melbourne for giving me access to the 10 volumes of the journal *Fun Letzten Khurben* whenever I had need of them.

To my husband Norman who was always willing to discuss my ideas and to make suggestions, I wish to express my great appreciation.

I thank those who gave of their time when I turned to them for help with an obscure word or phrase in the translations from Yiddish to English, thus ensuring the accuracy of the translated material.

# FOREWORD

It took half a century to challenge the myth of the postwar silence of Holocaust survivors. Since then numerous publications and projects have retrieved the early voices. Freda Hodge's collection of testimonies underlines this trend. Carefully selected and painstakingly translated, she has edited compelling survivor accounts, published between 1946 and 1948 in the Yiddish journal *Fun Letzten Khurben* ('From the Last Destruction') in postwar Germany. It is the first edition of its kind. The survivors were Yiddish-speaking refugees from Eastern Europe, classified as 'Displaced Persons' (DPs). They were waiting in DP camps in the American Zone of occupation for the arrival of travel documents and visas in order to continue their long journey to freedom. The title of the edition points to the dual nature of modern Jewish experience. 'Tragedy' refers to *Khurben*, the Yiddish term common at the time for the destruction of European Jewry. Others spoke of the Jewish Catastrophe, a term used since the beginning of the mass murder. The term Holocaust entered the discourse in the 1950s, in the English-speaking world, followed by the terms Shoah and genocide. Today there is a consensus that the annihilation of Jews during World War II was the ultimate act of genocide, unprecedented in history. 'Triumph' relates to the survival of the *She'erit Hapletah*, the remnants of European Jewry. With few exceptions, they succeeded in rebuilding their shattered lives. Survivor historians in Poland were, after liberation, at pains to restore the continuity of Jewish historiography, initiating Holocaust documentation, research and writings. By 1947 the number of Holocaust books published amounted to 38.

Let me briefly relate a few historical vignettes to shed light on the emergence and significance of early survivor accounts.

In August 1944 a handful of survivors established a Jewish Historical Commission in the liberated Polish city of Lublin – on the doorsteps of the deserted Majdanek death camp. Its first and most important task was to collect eyewitness accounts and other material, documenting the Jewish catastrophe which was still unfolding. In summer 1944 the 'Final Solution' dictated the mass murder of Hungarian Jews in the gas chambers of Auschwitz Birkenau. What started in Lublin continued in Lodz, Warsaw and other cities. From August 1944 to December 1945 some 1,500 testimonies were collected. By the end of 1947 the number had risen to 7,300. A country-wide network of Historical Commissions and branches, a bunch of officials and volunteers, among them the *Zammlers*, the collectors, created archival depositories preserving survivor accounts, German and Polish documents, Jewish records, letters and diaries, books and papers, pictures and photographs, songs and sayings, religious objects and other items. Relying on these sources, Jewish historians began to document and to reconstruct the history of the Holocaust, focusing on the annihilation of Polish Jewry. Having survived in ghettos and camps, or in hiding on the 'Aryan' side, they followed the patterns of their predecessors who had once established a flourishing Jewish historiography in Eastern Europe and fulfilled the ancient obligation of *Zakor* (Remember) – '*To keep the memory alive!*'.

Efforts to collect records documenting the German persecution of the Jews were already made during the Holocaust. German Jews, exiled in England, opened the Wiener Library in London in the prewar years. Material assembled in London on the Nazi occupation of the Netherlands was sent after the war to Holland to be housed in the state-funded Rijksinstituut voor Oorlogsdocumentatie, known as NIOD (The Netherlands Institute of War Documentation). In April 1943 Isaac Schneerson founded the Centre de Documentation Juive Comtemporaine in the city of Grenoble in occupied France. Extensive record collections filled the archives of the Jewish Agency or the JOINT, the American Jewish Joint Distribution Committee. Secret archives were set up in Bialystok, Kovno, Vilnius, Lodz and other Polish ghettos. Emanuel Ringelblum's underground Archive '*Oneg Shabbat*' (Joy of Shabbat) in the ghetto of Warsaw assembled the largest record collection. Only fragments survived the war, hidden in containers, buried and unearthed in the rubble of Warsaw.

After liberation, survivor historians such as Philip Friedman and Josef Kermisz, Rachel Auerbach and Leib Koniuchowski, Yisrael Kaplan and Nachman Blumenthal were the driving forces in developing a new distinct historiographical genre, termed at the time *khurben forshung* (destruction research, a Yiddish term) and *Vernichtungswissenschaft* (annihilation science, a German term). Philip Friedman introduced these terms to indicate that the persecution and murder of the Jews was a specific German crime. Indeed, the perpetrators never used the term 'murder'. They spoke of *Vernichtung*, as Dan Michman puts it, turning the Jews into '*nichts*', nothing. Laura Jockusch defines the *khurbn forshung* as a Jewish 'Historiography in Transit' based on the early voices of survivors and the first historical studies. The survivor historians laid the foundation for Holocaust scholarship. They speedily brought to an end their time 'in transit'. Many left Poland in the late 1940s and continued their work in the newly established state of Israel or in the United States. Arrangements were made to transfer archival material to other documentation and research centres abroad – to the YIVO Institute in New York and to Yad Vashem in Jerusalem. Those who stayed in Poland were forced to teach, research and publish under the strict control of a Stalinist state system. The Central Jewish Historical Commission in Warsaw ceased to exist. A new, smaller Jewish Historical Institute was permitted to preserve archival holdings and to conduct research. It still exists today.

Collecting survivor accounts and other documents served many purposes. First and foremost, they were a response to Nazi persecution, culminating in the 'Final Solution'. They offered a window into the destruction of Jewish life and recorded the experiences of suffering and survival. At the same time they were testament to the fact that the German murderers and their collaborators had not entirely achieved their final aims: to annihilate all Jews, to eradicate the 'Jewish spirit', to erase the evidence of the heinous crimes committed. Testimonies created 'substitute gravestones' (Laura Jockusch) for the murdered Jews who were denied a place in a Jewish cemetery, as well as a 'lighthouse' providing guidance for remembrance. Names and places contained in the early eyewitness accounts assisted the search for missing relatives and friends – a search which continues to this very day. Years later descendants of survivors relied on this data when tracing their family history. Apart from providing the groundwork for historical research, recollections later supported claims for compensation and restitution. Statements and affidavits of survivors, made in police investigations and war crimes trials, played a vital role in tracing perpetrators and bringing them to justice. The compilation of documents was also crucial to prevent denial or distortion of the Jewish tragedy. Jewish historians were convinced that the writing of the Holocaust should not be left in the hands of non-Jews alone. They shared the view that neither the Allies nor others, let alone Germans, could comprehend and explore the true nature of the Jewish catastrophe. Their documents, in particular perpetrators' records, did not permit the re-construction of Jewish history and reveal the Jewish dimension of the Holocaust.

There was yet another factor for the creation of archival depositories. Early survivor accounts could not capture post-Holocaust life in a way that recollections of later years could. However, many testimonies display at the very end, often in the last lines, a Zionist perspective, the desire of the stateless and 'Displaced Persons' to turn their backs on war-torn Europe and to rebuild their lives in the new Jewish state of Israel. Control of a people's own records has also been an expression of state sovereignty. The transfer to Israel of archival material gathered by Jews ensured ongoing access by Jews to their own history.

What happened in Poland also occurred in other countries. Wherever survivors were liberated and registered – in DP camps or refugee houses, in Jewish communities or relief organisations – they were asked to tell their stories, to sign protocols or fill in questionnaires. Altogether, almost 30,000 testimonies were recorded in the immediate postwar period – not only in Polish cities but also in Bucharest and Budapest, Bratislava and Prague, Paris and Amsterdam, London and Jerusalem and, most notably, in Munich.

Munich – a stronghold of National Socialism – became a hub of the She'erit Hapletah. Before the spring of 1945 the Allied forces conquered and divided Germany into four zones of occupation, they encountered a flood of almost 10 million displaced people, among them at least 80 000 Jews [available data varies considerably as it was almost impossible to register a constantly moving population. This number refers only to those who had survived the concentration and annihalation camps.] They had been liberated from overcrowded concentration camps, on roads and at railway tracks or at other sites marking the end of their death marches. With the help of members of the Jewish Brigade and Bricha [a clandestine organisation established by former Jewish partisans and soldiers from the Jewish Brigade to help Eastern European Jews to enter the Occupied zones and eventually to reach Palestine] the numbers of Jewish survivors in the DP camps eventually reached about 300 000. Jews in the Yishuv [the Jewish population in British Mandated Palestine] aided illegal Jewish refugees to leave Europe and to be smuggled into Palestine illegally.

Survivors in Munich quickly established a Central Committee of Liberated Jews in Bavaria to deal with the problems of Jewish survivors in the DP camps. The Central Committee, setting up 50 branches, represented all Jewish DPs in the US Zone. On 1 December 1945 the Central Historical Commission was formed, headed by Yisrael Kaplan, a Lithuanian survivor of the Kovno ghetto, and Moshe Joseph Feigenbaum, a survivor from the Polish town of Biala Podlaska. A manifesto was dispatched urging survivors to collect documents and to write and submit their stories of survival. Six months later, in August 1946, a historical periodical was launched entitled *Fun Letzten Khurben* ('From the Last Destruction'). The subtitle explained its mission: *A Periodical for the History of Jewish Life during the Nazi Regime.*

Kaplan and Feigenbaum served as editors assisted by Philip Friedman who had taken up the headship of the Education and Culture Department of the JOINT operating in Bavaria. At that time the number of the She'erit Hapletah was constantly rising as tens of thousands of 'new arrivals' sought temporary refuge in Germany. They had escaped the anti-Semitic campaigns and pogroms unleashed in Eastern Europe, altogether some 250,000. The DP camps in Bavaria attracted the largest number – around 170,000.

After overcoming some barriers – shortage of paper, printing problems and internal disputes – the journal *Fun Letztn Khurben* attained a circulation of 12,000 copies. Sold for 4 deutschmarks, it was sent to all DP camps in the US Zone as well as to Jewish communities and organisations both in Germany and abroad. It had to compete with other products of a booming survivor press which printed more than 100 periodicals in Yiddish and Hebrew, in Polish and German. Many DP camps had their own newspapers which contained hundreds of articles and reports on the Holocaust. *Landsmanschaftn*, representing survivors from the same city or geographic region, developed their own network of communication. The same applied to other Jewish groups and organisations. Last but not least, the publication of survivor memoirs commenced.

The activities of the Munich Jewish Historical Commission bore fruit. When it closed its doors at the end of 1948, 10 volumes of *Fun Letsten Khurben* had been distributed, covering more than 1,000 pages. The archival depositories kept a treasure trove of material (Ada Schein): 2,500 testimonies, 28,000 German documents, 1,081 photographs, 1,074 anti-Semitic books, 284 items of ghetto and camp folklore, 62 artefacts. As the survivor historians saw no future in Germany, the collections were placed in storage and later transferred to Yad Vashem. By then the early voices had already fallen silent. They had come against an impenetrable wall of indifference erected by postwar societies. In 1961 the Eichmann trial in Jerusalem caused international headlines. Survivor voices resurfaced when testifying in court to the horrors of the Holocaust. Several years later, as part of the explosion of Holocaust history and memory, a new massive wave of personal testimonies emerged.

The eyewitness accounts, translated by Freda Hodge, represent only a tiny fraction of the huge, largely unexplored, dispersed and fragmented body of early testimonies. Collected in German DP camps and published between 1946 and 1948, they were part of the second wave of survivor accounts. The first wave started in August 1944 and lasted until spring of

1945. The so-called *Bucharest Testimonies* serve as an example. In the spring of 1945 over 1,000 survivors arrived in the Romanian capital, representing the mosaic of nationalities within the She'erit Hapletah. They came from The Netherlands and Norway, France and Germany, Czechoslovakia and Hungary, Poland and Lithuania, Latvia and the Soviet Union. Accommodated in a 'refugee house', they were asked to tell their story of survival – in their mother tongue. The 'protocols' were typed and signed, often translated into English or other languages. Only copies of copies have been traced. Efforts to find the originals have been in vain.

Freda Hodge's collection mirrors *Fun Letzten Khurben*'s focus on the destruction of Jewish family ties and communities, located in Yiddish centres of the 'Blood Lands' of Poland, Lithuania and Belarus. Written by men, women and children, they reflect episodes and experiences of deportation and ghettoisation, forced labour camps and death camps, death marches and liberation. There is no mention of the Warsaw ghetto uprising – the most significant act of Jewish resistance and heroism – nor any reference to the underground activities of Jewish youth organisations. No voices are recorded criticising the Jewish Councils. Emphasis is placed on smaller ghetto rebellions and Jewish partisans fighting in forests. The centrality of Yiddish-speaking Jews excluded the incorporation of eyewitness accounts from Jews persecuted in Western Europe or other occupied territories. Only two testimonies from a German and Hungarian survivor are included. Finally, there was no place in the periodical for recollections of Jews who on the eve of the Holocaust had been deported by the Soviets in Eastern Europe to remote settlements or forced labour camps in Inner Asia. Many of them arrived after the war in Germany as 'Displaced Persons'. Labelled at the time often as 'Asiatic' Jews, they formed the largest group among the Yiddish-speaking DP population. Research on the fate of this distinct survivor group has recently commenced.

Despite these limitations, the selected testimonies share the features of other early survivor accounts. They graphically reveal the brutalities, barbarism and extreme terror survivors encountered. In their immediacy and rawness, they often show their authors' aggression and anguish at their recent suffering and loss. They are also testament to courage and endurance, resilience and resistance. The eyewitness accounts, collected in the immediate postwar period, constitute, as Feliks Tych points out, the most important body of Jewish documents pertaining to the history of the Holocaust, at a time when memory was still fresh. These features make the early voices profoundly different – and historically more significant – than

# Foreword

later recollections gathered in 'oral history' programs or the monumental Spielberg audio-visual project. Today more than 100,000 testimonies have been collected, dispersed throughout numerous archival depositories. With the passage of time there will be no living witness of the Holocaust left. Here, Freda Hodge presents 30 voices of Yiddish-speaking survivors, retrieved from the largely unexplored depths of Holocaust history.

Konrad Kwiet<br>
Emeritus Professor<br>
Resident Historian at the Sydney<br>
Jewish Museum

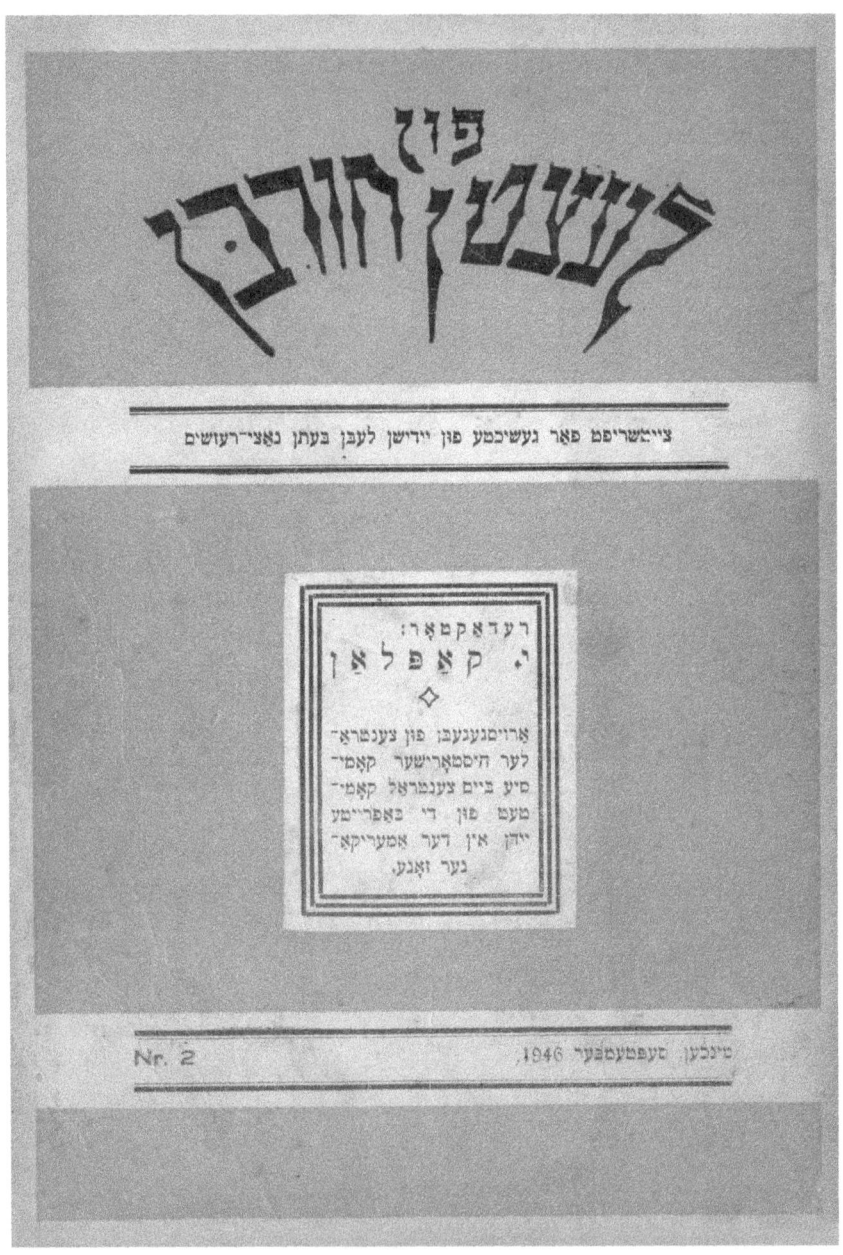

Front cover of the journal *Fun Letzten Khurben*, in which the survivor testimonies appear written in Yiddish

# INTRODUCTION

## The Early Testimonies of *She'erit Hapletah* in the Aftermath of World War II

### Freda Hodge

I have selected and translated these captivating and, very often, harrowing stories of survival because each one is a reflection of the indomitable courage and endurance of the Jewish people during a period of their unparalleled suffering at the hands of the Nazis, together with their collaborators, during the German occupation of 21 European countries in World War II. These eyewitness testimonies, which were originally published in Yiddish, have lain in obscurity for too long and cry out to be read and remembered and to find their place in the history of the Holocaust. It is our responsibility to pay homage to survivors who were courageous enough to give their testimonies to the world so soon after having survived Nazi atrocities. These testimonies, together with the others published in the same journal, *Fun Letzten Khurben*, stand as a memorial to the living and the dead, and will always serve to remind us of the role played by ordinary people in the nightmare of World War II. In his report about the first conference of the Historical Commission in Munich, Moshe Feigenbaum, Chairman of the Organisation of Liberated Jews in Bavaria, stressed the importance of recording the tragedy of the Holocaust, putting it above every other concern: 'The generation of the catastrophe is no longer alive, and we survived only by a miracle; we are the witnesses of the tragedy ... Therefore we must not refuse to document it ... While creating the documents we must not be afraid that this will reopen wounds in many people. The duty to document everything is greater than individual sorrow.'[1]

The early testimonies are characterised by their immediacy, the detailed nature of their narratives and their matter-of-fact, even detached tone. The fresh memories provide a more reliable perspective of what occurred

---

1   The conference took place over a two-day period in Munich from 11–12 May 1947.

and for the historian they are a mine of information. Later testimonies do not duplicate these characteristics. They are affected by the the temporal distance from the actual experiences and the changeable nature of recall. Confusion about what the survivors have personally experienced and what they have absorbed over a period of time from the media and from other testimonies can influence the veracity of the testimony. Sometimes there is an obvious desire on the speaker's part to present themself in a favourable light or even to shape the discourse with an element of self-aggrandisement. This can and does affect the accuracy of the testimony.

The testimonies were originally written in Yiddish, the *lingua-franca* of the majority of the Holocaust survivors. This, no doubt, made the testimonies inaccessible to large numbers of historians and researchers who did not know Yiddish or were not aware of the testimonies as a significant source of historical information. There exists a vast corpus of work about the Holocaust and World War II in general, but the individual tales of survival in the face of impossible odds tell us far more than just the facts of what took place. They demonstrate the spirit that enabled people not only to survive but to rebuild their lives after liberation. The Jewish survivors felt the need and the moral responsibility to document their experiences during the Holocaust, both as evidence against the perpetrators, and to record this agonising period in Jewish history for future generations. Their testimonies stand as a memorial to the murdered six million Jewish victims of Nazi hatred.

The Allied forces in the West, under the command of General Dwight D. Eisenhower, defeated the Nazi regime in the spring of 1945, the official conclusion to the war being VE Day, 8 May 1945. The Allied forces liberated different areas in Germany at different times, as they came from four directions: the Soviets from the East, the Americans from the West, the British from the North West, and the French from the South West. When they arrived at the Nazi concentration and extermination camps they were completely stunned by the unspeakable scenes which greeted them. The troops, in most cases, were ignorant of the true nature of the Holocaust and the extent of its bestiality. They were also unaware that, not only the Germans engaged in violent actions against the Jews, but that they were aided and abetted by Ukranians, Lithuanians, Latvians, Hungarians and Poles in addition to others. The liberators saw thousand of bodies piled one on top of another, discarded as if they were refuse, while the victims who were still alive wandered aimlessly in their striped uniforms or stared unbelievingly at their saviours. The stench in the camps assailed the soldiers like a poisonous miasma. When General Eisenhower entered Dachau, he issued the order to his troops: 'Get it all on record now – get the films, get the witnesses – because somewhere down the track of history, some bastard will get up and say "This never happened"'.[2]

Liberation would bring temporary relief for the survivors, but soon enough the stark reality of their position made the future look bleak. The anguish of facing an uncertain future, without family, without a home, without a country, was perhaps made bearable by the spirit inherent in their narratives as they looked to the future. The Allied forces had to face the enormous task of caring for the almost 10 million Displaced Persons of different nationalities who had been uprooted by the war.[3] The number of Jewish survivors was an estimated 300,000, most of whom were deemed to be stateless.[4] As Michael Brenner notes, 'The Jewish survivors of the Holocaust were in reality stateless people, desperate to begin a new life, hopefully, with family.'[5] For them Europe, particularly Poland, was a graveyard where all that had been dear to them, their families, their homes and possessions, and their culture of many hundreds of years, had been consumed by the Nazi hell. Even though Poland was the country of origin of most of the survivors, they refused to be repatriated to a land where, even after the Holocaust, they were not welcome. When some made an effort to return to Poland in order to search for family, they were met by anti-Semitism, which culminated in many pogroms and other acts of violence. For many Jewish survivors, the murder of 47 Jews in Kielce in July 1946 was seen as the final act of horror in a country which had been home to most of them. The majority of the Jewish survivors came to believe that the future of the Jewish people lay outside of Europe; the further away the better. They would have to find new directions in an unknown future. Their lives which had been for centuries Euro-centric had now to be focused elsewhere, hopefully on a Jewish homeland in Eretz Israel. The survivors

---

[2] See www.teejaw.com/eisenhowers-prediction-some-bastard-will-say-this-never-happened.

[3] A.J. Patt and M. Berkowitz, *We Are Here: New Approaches to Displaced Persons in Post-War Germany*. Detroit: Wayne State University Press, 2010.

[4] Margarete L. Myers, 'Jewish Displaced Persons Reconstructing Individual and Community in the US Zone of Occupied Germany'. *Leo Baeck Institute Year Book* 42:1, 1997, 304. However, as Myers notes, 'there is often some disparity between the figures quoted by historians. The numbers constantly fluctuated as the survivor population frequently moved from one camp to another or wandered from place to place searching for family members'.

[5] Michael Brenner, *After the Holocaust*. Princeton: Princeton University Press, 1999.

called themselves collectively 'She'erit Hapletah', a biblical term meaning the 'Surviving Remnant'.[6]

After the war, Germany was divided into zones of occupation, the American Zone containing the largest number of Displaced Persons and DP camps. Five-hundred DP camps were established in the American and British zones.[7] The Americans were at first determined to repatriate as many refugees as possible, regardless of their experiences during the war and the unwillingness of Jewish survivors to return to their country of origin. They refused to recognise the Jews as a separate ethnic group which had been the victim of discrimination based purely upon their ethnic origin. Ironically, General George Patton, a virulent anti-Semite, was placed in command of the American Zone, where the majority of the 'She'erit Hapletah' were. Among the many derogatory comments made by Patton about the Jewish survivors, his diary entry for 17 September 1945 reads: 'we entered the synagogue, which was packed with the greatest stinking bunch of humanity I have ever seen. When we got about halfway up, the head Rabbi … was dressed in a fur hat similar to that worn by Henry VIII of England and in a surplice heavily embroidered and very filthy … The smell was so terrible that I almost fainted'. Referring to Earl Harrison, Dean of the Pennsylvania School of Law, who had been appointed by President Truman to report on conditions in the DP camps and the treatment of the Jews by the American troops, Patton declared: 'Harrison and his ilk believe that the Displaced Person is a human being, which he is not, and this applies particularly to the Jews, who are lower than animals'.[8]

The general was soon removed from his command by Eisenhower for trivialising the US policy of de-Nazification and for his scandalous statements about the Jews, whom he regarded as vermin. In the DP camps Jews frequently found themselves together with former SS guards and kapos [Concentration camp prisoners selected by the Gestapo to supervise fellow inmates in return for privileges. Their treatment of the other prisoners was very often extremely brutal], even SS men who masqueraded as former prisoners in order to escape justice. Poles, Lithuanians and Ukrainians continued to openly treat the Jews with great hostility. A number of camps were surrounded by barbed wire and were guarded by the military. For the Jews,

---

6   Ezra 9:14; 1 Chronicles 4:43.
7   A. Grossman, *Jews, Germans and Allies: Close Encounters in Occupied Germany*. Princeton: Princeton University Press, 2007, p. 133.
8   'General George S. Patton on the Jews & Conquering Bolshevism' (sic), www.churchoftrueisrael.com/identity/patton.html (accessed 5 February 2017).

this was reminiscent of the concentration camps, an unwelcome reminder of what they had been forced to endure. While Jewish DPs attended a Sabbath service in the DP camp of Hohne-Belsen, Polish DPs demolished the newly created Jewish prayer house, destroyed the Torah Scrolls and fired shots at the Rabbi.[9]

Conditions in the DP camps were intolerable in many other respects as well. There was overcrowding and shortages of food, clothing and medical supplies. The Jewish DPs sometimes encountered violence from non-Jewish camp inmates and, in addition, they had to cope with the inherent anti-Semitism among many of the American soldiers who had grown up in the 'WASP' climate of the United States during the interwar years.[10] American troops were primarily young men of 18–25 years of age, who found the ragged and fractious Jewish DPs strange and even repulsive. The Germans seemed to them to be civilised and polite by comparison with the loud and frequently uncooperative Jewish survivors.

For some months organisations such as the United Nations Relief and Rehabilitation Administration (UNRRA) and the American Jewish Joint Distribution Committee (JOINT)[11] had to struggle against the chaos in their own organisations before meaningful relief could reach the DPs. Apathy and disorder characterised the DP camps in 1945, and members of the She'erit Hapletah felt disappointed and aggrieved at the lack of understanding and insight into their situation by their American liberators. Not surprisingly, the survivors were not willing to work for the benefit of Germany, nor did they wish to undertake the necessary work in the DP camps. They felt that it was now the turn of the Germans to work for them. They focused on their first concern which was to look for family members who might have survived, and the leaders of the She'erit Hapletah realised that the demoralisation, anger and frustration among survivors must be channeled into affirmative action which could bring about new hope. They saw 'a future-oriented Zionist political' path as the way forward.[12] Though their immediate concern was to improve conditions in the DP camps, their central commitment was to a national rebirth of the Jewish people with their own country in Palestine. When David Ben-Gurion, who would

---

9   M. Brenner, *After the Holocaust*. Princeton: Princeton University Press, 1999.
10  White Anglo-Saxon Protestants, deemed by some to be the elite in American society.
11  JOINT was also known as the JDC, dedicated to giving aid to refugees and other victims of disasters worldwide.
12  A. Grossman, *Jews, Germans and Allies: Close Encounters in Occupied Germany*. Princeton: Princeton University Press, 2009, p. 158.

become prime minister of the newly formed state of Israel in May 1948, visited the DPs in 1945, he 'was unabashed about the survivors' significance for the future of Zionism' and he inspired the survivors by referring to them as 'a political force'.[13] Zeev Mankowitz records 'the willingness of tens of thousands of survivors to vote with their feet',[14] willing to brave the British blockade of Palestine in fragile and makeshift boats, facing the strong possibility of being incarcerated by the British in Cyprus. To the She'erit Hapletah their task was to 'bear eloquent witness to their affirmation of life and their undiminished humanity'.[15]

In the American sector it did not take long for the Jewish survivors to organise themselves for the purpose of representation and advocacy, especially vis-a-vis the Americans. They needed a voice to convince the Americans that the Jews were a separate ethnic group whose needs were different from those of the other DPs. The indifference of many of the postwar governments to the plight of the Jews, frustrated in their attempts to obtain entry visas for emigration to other countries, further galvanised the Jewish leaders to fight for a Jewish homeland in Palestine. Most of the Jewish DPs continued to adhere to the same political ideologies which they had followed before the Holocaust, as is clearly illustrated by the emergence of a DP press in the camps which reflected the survivors' many political ideologies. However, the appeal of Zionism to the She'erit Hapletah was strengthened by the apparent indifference of the world to their plight. It seemed that only a separate and independent homeland in Palestine could offer the Jews any security and a sense of belonging in the future.

In the immediate postwar period, as the 'Iron Curtain' descended upon Eastern Europe, and Russia evolved quickly into the Soviet Union, creating communist states in the Baltic, Poland and Czechoslovakia, the Cold War became a struggle for dominance between the Soviet and US superpowers. Given these circumstances, the focus of the United States turned to the battle against communism, which posed the greatest threat to Western power. The Americans believed that it had to be fought at all costs. They became determined to bolster the German economy, regarding a stable Germany as a strong bulwark against communism. The American Secretary of State, James Byrne, made 'a conciliatory speech' in Stuttgart on 6 September which 'had signalled U.S. support for German

---

13  Ibid.
14  Z. Mankowitz, *Life between Memory and Hope: The Survivors of the Holocaust in Occupied Germany*. Cambridge University Press, 2002, p. 300.
15  Ibid, p. 303.

reconstruction and the Cold War turn away from denazification. It also marked the upcoming end of the brief (relatively) golden age of special DP access to American power, protection, and rations that had been inaugurated by the Harrison report.'[16] The Americans were less concerned about the Jewish DPs and combatting German anti-Semitism than they were about the Cold War. Laura June Hilton argues: 'Analysis of the material conditions of postwar Germany provides insight into the fluctuating position of DPs in society, the shifting priorities of the US Government and its occupation forces, and the rehabilitation of Germany and Germans in light of the growing threat of communism'.[17] The American Government turned to recruiting German nuclear and rocket scientists, who had worked for the Nazi regime, to emigrate to the United States where they were accepted as citizens to work on the American nuclear and missile program in their arms race against the Russians.

Historians were primarily researching World War II and its universal ramifications, while the Holocaust was not researched in real depth until the 1960s, after the Eichmann trial in Jerusalem suddenly awoke the conscience of the world and a flood of Holocaust historiography began to appear.[18]

The She'erit Hapletah grew in number as Jewish refugees escaped from Eastern Europe, Czechoslovakia, Romania and particularly the Soviet Union, where they had spent the war years. They were helped by the Bricha movement, an illegal organisation established to help Jewish refugees make their way to Germany and from there to Palestine. The Bricha, established by the heroic Jewish poet and partisan Abba Kovner, among others, attracted former partisans, soldiers from the Jewish Brigade in Palestine and other Zionist volunteers. It was the Bricha who provided small, sometimes barely seaworthy boats, in which the passengers and crew attempted to break the British blockade of Palestine. This wave of illegal immigration came to be known as *Aliyah Bet*.

When the Jewish survivors of the Nazi concentration camps were housed in the DP camps, the majority of them were young people; the absence of children and the aged among them was starkly evident. Most survivors had

---

16  A. Grossman, *Jews, Germans and Allies: Close Encounters in Occupied Germany*. Princeton: Princeton University Press, 2009, p. 167.
17  L. Hilton, 'Prisoners of Peace: Rebuilding Community, Identity and Nationality in Displaced Persons Camps in Germany, 1945–1952'. PhD thesis, Ohio State University, 2001, p. 149.
18  M. Marrus, *The Holocaust in History*. Toronto: Key Porter Books, 2000, p. 200.

been used as slave labour. Hitler's policy was to exterminate the old and the children who were considered by the Nazis to be useless burdens on the German economy. The children also posed a danger, as potential future avengers for crimes perpetrated against the Jewish people. This created the particular phenomenon of a largely young adult population of survivors in the DP camps. However, when the Jewish refugees in other zones were led by Bricha to the American Zone, they swelled Jewish numbers in the DP camps and changed the camp demographic to include Jewish families with children.

Truman's special envoy, Earl Harrison, was scathing in his condemnation of the treatment meted out to the Jewish survivors. Although his report was met with consternation in Washington, it led to many changes for the better. An oft-quoted point in his report reads as follows: 'As matters now stand, we appear to be treating the Jews as the Nazis treated them except that we do not exterminate them. They are in concentration camps in large numbers under our military guard instead of SS troops.'[19]

Harrison recommended that the Jews should be allowed to have separate camps with a wide degree of autonomy, to be run by their own personnel. This was precisely what the Jewish leaders had lobbied for, and as a result of the report the Jews were recognised as a separate ethnic group with their own specific needs. Following the implementation of Harrison's recommendations, and the improvements in living conditions in the camps, it was not long before morale improved among the She'erit Hapletah and they began to look to the future with more hope.

Dr Samuel Gringauz, Moshe Feigenbaum, Israel Kaplan, Dr Zalman Grinberg and Dr Philip Friedman, all of whom had played significant roles in their prewar communities, were key figures in initiating the idea of a representative body to act as the voice of the She'erit Hapletah in dealing with the American military, and to extend their representation even further. They and others created the infrastructures for health, education and religion, as well as structures to meet the cultural and social needs of the survivor communities. Members of the She'erit Hapletah began to reconstruct their lives.

American Jewish army chaplains and soldiers of the Jewish Brigade were of invaluable help to the survivors, often obtaining supplies for them despite great shortages of most things required in daily living. Dr Abraham Klausner witnessed the horrors of Dachau when he arrived at

---

19   www.ushmm.org/research/library/bibliography/displaced persons/HarrisonReport

the extermination camp with the American troops. He decided to devote himself unconditionally to the cause of the Jewish DPs. He was not intimidated by lack of official cooperation, and would scrounge supplies, requisition army resources, and generally act with great courage and initiative for the benefit of the Jewish DPs. In order to remain in Munich when his unit was moved onwards, he even went AWOL (absent without official leave) despite threats of court martial. He became a pivotal figure in the establishment of the representative body for the Jewish DPs, the Central Committee of the Liberated Jews in Bavaria. He was the first person to publish lists of survivor names, six volumes in all, to enable the Jewish DPs to search for family members in a more effective way. The lists were distributed throughout Europe and America.

Many Jewish marriages took place in the camps and elsewhere as people sought to re-establish family life. The survivors were desperate to again enjoy the intimacy and warmth of a family, as many of them were entirely bereft of any immediate family at all. The birth rate in the DP camps was for a few years considered to be the highest in the Western world. The lives of the newborns were seen as a telling form of revenge against Hitler's ideology, as well as being a precious gift to their parents. The babies and children were regarded as the living hope for the regeneration of the Jewish people. The JOINT and UNRRA acquired the religious items and wedding rings necessary for the frequent wedding ceremonies which took place in the DP camps.

Some of the survivors requested permission to live outside the camps, and the Americans at times obliged by confiscating German properties which were handed over to the Jewish survivors. The Americans billeted others in German homes. Hilton points out that 'the issue of assigning German billets to DPs was very prickly'.[20] Officials approached this task with considerable caution. A fragile working relationship existed between US troops and the Germans, and army officials were usually not willing to risk antagonising the local German population to obtain better housing conditions for DPs. This ambivalent attitude was not conducive to a sense of security among the DP population. For the She'erit Hapletah this was no answer to their view of the future, and it became increasingly obvious to the survivors that their rehabilitation and the restoration of their dignity could be achieved only by their own initiative.

---

20  L. Hilton, 'Prisoners of Peace: Rebuilding Community, Identity and Nationality in Displaced Persons Camps in Germany, 1945–1952'. PhD thesis, Ohio State University, p. 163.

Further compromising the relationship between the Jewish DPs and the Allied forces was the survivors' need to supplement the supplies provided by UNRRA and the JOINT by engaging in black marketeering activities. Both refugees and the German population in general were actively engaged in illegal trade and barter. Shortages of food and clothing were so acute in 1945 that the American army had to issue orders which strictly rationed food for the survivors. Jewish DPs were widely accused by the Germans of being the worst among the profiteers in the black market. The military government was persuaded to act on German information and raids on the DP camps were frequent, exacerbating tensions between the authorities and the Jewish survivors. In reality both the Jewish DPs and the local German population used the black market to supplement the meagre rations obtained from the Americans, to meet their elementary needs. Inevitably there were also those who dealt in the illegal market in order to enrich themselves. Black trade soon became an integral part of the German economy.

In the face of so many seemingly insurmountable problems, the elected Jewish leadership felt that the provision of a strong representative voice for the She'erit Hapletah was of the utmost necessity. A conference was arranged to take place on 25 July 1945 in the St Ottilien hospital, not far from Munich. [The hospital was a monastery, converted after liberation]. Ninety-four Jewish delegates from Germany and Austria were brought together. Many dignitaries were among those who attended the conference where the elected representatives [the delegates had been elected previously by the camp populations in preparation for the St Ottilien conference] of the She'erit Hapletah met to discuss which path to take to secure the future of the Jewish survivors.[21] The conference focused on two issues: free and open immigration to Palestine and autonomy for the Jews in the DP camps. Building on the success of the St Ottilien conference, the newly named Central Committee of the Liberated Jews in Bavaria elected a group of survivors to act as the true representatives of the She'erit Hapletah. They served as a bridge between the Allied authorities and the DPs, and also took upon themselves the task of ensuring the general welfare and rehabilitation of the survivors.

The Central Committee's functions were many and diverse. One of their immediate aims was to create Historical Commissions whose purpose was to record the history of the Holocaust, collecting as many eyewitness

---

21   The official representatives of She'erit Hapletah, who had been elected at the St Ottilien conference, later formed 'The Central Committee of the Liberated Jews of Bavaria'.

accounts as possible of the destruction of Jewish communities. Documents, testimonies, artefacts and photographs of both prewar Jewish life and the period of the Holocaust were widely collected. The Historical Commissions hoped that testimonies and captured German documents would be used by the Allies as evidence against the Nazi perpetrators during the Military Tribunal and the Nuremberg Trials. However, they also saw this material as an essential resource for researching and recording the Holocaust from the Jewish point of view, or, in Philip Friedman's phrase, presenting a Judeo-centric understanding of the Holocaust, in contrast to the general focus at that time on the war as a whole.[22]

After the meeting at St Ottilien, Levi Shalit, journalist and poet, and one of the driving forces among the She'erit Hapletah, suggested that the Committee should publish a newspaper, an official organ that could keep the Jewish survivors informed about current news and in touch with other Jewish communities in all parts of Germany and even further afield. The idea was met with surprise and even diffidence by the newly elected committee who were aware that, if the suggestion were to be implemented, practical difficulties around paper, typesetting and means of distribution, among others, would have to be overcome. In addition, they would need the permission of American authorities.

Newspapers of every political shade had always been an integral part of Jewish culture and reflected the political ideologies of the people, their literary and dramatic interests, world affairs, and the many aspects of everyday life. The camp newspapers would play no less an important role in the lives of the She'erit Hapletah by giving them a voice, conveying information, and making the DPs feel less isolated. Among the camp leadership there were very able writers, such as David Wolpe, the poet; Israel Kaplan, the historian who was to become the editor of *Fun Letzten Khurben*; Moshe Feigenbaum, future Chairman of the Central Committee of Liberated Jews in Bavaria; Dr Gringauz and many others who could play a role in establishing and maintaining a newspaper or journal. By reflecting the revival of Jewish culture in their theatre reviews, literary discussions, and world political interests, these publications encouraged the rehabilitation of the Jewish DPs and contributed to their being able to feel that they again belonged to

---

22   Dr Philip Friedman, a Polish-Jewish historian, was the author of several books on history and accounting. In the late 1950s, Friedman urged Holocaust researchers to focus more on a Judeo-centric perspective of the Holocaust as opposed to the Allied point of view which was Nazi-centric, and which encompassed the war in general.

the community of mankind. An extremely important role of the newspapers was to help reunite families by regularly publishing the names of survivors seeking family members.

Within a remarkably short time more than 100 assorted newspapers and journals were published in the camps. Leo Schwarz, an American citizen who was directing the work of the JOINT in the American Zone of Germany, felt compelled to improve the lot of the survivors by any means at his disposal, and he and the Jewish Chaplain Klausner were invaluable in their efforts to help set up the newspaper *Unzer Veg* (Our Way) which became the voice of the Central Historical Committee, and the journal *Fun Letzten Khurben*, which was first published by the Central Historical Commission in Munich in August 1946.

The journal was unique in its diversity. The editor, Israel Kaplan, referred to it as a journal of the people, a publication in which he wished to publish material which reflected prewar life and culture in the towns and the villages of Eastern Europe, as well as the Jewish experience during the Holocaust.[23] His aim was to preserve as much as possible of the rich and varied culture of the Jews which was destroyed by the Nazi regime. He saw the preservation of Jewish culture as a means of enabling the survivors to 'give shape'[24] to their experiences during the Holocaust, and to cope with the present. His focus on Jewish culture helped to restore a sense of pride and dignity in his readers, a reminder that they came from an enduring culture. This helped to reinstate the survivors' sense of self worth. The journal series was very different from other publications of the time as it did not adhere to any particular political ideology. While it reflected the past, it also focused on both the present and the future. Kaplan did not shy away from acknowledging the difficulties in persuading people to write their testimonies, as much of the She'erit Hapletah was already 'sitting on their suitcases', as it were. This phrase was used by Kaplan to describe the DPs impatience to emigrate to other countries.

The Munich Historical Commission and its journal, *Fun Letzten Khurben*, functioned to preserve significant historical material relating to the Holocaust. In Volume 1 Feigenbaum emphasised the importance of the role of the Historical Commission: 'We, the surviving remnant, the living witnesses, must create for the historian the fundamentals which will serve

---

23   *Fun Letzten Khurben*, Munich Central Historical Commission, Vol. 1, p. 1.
24   L. Langer, *Holocaust Testimonies: The Ruins of Memory*. New Haven: Yale University Press, 1991.

in place of the above listed sources from which he will be able to derive a clear picture of what happened to us and amongst us'.[25] Remarkably, the Historical Commission managed to collect 3,500 testimonies, as well as 'hundreds of thousands' of other documents, including Nazi documents, Jewish artefacts and photographs.[26] When its role came to an end in 1949 the entire archive was sent to the newly established Yad Vashem, the Jerusalem-based Holocaust remembrance centre.

In a report about their activities, the Central Historical Commission described Kaplan's work and his role as editor of *Fun Letzten Khurben* in glowing terms: 'A new spirit of life was brought into the work of the Central Historical Commission by the "literateur" and historian Israel Kaplan'.[27] Feigenbaum explained also that Kaplan gave up a far more comfortable job in order to take part in the difficult work of the Historical Commission.

The format of the journal series was the same in all 10 volumes, except for Volume 1, which is larger in size than the editions which followed. Kaplan obviously placed great historical value on survivors' testimonies and, in all, he published 100 Holocaust survivor accounts in the journal series. They took precedence over the other material in the journal and always appeared in the first section. Kaplan devised a methodology for use by the collectors of testimonies in order to improve the quality of eyewitness accounts. In the first volume of *Fun Letzten Khurben* he exhorted readers to: 'Describe and send in to us your experiences during the Nazi period. Write clearly, provide as many facts, dates, and names of people who, during that time, took part in public life. Give us also the names of our murderers.'[28]

Kaplan requested readers to describe life in the big cities as well as in the villages, and, when naming perpetrators, to include as much information as possible about their personal history as well as their deeds. Some of the volumes contain the following request: 'If you have a photograph or a document from the dark tragic time, don't keep it solely for yourself. Hand it in to the Historical Commission. After it has been copied, it will immediately be returned to you with thanks.'[29] He stressed the need to gather objects

---

25 M. Feigenbaum, 'Why Do We Need Historical Commissions?' *Fun Letzten Khurben*, Munich Historical Commission, Vol. 1, p. 1.

26 Report about the Historical Commission's activities. *Fun Letzten Khurben*, Munich Historical Commission, Vol. 4, p. 4.

27 Kibbutz Lochamei Hagettaot (Ghetto Fighters Kibbutz). Israel, Archive Collection Israel Kaplan, File No. 6483, pp. 4–5.

28 The editor. *Fun Letzten Khurben*, Munich Historical Commission, Vol. 1, p. 13.

29 The editor. *Fun Letzten Khurben*, Munich Historical Commission, Vol. 9, p. 77.

like concentration camp clothing, shoes, hats, eating implements, work equipment, and also 'recipes' from camp and ghetto food. He emphasised the vital role of folklore in the ghettos and camps, such as songs, poems, expressions, jokes and anecdotes. Code words and sayings which prisoners used in the Nazi labour camps were an essential means of communication amongst the Jewish prisoners, and served as timely warnings of impending danger. In several editions Kaplan exhorted the survivors to respond to the Historical Commissions, stating: 'History today is on the tip of every Jewish tongue; history emerges from every fold in our memory. One must only have an ear to catch words. Let us heap up, create. Collect – save!'

Each section in the journal covers a different theme. These are:

- Testimonies
- Children's testimonies
- Folklore
- Document archive
- Photographs from the Nazi period
- Report on present activities of the Central Commission
- Bibliographical lists of relevant articles in other publications of the time

A copy of the first volume of *Fun Letzen Khurben* was sent to scholars at YIVO, based in New York, and acknowledged as the leading institute of Yiddish scholarship and history.[30] They commended the journal highly and expressed the hope that it would be expanded as they felt that it had a significant role to play. In their letter to the Munich Historical Commission and the Central Committee of Liberated Jews in Bavaria, YIVO stated: 'We are even more amazed when we consider that the publication appeared in a place and a time when you have to take care of a thousand other matters, and despite this, you are aware of the importance of collecting and researching the catastrophe experienced by our people'.[31] Much encouraged, Kaplan and the Historical Commission pressed on. The hopes of YIVO came to fruition as the journal grew from 36 pages in Volume 1, to 185 pages in Volume 10. The Commission kept in close touch with YIVO

---

30   The acronym for the Jewish Institute for Research in New York.
31   Letter from YIVO to the Central Historical Commission in Munich and the Central Committee in the American Zone of Germany, dated 18 November 1946.

between 1945–1949, and consulted with YIVO scholars as the need arose. The Hebrew University of Jerusalem also praised the journal highly.

The testimonies appearing in *Fun Letzten Khurben* have not been translated before, except for abbreviated excerpts of three of the testimonies in a book edited by Leo Schwartz in 1949.[32] Ze'ev Mankowitz's comment from 1988 remains broadly true: 'The collective enterprise for the people of *She'erit Hapletah*, articulated in Yiddish, remains a closed book for most'.[33] The testimonies in the present publication have been selected with the aim of providing as broad a spectrum as possible. The originals vary in quality, but an attempt has been made to retain the spirit and the tone of the original documents. At times, the chronology of events described in the testimonies may be confusing, but they follow the original way in which the narrator told his or her story.

## A Note on Personal and Place Names

The spelling of place names calls for some difficult decisions. Many of the multinational names in Europe during the war have different spellings for Jews, Lithuanians, Russians, Germans and others. Wherever possible this book uses the Yiddish version of personal and place names. For example, the number of different spellings for Koldyczewo and also Mielec illustrate the nature of this problem: Koldyczewo, Kaldycheva, Kuldychevo; or Mielec, Mellitz, Mayliyk, Meleck.

---

32  L. Schwartz, *The Root and the Bough: The Epic of an Enduring People*. New York: Rinehart & Company, 1949.

33  Ze'ev Mankowitz, 'The Affirmation of Life in She'erit Hapleita'. *Holocaust and Genocide Studies*, Vol. 5, No. 1, 1990, 13–21. Presented at the Remembering for the Future Conference, Oxford, 10–13 July 1988.

# WHY DO WE NEED HISTORICAL COMMISSIONS?

By M.Y. Feigenbaum, Leader of the
Central Historical Commission, 1946

Published by the Munich Historical Commission in the Journal Series
*Fun Letzten Khurben*, Vol. 1, 1946

Many of us still ask: for what purpose do we need Historical Commissions? We are flooded by a deluge of documents about Jews for the Nuremberg Trials; what more can we add to what has been said amongst ourselves? Furthermore, the superpowers have put together a huge amount of material about the Nazi epoch, so what sort of a role can a few more documents which we will manage to collect play?

And, truthfully, during the Hitler occupation, we never dreamt of undertaking such a task. It was hard to believe that any one of us would survive. We thought to ourselves that those who might undertake to write the history of our tragic time will not have a difficult mission. The horror which the brown shirt murderers so openly inflicted upon the Jews will have enough living witnesses in the countries in which we were tormented. They will already have recorded our tragic lives quite objectively, the history of those times, and also the annihilation. This is what we thought.

But almost immediately after our first steps into freedom we were disappointed. It became apparent that our neighbours are not only unwilling to pass on the objective information, facts and impressions, but the opposite; they make an effort to diminish the Jewish tragedy, even to obscure it.

And we don't have far to look for this. We don't have to record any facts from Poland. For example, it will be enough only to quote the statement made by the former Prime Minister, Churchill, in front of the English Parliament in February 1945, in which Churchill declared that, as we have said, the Nazis murdered approximately three million Polish Jews.

This is stated by the Prime Minister of an empire which holds the whole world in the clutches of her espionage, and which is aware of the smallest occurrence in the world; this is said by a military man at the time when, as far as the river Vistula, Poland had already been free for seven months. First, the Jewish Central Commission in Poland must take the credit for directing attention to Churchill, presenting him as not only saying 'as we have said', but declaring that it is unfortunately a tragic truth, that the Nazis murdered 3,200,000 Polish Jews.

This fact alone says enough, and it remains unnecessary to cite others.

The superpowers truly collected a mass of documents; but the Jewish problem was far from their minds. First of all, they had in mind their own interests. We don't know at all whether these secret documents will always remain secret. Along with this, there is considerable doubt about whether a Jewish historian will have access to them. Many documents, which are directly connected with us Jews, are not being collected by the great powers at all, so whose duty is it to do so?

However, let us now accept that all the documents are being collected by them – and the Jewish researcher has access to them – but what do these documents indicate?

All these documents still convey only a fragment of our tragedy. They show only what the murderers' attitude was towards us, how they treated us and what they did to us. Did our lives in those nightmarish days consist only of such fragments?

On what grounds will the historian be able to create a picture from them (the documents) about what happened in the ghettos? In what way will we be able to preserve the record of our suffering and painful lives? By what means will we be able to know about our heroic fathers, and how will we convey our attitude to our torturers?

Before the war, in order to preserve Yiddish life, there was at the disposal of the historian the Yiddish press, folklore, notebooks, literature, archival materials, photographs and so on. Today, for us, it is as if all of this is destroyed.

We the remaining remnant ('She'erit Hapletah'), the surviving witnesses, must create for the historian the framework which will represent the above mentioned oppression, from which he will be able to create a clear picture of that which happened to us and between us.

Therefore, for us, every eyewitness account from a surviving Jew, every song from the Nazi period, every saying, every story and joke, every photograph and whichever creation, from both literature and art, in short, all that can shed light on the martyrs' path of our tragic generation is important.

It is clear then that we Jews alone must document this bloody epoch. Moreover, Historical Commissions are necessary.

But the Historical Commissions are not only collectors of documents for the scientists and researchers; they are also an instrument which must be used by our Jewish organisations, which are struggling for our future in the international arena.

In the Historical Commissions there is material which can be used by the organisations as ammunition for the benefit of our interests. It is the duty of every Jew who managed to tear himself away, while still alive, from Hitler's nightmarish, murderous grip to place himself at the disposal of the Historical Commission whenever he is asked to do so.

# PART ONE

# 1

# MIELICE LABOUR CAMP

Eyewitness Account by Josef Kas

Collected by the Munich Historical Commission.
Published in the Journal Series
*Fun Letzten Khurben*, Vol. 2 1946

On 19 June 1942, we arrived at the SS labour camp Mielice (district Krakow). The labour camp was designated for Jews only, and was situated in the grounds of the Heinkel aeroplane factory. At the time of my arrival, the number of Jews working there was approximately 100. About 5,000 Poles and 500 Germans worked in the factory proper. Every day after work, the Poles and the Germans would go back to their homes; but the Jews had to return to their camp barrack. The aeroplane factory had very modern installations; before the war it was the largest Polish aeroplane factory. The Jews here were divided into two categories according to their work: production Jews, that is, those who were involved in actual production; and the unproductive ones who were the 'assistant workers', who were assigned to garden work, transport and so on. Also, those Jews who were assigned to 'greater' Berdichev (the region of Volhynia, now the disrict of Zhitomir in Ukraine) which belonged to the factory were designated 'unproductive' workers.

The food was appalling. The factory kitchen cooked three types of food:

1. For Germans, two first-class types of food to eat
2. For the Poles, a soup, of reasonable quality
3. For Jews, soup, but only from dregs which could not be utilised for anything else.

Months later the range [of food] was only wormy cabbage, garbage, grass and rotten potatoes, cut up with their peels. The food often stank terribly; even the really hungry were revolted by it.

At that time the camp was under the leadership of a Pole, Polerovski. He wanted to use his position as the camp commander only to become rich, easily and quickly. After a 12 hour work day, when we would finally return to the camp, we had to sit for hours in the *appel-platz* [place where roll call was held] with legs crossed, and on Sundays for the whole morning with almost no break. At that time, Polerovski would search all the barracks, and would rummage through everything in case he might find some items which he could take with him. All newly arrived Jews (at that point new transports arrived regularly) were thoroughly searched and everything that had even minimum worth was taken. The post was under Polerovski's control; the parcels were opened and for the most part were taken away. The first shootings occurred before this time. It happened when two Jewish youths were suspected by Polerovski of wanting to escape. He had them arrested and handed them over to the Gestapo to be shot. Even earlier Polerovski sent five Jews to the extermination camp Pruszkow, to their inevitable death, as a punishment for escaping from a camp.

In October 1942, the regular distribution [of food] continually deteriorated. At first, every person was given a loaf of bread weighing 2 kilos for a week, then they decreased the ration to 180 grams per person. With hard labour in which most of the camp inmates were engaged, it was absolutely impossible to live from this regular allocation. Pulerovski had already confiscated everyone's belongings which people could have sold to the Poles in the factory. The Jews, not having any other means by which to sustain life, had to create various ways and combinations with other objects even though doing so was subject to a death sentence.

The extremely cruel behaviour towards the camp inmates increased daily. The 'work guards', who were mostly from Silesia, would upbraid the workers for laziness at work and use rubber truncheons to 'honour' a few Jews (very often 20 to 30 men) with the infamous 25 on the buttocks. In this respect, the German and often the Polish overseers and foremen would frequently outdo the Gestapo. The Jews were beaten at work with or without an excuse, all with the approval of the relevant overseer. Beatings were for all these 'gentlemen' a sport. Often foremen would demand from the Jews impossible 'tasks' just to have a good excuse for beatings. An additional favourite of theirs was first to beat the victim until he was half dead, and after that to give him to the 'work security' unit with the excuse of balancing out the work, which was almost a death sentence with the '25'.

But also in the camp itself the Jewish police mistreated the Jews badly. The contemporary Kommandant of the Jewish police, Khilowitz, had during the five months in his position beaten to death at least five Jews; also, the majority of the Jewish police personnel did not differ from their Kommandant in this respect. For roll call Khilowitz would whistle three times, and all the Jewish police would immediately charge into the barracks, and with a deluge of blows they would drive the inmates out. In this regard it must be noted that in previous times there were regular rollcalls. Often all the groups which had already returned from work would be lined up in the *appel-platz* and then would come the command 'about turn', and we would have to march back to work, often until 11 at night. In the morning, we were woken at five thirty. Woe betide anyone who did not spring out of bed. The Jewish policeman, Rosenzweig, who was an absolute sadist, followed this method: he would enter the barrack and call out quietly 'get up', and then he would call out loudly: 'What, you don't want to get up?!' And before one could manage to get out of bed, he would immediately pounce upon people handing out beatings in every direction, then overturn the beds, and pour water over those Jews who were in the process of getting dressed. He behaved in the same way at every opportunity.

Sunday was the worst day for the camp inmates. On this day most of the groups from the factory did not work, so the Jews remained in the barracks. This opportunity was used by the members of the Jewish police to create utter chaos. They caught Jews and sent them to work. While they lined up for rollcall there was no shortage of beatings.

Finally, however, the Poles informed on their Polerovski. The Germans carried out a house search in his home, and found goods and money worth hundreds of thousands of zlotys, which he had confiscated from the Jews for himself, instead of handing it over to the Gestapo. He was arrested and from then onwards no more was heard from him.

Now a Polish judge, Novitski, took over the camp. In December 1942, almost at the same time as he arrived, there was a serious typhus epidemic. From the more than 600 Jews, generally about 100 in the camp would lie ill. The place for the sick was in the so-called 'infectious diseases room', in their filthy condition, on plank beds with one thin cover over them during the frosty days of January 1943. The person responsible for the situation in the camp was Meier Stein. He was the chief of the 'Work Protection Unit' and at the same time head of the Jewish camp, the master of life and death over all the camp inmates. He ordered the judge, Novitzki, to fight the typhus epidemic by means of bursts of shooting. Novitzki, an old man, who could not move himself without a stick, crept around the sick bay all day, in the dining room and the *appel-platz*, and noted down anyone whose appearance he did not like. In this respect, it must be observed that every Jew had a number marked on his back. In this way Novitzki was able to make a note of the selected people, and they were not even aware of this. On the second day, the well known 'Berdichev wagon' would arrive in the camp; they would search for those Jews who were marked and in the freezing cold they were told to undress. Then each one would receive a sheet, and they would be loaded onto the wagon. Anyone who saw this horrifying scene even once, in 20 or more degrees of frost, could not forget this in a lifetime. Some tried to get away, but the work overseers did not allow even one to disappear. The graves were already prepared earlier by the Jews themselves. Whoever did not want to dig the graves was shot together with the other unfortunate victims. The place where the mass graves were situated was a field near the Berdichev airport, and was named by the camp inmates 'Berdichev lawn'. Jews were brought to the field by wagon, and had to kneel in the prepared grave; then the work overseers would finish them off with a 'neck shot'. After every such action our own Jews had to cover over the graves.

In about the middle of January, when 250 Jews were exterminated in the above manner (the approximate number of Jewish victims at the beginning of the typhus epidemic was more than 600), the camp Kommandant himself suddenly contracted typhus. Novitzki died within three days. His successor was called the 'Jewish Policeman' Drozdze from Katowice. In the beginning there was an enormous improvement in conditions, as the terrible shootings stopped almost completely. The appalling state of shock diminished. The camp inhabitants could breathe more freely. Drozdze made an effort to curb the desire of Meier Shtein to starve and shoot the Jews. Approximately two months later Drozdze was appointed as Chief of the Jewish Police and, because of this, apparently his desire to advance increased. Besides this, he also began drinking. In addition the German chiefs and officers brought him various complaints. Here a Jew stole potatoes, there a Jew bought bread, again a Jew did not work hard enough. Once more the shootings began. As labourers, Jews began again to escape from the camp. At first, for every man who escaped, five others were shot and later 10 Jews. Drozdze himself directed the shootings. He would bring the victims to Berdichev and there he would immediately 'take care' of them. The situation became even worse when the management of the whole factory was taken over by the Gestapo. For the smallest transgression of which a Jew may have been guilty, the Gestapo had to be informed, and this always ended with shooting. When a Jew escaped, the whole camp had to assemble and the Gestapo would choose 20 men to be shot. It happened more than once that, for the same effort, they took a few more. It is easy to imagine how the camp inmates felt when the Gestapo moved through the rows and called out: 'Come, come!' During the shooting a certain Zimmerman stood out because of his pleasure in taking part in the selections, and mostly he chose more people than were necessary. The shootings were carried out mostly by the Gestapo Chief Tonmeier from Mielice, and the Jewish Police Chief Shtein or the factory manager.

In September 1943, the Mielice camp had grown enough to house 1,500 Jews. However, more Jews from the neighbouring, smaller camps which had been liquidated kept on arriving here. Then the camp was taken over by the SS. Amongst the Jews there were 150 women who, shortly before the camp was taken over, arrived there. This was the only female transport (except for 20 women in October 1943) who were sent to Mielice.

With the takeover by the SS, everyone became very frightened. The new regulations, however, put an end to the very bad state of the camp, which could have led to the complete eradication of the Jews. The food, which until now was cooked from garbage only and was too bad even for cattle food, began to improve. The camp was given its own kitchen (until then the food for the Jews was cooked in the factory kitchen) and received the necessary life-sustaining goods directly from the SS stores in Pustkow. It was not much, but at least it was really life-sustaining and not just garbage. The food was then far from good, and very watery, but it did not stink and it was possible to eat it.

The Gestapo no longer had to make decisions about Jewish affairs, and likewise also the Jewish Police Chief, Meier Shtein. By the way, Meier Shtein (appropriately from the Wehrmacht) would chase the Jews every few weeks all over the courtyard in order to see who was no longer able to remain on his feet properly, and would immediately shoot them. At the end of 1943 this same Meier was denounced because of theft, and someone else came in his place. SS Sergeant Major Herring who now took over the camp had an athletic build. It was said that he had emptied many Jewish camps amongst which there would have been a large Jewish labour camp in the region of Przemysl. His large dog would accompany those who were sentenced to death, and maul them until they were half-dead. Herring had apparently seen more than enough Jewish blood flowing, but he vented his sadism in his beatings. He was happy when he counted 100 lashes with a whip; then he would set his dog on the victim. The 100 beatings lasted for two to three hours, and he himself would inflict the beatings on his victims in his office. The doctor had to treat the victims and attempt to get them ready to return to work within three days. For every little transgression, he would flog them with the cane – for having money (even small change), for stealing potatoes, for exchanging something, for falling asleep at work and so on. Herring sentenced to death two Jews who were captured in the forest, and a child, just six years old, whose parents, in the face of incredible danger, had managed to conceal him in the camp for one and a half years.

In approximately six months time, in February 1944, Herring was transferred to Cracow and Sergeant Schwamberger took his place. He brought his wife and child and three trucks full of furniture. He gave orders for the building of a new barrack at the entrance to the camp where he placed a Ukrainian Kommando [a work unit] of the SS which took over the guarding of the camp. The Head of the Guard Kommando was Police Sergeant Hartmann from my district, Schwamberger, and a man from the Tyrol. They were the two appropriate people for their set task. Schwamberger had previously been stationed in Przemysl where he ostensibly liquidated two Jewish camps. He brought to Mielice a huge number of boxes and baskets full of looted Jewish belongings – about 200 dresses for his wife, 30 to 40 outfits for his three-year-old son, Persian rugs and other beautiful objects. He had magnificent furniture and lived like a duke. His home was arranged like that of a millionaire. He had his own carriage which was drawn by two beautiful white horses. About 10 camp inmates were assigned to keep his home in order. Schwamberger's sole aim was to become wealthy. He used to steal right and left from the camp. He wanted to steal a fortune which would be enough for his lifetime.

The worst, the most unforgettable day in the camp during Schwamberger and Hartmann's time, was 20 April 1944. Drozdze, the former head of the camp, still had some lesser duties, and he made that tragic day infamous. On 19 April, it was reported to the camp leader that during the night shift four Jews had escaped. A terrible panic overcame the camp. A few days earlier someone had escaped and it was barely possible to persuade Schwamberger and Hartmann not to punish innocent Jews for this. This time, however, Schwamberger was determined to punish someone. On 20 April, after work, silence reigned in the camp, a silence before the storm. No one dared to leave the barracks. People hid beneath the planks or elsewhere.

Suddenly a shot was heard, then several shots, then an interval and again several shots. Then it became quiet. In the SS barracks, a drunken orgy began to take place. This 'heroic' behaviour had to be lubricated. In addition, it was Hitler's birthday. All night, noise and shouts and singing and fooling around were heard. That night no one in the camp slept. Everyone waited to hear renewed shooting, and each one was prepared for death.

At approximately five in the morning two shots were heard. There should have been a rollcall at five thirty, but no one wanted to take the responsibility, because they were anticipating mass shootings. The SS personnel drove the inhabitants out of their barracks, and here a miracle occurred for which no one was prepared: the march out of the barracks took place without any shootings. The workers had barely marched off to the factory when Hartmann, with a revolver in his hand, ran around the barracks where the night shift workers and those who worked in the camp itself were to be found, and decided to pay back those who had escaped from the camp. He hunted for three victims, not taking into account that the escaped Jews had run away from their work place, and he placed the responsibility instead on three barrack Elders, because the escapees were from their barracks. Accountability actually lay with the German masters who should have guarded the Jews more carefully, but it was not possible to put the blame on them. Thus Hartmann sought out a few innocent Jews. He gave an order to hang the three barrack Elders and one Security Service man by their arms. Each one of them hung for 20 to 30 minutes, and Hartmann went back and forth with an embittered look on his face. The whole night shift had to look upon this horrible display. After the victims were taken down it became quiet again.

Little by little, at about midday, we began to find out the details about the nightime shootings and the victims of the Aktion [the organised rounding up of Jews for transportation to a concentration or labour camp, or immediate extermination]. A shoemaker who had hidden himself in the factory was discovered by Hartmann's dog, and was so badly bitten that Hartmann did him a favour by shooting him. Two Jews were shot inside the barrack because they carelessly got in front of Hartmann. A large number of shots in the barrack were blindly discharged; from these there was also another death. The following day, Drozdze, the Jewish policeman, finished off the best woman doctor in the camp, the wife of the shot man from Bitkow. No one amongst the victims knew about the escapees. They did not even know them. During the Aktion, Hartmann had several Jews torn from their beds, whom he then 'honoured' with 30 lashes each with the rubber whip.

For weeks after the Aktion the Jews still trembled at a mere glimpse of Police Sergeant Hartmann. People also started to talk about the camp being transformed into a concentration camp. The rumour was spread by the Jewish arrivals from Bedzin, who stated that there too the same thing had happened. All the Jews there received striped prisoner garb. In contrast to the pessimists' news, the optimists had a different version of the news which stated that we would soon be liberated by the Russians. Nothing materialised to confirm the creation of a concentration camp [in place of the labour camp], and the probability decreased as liberation from the Red Army came closer.

In June 1944, a certain Sergeant Major Landsberger, who came from Plaszow to Mielice, was assigned to reorganise the camp into a concentration camp. The bad news became reality. The first assignments to be carried out were to encircle the camp with electrified wire, and to erect guard towers quickly, to give the camp the appearance of a real concentration camp. Prior to this there were also watch towers, but they had been only provisionally erected. Landsberger took to his work with devilish zeal. Day and night the Jews had to work for hours after their normal daily work. Within six weeks the concentration camp was completed.

Approximately eight days before handing over the camp administration to concentration camp Plaszow, a superb specimen of a horse belonging to camp leader Schwamberger ran into the electrified fence and dropped dead because of the irresponsibility of a few Jews. Again the camp inmates were violently set upon. We were prepared for a new Aktion over this incident but luckily Schwamberger allowed himself to be placated when another horse was purchased for him using the camp finances.

On 12 July 1944, the handing over of the camp, from Schwamberger to Landsberger, who became the camp Kommandant, took place. As leader of the SS Guard Kommando, Sergeant Foyer, a mass murderer from Plaszow who had shot at least 54,000 [sic] Jews, was appointed. The Jews had to exchange their clothes for inmates' uniforms. A new Jewish camp Elder [the Elder's task was to maintain order in the camp barracks], Yorke, came from the Plaszow camp – he was one of the most honourable of the camp elders that we had ever met. He used all the influence he had with the SS for the benefit of the Jews.

The greatest fear was that the handing over of the camp would radically change the situation for the worse, which did not happen. On the contrary, many things changed for the better. Food and treatment improved. The managers in the factory were forbidden to deal with the Jews in a harsh way which had hitherto cost the Jews their health and, no less, their lives.

On 24 July 1944, there was an order to evacuate the camp. The Russians were getting closer. On the day of the evacuation they were already 35 kilometres from Mielice. We were ordered to pack everything and to get ready to march. They handed out supplies for two days, emptied out the warehouse and packed everything into two wagons. Then the Jews were loaded onto a waiting train with 70 people in each wagon. At six in the evening the transport left. No one was able to eat because of the terrible heat. There was no water. The wagon in which we rode had one small window strung with barbed wire, and we could barely breathe. One person lay upon another. Every hour someone fainted. We were unable to exit from the wagon. We used conserve cans to do the necessary, and then poured it out through the window, but when it was noticed by the SS men, they straight away fired shots into the wagon. Luckily, in the afternoon of the second day we reached the destination of the journey, the main camp of the concentration camp Plaszow-Wieliczka (Poland); and the number of dead was only two or three.

This was the end of Mielice camp. The few who were sick, unsuitable for the transport, were shot by Sergeant Feier even before the train was on its way to Wieliczka. After a few days partisans set fire to the camp. Fourteen days after we were transported, a German army newsletter reported that: 'after a great struggle the aeroplane factory in Mielice was left to the enemy'. In fourteen days time … [The original testimony in Yiddish ends with this incomplete sentence.]

# 2

# LIFE AND DEATH OF THE JEWS IN DUBNO

Eyewitness Acccount by Moishe Weisberg

Collected by the Historical Commission in Landsberg.
Published by the Munich Historical Commission in the Journal Series
*Fun Letzten Khurben*, Vol. 2, 1946

The regional town of Dubno is situated next to the river Ikva, at the crossroads of Kiev, Brod/Lemberg and Rovno. It is an old town which has existed for hundreds of years. Until the outbreak of the German–Soviet war, life flourished in all ways. The Jews who lived there numbered about 12,000, 60 per cent of the general population. In 1941, at the beginning of the Nazi occupation of Dubno, 13,000 Jews lived there.

On 25 June 1941, the Nazi hordes descended upon Dubno. The Jews were overcome by a terrible fear. Jewish businesses were robbed by the Germans and by the local Ukrainian population. Looting of Jewish private possessions also began. The bread ration for Jews was reduced to as low as 100 grams daily. It was decreed that Jews had to wear a white band, 15 cm wide, on which there was a blue Star of David. On 17 October 1941, the white bands were changed over to yellow patches which had to be 8 cm in diameter, and had to be worn on the left side of the chest and also on the right side of the back. The elected Judenrat [the Jewish functionaries arbitrarily selected by the Nazi administration in every ghetto, whose task was to carry out German orders vis-a-vis the ghetto inhabitants] formed a collaborative group with Magistrate Konrad Taubenfehler at the head; they had to bring in money and possessions to the Germans as daily contributions; for example, clothes, linen, bedding, furniture, crockery, instruments and so on.

On 22 July, a month after the arrival of the Germans, there occurred the first death-roundup of the Jews. It was a Tuesday afternoon. A few vehicles with SS personnel arrived in Dubno. They mobilised Ukrainian militia to help them and began the first murderous Aktion or extermination. The Ukrainians captured up to 150 men. From the house where I lived (Zabrama Street, 5) they took away all the men. I and another three men (Lazar Weisbaum, Michal and Hirsch Bortnik) were successful in hiding. The captured Jews were brought to the assembly place where the SS murderers were already waiting. They threw themselves upon the Jews and beat them viciously. Seventy men were sent back home, and the remaining 80 were packed into the trucks and driven to the Jewish cemetery (not far away from where I lived). There was already a prepared grave there. They were told to undress completely so that they were completely naked; then they were beaten again. Their gold teeth were torn out, and finally they were placed at the edge of the grave and shot. On the following day my Ukrainian neighbour, Chernikow, brought home various photos and documents and eyeglasses plus other items which he had found in the cemetery next to the mass grave.

In the middle of August the Wehrmacht ordered the Dubno Jews to give up their gold and silver and all other valuable possessions. The order was followed with extraordinary thoroughness.

The second Aktion took place on 21 August 1941, two months after the arrival of the Germans, and a month after the first Aktion. This Aktion was also only for men. It was on a Thursday at about half-past 10 in the morning. Different rumours circulated and then an extraordinary panic set in. Jews started to rush into their houses. In the streets one could see groups of Ukrainian police who had been brought into Dubno. They were armed with pistols, iron bars, sticks and other types of murderous weapons. Their eyes and portions of the faces of these Ukrainians were covered with black masks. The local Ukrainian thugs tried to cover themselves up in front of the Jews, because they knew them well as former school friends, and as soldiers, and from a number of social groups. Like wild animals they plunged into Jewish streets, yards and houses. They looted in the cellars and in the attics. They pulled out people who were hiding, old and young men. They beat them and wildly chased the wounded and defenceless Jews.

On that bloody day I was at the Judenrat. The murderers came back up to 20 times and searched everywhere for hidden officials. Out of 42 officials,

37 were taken away. A few saved themselves thanks to the fact that they had locked themselves in a little hidden 'shul' (synagogue; shtiebel) which I too used to attend. From this little shul we could see the assembly place to which the Jews were driven. They were taken away to the local jail in groups. In the courtyard and corridors of the jail there were two rows of Ukrainian police armed with sticks and iron bars. Every Jew had to pass between the rows, and was drenched in blood from the beatings. The German murderers were waiting in a hall. They took some people from the group of Jews; almost everyone was condemned to death. Only a few were set free. Those who were sentenced to death were taken in trucks to the Jewish Cemetery where everything was taken from them; they had to strip naked, and were then shot. This Aktion took 10 hours, until seven in the evening, and 1,000 Jewish men lost their lives.

From that day, for about half a year, no big Aktion in Dubno took place. There were only incidents when individual Jews or small groups who were accused of suspicious activities were shot. The Jews were kept busy with various civil duties or military forced labour. In addition, morale was eroded by beatings and by Jews being forced to do the most difficult work. The largest proportion of the Jewish population became semi-starved skeletons, morally depleted, physically and psychologically deprived to the greatest degree. The Jews tortured themselves with all sorts of invented rumours. The rumours, however, grew from day to day, mainly because the German Army was victorious on all fronts. In the town, thousands of Soviet prisoners were brought in and tortured by beatings and by hunger as badly as the Jews were. During the winter months of 1942, in Rovno and Dubno, 55,000 of them [Russian prisoners] died.

The Germans also literally and systematically brought ruin to the Jews. As a rule they expected the Judenrat to hand over Jewish possessions and goods. These expectations were impossible to fulfil, and it was very hard to carry them out. The deprivation increased from day to day, and the different news which circulated among towns and villages about the ongoing destruction increased the feeling of an impending catastrophe. From Rovno there was the tragic news that on 10 and 11 November 1941, 18,000 Jews were murdered and buried in nine mass graves in Sosenki forest, five kilometres behind Rovno. Other snippets of news came from other towns.

On 5 March and again on 23 March 1942, two big Aktions took place; they were supposedly part of the preparation for creating a ghetto. To help with this Aktion the Germans mobilised thousands of Ukrainians and Poles from the surrounding towns. Hundreds of Ukrainian police removed all the finest possessions and goods like furniture and food from Jewish homes. They left only rags and broken dishes. For the Ukrainian folk, robbing the Jews was a significant event. The Poles were also not hesitant about looting.

On 2 April 1942, a ghetto was established (in Dubno). Ghettos were established in almost all towns but it was different in the eastern Ukrainian areas. In those areas there was no longer a Jew to be seen. In Dubno they (the Germans) selected the dirtiest little streets [in which to situate the ghetto.] They added another few small areas and streets which lay at the edge of the river Ikva. The place was surrounded by a high wooden fence with barbed wire. In the space of one day all the Jews from the town had to move into the ghetto. For the 11,000 Jews who lived at that time in Dubno, the space was too small, and overcrowding was unbearable. In addition to this, poor hygiene brought a number of epidemics.

From the ghetto every morning various guarded groups marched out to work; and in the same order they came back at night. Not a single Jew was allowed to be seen outside the ghetto. Often, either Germans or Ukrainian 'gendarmes' in the ghetto would carry out searches among the groups which had returned. For finding on anyone a few grams of butter or other foodstuffs, the person concerned would be beaten murderously and, in addition, he (or she) would be arrested. Such an incident, for example, happened to my friend, Klara Tenenboim. An agronomist by profession, she worked as a gardener in the leader's area. Once, when her group had returned from their work, suddenly the Kommandant of the gendarmerie, von Papke, came out of one of the houses, together with several Ukrainian policemen. They stopped the group and carried out a search. They found 10 grams of butter on Klara Tenenboim. Von Papke beat her mercilessly, trampled her with his feet, and together with a number of other girls she was taken to the police station. There he again searched her, and he found on Klara certain identity papers; when he found them, he cynically tore them up, screaming out: 'You may not have any photographs.' For this slight transgression he decided to shoot her. Thanks to the great efforts which were made by the area leader, for whom she worked, he managed to save her from death. By the way, Klara Tenenboim survived the Nazi regime and lives at present in Vienna.

Life in the ghetto became hopeless, while waiting tensely for some order to be given. An end did come, but it was a very tragic one. In the middle of May 1942, six weeks after the ghetto was established, the Germans divided the ghetto into two parts. On the one side tradesmen and artisans who received special work passes lived; the other side was for the non-workers. In reality, the number of work permits which were given out were not only for the workers, but also for those who had considerable protection, or who paid heavily for the papers. I personally was classified as a building technician in the area of the Kommandant's offices, and thanks to that I was successful in getting a work permit. I was able to obtain 25 work permits for Jewish boys who were working in the Ukrainian industries in the Kommandant's area. The Jews soon understood that a great catastrophe awaited them, and that was exactly how it was. May 27 1942 was for the Jews of Dubno a day of mass slaughter which took the lives of about 7,000 persons. It seems that the main murderers of the Jews were the Kommandant of the gendarmerie, von Papke, the leader of the German work groups named Hammerstein, the Area Kommandant Broecks who was his aide, the City Kommandant, Aleter, and Inspector Wiese. von Papke was a sadist with a horribly wrinkled and lined face, always with his riding crop in hand. All of this characterised his evil personality. Hammerstein, who came from the Sudentenland, was a tall man with a fairly refined face and a pleasant voice. He wore glasses on his nose. Whoever spoke to him for the first time could not have imagined that this person could be such a bestial murderer on an extraordinary scale. The Area Kommandant, Broecks, spoke less. He would sign orders or give his agreement. His bloody orders were carried out by his German soldiers and by the Ukrainians who were ordered to do so. After the decrees were followed, he used to come out to inspect the place where the carnage took place. His subordinate, Aleter, was a short man. In a very organised and unemotional way he carried out the orders. He was the chief torturer of the Dubno Jews. Inspector Wiese was like von Papke, a criminal type, a sadist who always used to beat every passing Jew for no reason or transgression. He took part in every Aktion.

In addition to the Germans, prominent Ukrainians helped with the torture of the Jews. The senior Ukrainians were the mayor, Burka, the deputy-mayor, Servas Stariste Siderovich, as well as others. And senior to these leaders was a district leader. These prominent Ukrainians were trade teachers who taught with me in Soviet schools from 1939 to 1941 and who pretended to be dedicated communists.

The Aktion proper happened in the following way. On 26 May 1942, in the evening, the Jewish ghetto police received an order not to let anyone from the non-working side go over to the workers' area. At midnight, one heard three shots at the gates of the non-workers' side, after which the barbaric German SS tore into the ghetto with several hundred Ukrainian police. Outside, the ghetto was encircled by armed police who all wore helmets. The Germans also had dogs. They started chasing the Jews out of their homes and these victims were beaten without mercy. Many women fainted when they saw their children being stomped on by the murderers' boots. The sick, the crippled and the aged were shot on the spot. Other Jews jumped into the river Ikva, preferring to die this way rather than to give themselves up to the murderers. Many people simply went mad, losing their sanity. One woman, Chaya Feinblit from Rovno, who had not had children for the first 14 years of marriage, had given birth to her first child just at the beginning of the German occupation. During this Aktion, when the murderers wanted to take away her baby, she threw the child into the river, shouting out: 'Should I see the death of my long-awaited child?' And then she swallowed poison. The barbarians near her just laughed and carried on with their bloody task.

The harried, unfortunate Jews were brought together near the exit of the ghetto where trucks had arrived. From the group of Jews there came a loud cry which cut into the deathly silence. The Germans had packed the unfortunate victims into the vehicles and taken them away, and those who couldn't fit into the trucks were herded on foot like cattle. The men were driven into the Jewish cemetery, and the women and children into an area at the back. There were 800 children of school-going age. The most beautifully-dressed children were set apart in front in rows of four. They were given little bouquets to carry, and in a great irony of fate, our beautiful children went in the most beautiful month of May to their own funerals with flowers in their hands. They were herded by Ukrainians, German men and German women with dogs which were set upon the children, and many children were torn apart by the dogs on the way. This is what was done by German women and mothers who had their own little children.

The group of Jews was brought to deeply-dug pits or graves. Everybody had to undress completely. The Germans tore the gold teeth out of the mouths of victims. Very rarely did one hear a cry or a moan. The men and women were very thin and had yellow, pale faces. They looked more like ghosts than humans. For them everything was the same, whether alive or dead. The naked people – women, men and children – had to remain on their knees with their heads bowed facing the already-dug graves, with their hands behind their necks. In a corner of the pit was a German with a loaded machine gun. He kept his feet dangling over the edge of the grave, and in his mouth there was a cigarette. Every few minutes one could hear the firing of the machine gun, and 20 people would fall into the grave. In this way, every few minutes 20 new victims fell into the pit. The people who were not killed by the first shots were killed by a second. A number were suffocated under all the newly fallen-in corpses. The full graves were covered with lime. The blood seeped out of the earth and even the next day the Ukrainians could see how the earth of the grave moved.

The Aktion lasted until the morning of 27 May. The Jews from the workers' section of the ghetto were driven to work on that day as if nothing had happened. These were the remaining tradesmen who were saved from death for a while by a piece of white paper (a work permit). It is impossible to imagine the psychological state of these people who had lost the largest portion of their families in one night, together with friends and near ones with whom they had mingled and lived. From time to time they observed vehicles loaded with various goods. It was Jews themselves who took these goods belonging to their fellow Jews from the places where the others had met a gruesome end. In a number of places, Ukrainian and Polish passers-by stood and looked at the tragic Jewish groups who continued on their way to their work. They remained standing and smiled ironically. At best, one of these figures might shake his head and then continue on his way.

The next day many of the local Jews quietly told others how the majority of their so-called non-Jewish brothers had helped the bestial Germans to capture hidden Jews and hand them over to their deaths. A friend of mine, a teacher, a Ukrainian, Wolodka Drutshenko, with whom I had worked, had personally caught or captured hidden Jewish children and handed them over to the Germans. The most successful person at searching out hidden Jews was Vanka Hoffman whose father was a lawyer, a Russian. With the arrival of the Germans he and his family became Volksdeutsch!! [Members of the German race living outside Germany] One of his sons was a Kommandant in the Ukrainian police, and at every Aktion he personally shot hundreds of Jews. The daughter worked in the Kommissariat. The above-mentioned Vanka played a black role which gave much grief to the Jews. In this role he asked to have the artisan group split up and he took huge sums of money from the artisans for every work permit; then later he would look for certain individuals [who had received work permits from him] and hand them over to the Germans. He even handed over his own school friend, Mischa Spritzman (it is worth noting that Vanka Hoffman was later seen by Klara Tenenboim in Vienna).

After this Aktion, the beautiful summer days became more and more difficult for the Dubno Jews. More than 3,000 Jews remained alive, but they lived in constant terror, and were convinced that they were being kept alive only to draw out of them the last bit of skilled work, and that their fate would be a tragic death. There were a few naive ones, optimists, who comforted themselves with various spurious news reports about the battlefront, from overheard discussions amongst the Germans, and from the radio. When a German would occasionally allow himself to say a word against Hitler or his forces, it was enough to make Jews feel that they could build a mountain, and for a whole week to hope and to be encouraged.

Meanwhile the Germans created trade schools in the Ukrainian states, so that skilled Ukrainians, when necessary, would be able to annihalate the Jews and take their places. Foreseeing that the end of the remaining Jewish population was getting close, the Ukrainians and Poles started stealing from the Jews, taking anything of value, promising that it was for – so to speak – 'help' in a time of danger. The Jews gave away to their non-Jewish neighbours all of their best goods, saying 'If we survive, then perhaps we will get something back'. A Polish woman, a friend of mine, Zofia Stefanowitshova, whom I saw almost daily, took Jewish-owned goods from the house of two former Jewish neighbours in order to hide them: they were Eigentimmer Bronshtein, and a Jewish girl, Adela, and her mother. She (the Polish woman) filled a cellar full of Jewish belongings, amongst them two cupboards filled with goods. When the above-mentioned Adela came once because she wanted the things in the cupboard which were with this woman, and to take a dress out of the cupboard, she was abused and chased out of the house. The same thing happened to Mrs Bronshtein when she wanted to take a small amount of her washing. This is how almost all of the Ukrainians and Poles behaved: they became rich from our tragedy.

I myself heard a conversation at Zofia's place. I was sitting in a room in her house. A Polish dressmaker, Kolova, came into the house. She did not know that I was in a second room. She started to speak in a cheerful voice to Zofia: 'Mrs Zofia, are you not able to take away from a Jew a pram for your little daughter, Dzitka? The Jew will be killed in any case and you, my friend, would have a pram for your child. I have already taken a piano for my child, and that Jew has already been allowed to go to his Maker! So I know now that it is mine.' And this Kolova talked on: 'I must get hold of two good fur coats for myself and my husband. I already have some ordinary coats from the Jews, but I want to get a Karukul fur coat – and I will have it. One must not be asleep and one must do what one can for oneself in comparison with what others have already done. Compared to what the others have, we have very little.'

The above-mentioned Dzitka (the daughter) for whom she took the piano was only one year old! Zofia, to whom she spoke in this way, showed Kolova by placing her finger on her nose not to speak further (knowing that I was in the next room). I then came out of the room, furious, but in a cold and stern voice I said to this Kolova: 'You, lady, will play mazurkas on the piano after the Jews are gone, but I don't know if you won't also play a tragic march after the Poles are also murdered!' The fact is, that's what really happened. After destroying the Jews, the Ukrainians started on the following day to attack the Poles, using violence and robbery against them. These are just small episodes which characterise the relations between the Ukrainians and the Poles towards the Jews in the Ukraine. A decent attitude towards the Jewish tragedy, shown by sympathy and help, was a rarity. Such Ukrainians were practically non-existent. The local Russians were also no better. A friend of mine, a Russian called Kazakh, with whom I worked in the Kommissariat, later showed his real face when I was away from Dubno trying to get Aryan papers. For a time he kept track of me in order to hand me over to the Germans. Only the local Christian Czechs did, in certain circumstances, show sympathy and helped friends. All the local Christian residents who were very pious would hang their heads in sorrowful prayer in their churches. Those who repeated the holy words 'feed the hungry and the thirsty' were shown, in practice, to be the most gruesome and bloodthirsty murderers, looters of Jewish goods and helpers for the Germans to exterminate the Jews.

Meanwhile in the ghetto, each day was more sorrowful than the next. In the evening every Jew lay on his hard bed with the feeling that this could be his last night. Often, because of different rumours, they didn't sleep at all. Many Jews prepared underground hiding places, believing that they would give some protection and that in a dangerous time they could save themselves from death in these places. The bunkers and hiding places were cleverly camouflaged so that they really thought that it was impossible to detect them. And yet they later found out that it was all for nothing, thanks to the collaboration of the non-Jewish population with the Nazis.

Life in the ghetto steadily deteriorated, bringing the worst of poverty and misery. The bread ration was very small, and no other food was distributed. Whoever had the means bartered his last possessions for food in order to stay alive. For a tiny piece of butter or meat, the finest clothes or valuable items were given away. Very often Jews paid with their lives.

With the passage of time no cultural or political activities were seen to take place in the Dubno ghetto. The reason is that, immediately after six weeks of its existence, the greatest number of ghetto inhabitants were killed; the survivors suffered for another six months.

From the first big Aktion in Dubno until the final liquidation the Germans made use of the skills of the Jews. German demands were great and the Jews were unable to meet them. The head of the Judenrat, Magistrate Konrad Tyberfeld, and the leader of the Jewish Labour organisation, Rozenboim, lost their positions as they were unable to find a solution to the impossible demands; also, they did not wish to give the other side [presumably the Germans] an opportunity to berate them and cause trouble. They did everything they could in their official roles. The majority of the Jewish craftsmen were rotting in the ground. The leader of the German work detail, Hammerstein, used to come to the ghetto to chase the Jews out to work, beating them and torturing them. There were instances when individual Jews escaped from the ghetto into the forest or to stay with non-Jews whom they knew, and lived there with Aryan papers.

In the summer of 1942 rumours started to circulate in the ghetto about the liquidation of other ghettos in the Volyn states. Two Jews who escaped from Kremenetz informed us about an Aktion on 14 July 1942, which took place in their ghetto. Up to 12,000 Jews died in that Aktion. According to what they told us, the Kremenetz Jews experienced an even greater hell than the Dubno people until their deaths. From 50 to 100 people died daily from starvation. A second escapee from Rovno informed us how, in the beautiful July days, the Germans murdered the remaining 7,000 Jews in the Rovno ghetto. This tragic news foreshadowed the fate of the Dubno Jews. In August 1942, about 4,500 Jews were crammed together in the Dubno ghetto. Their number was increased by Jews who were expelled from the surrounding areas. Although they were people who were descendants of generations of field workers and farm labourers, these Jews were allowed to take almost nothing of their possessions into the ghetto. The hunger and suffering of the Dubno Jews became even worse after the Aktion of August 1942. The Aktion was for the purpose of confiscating all food products from the surviving Jews. The Jews were forced to take all remaining food – flour, cooking oil and other products – to a specific location where these were then removed from them and put in trucks.

On 5 October 1942, the tragic end came for the remainder of the Jews in the ghetto. I then had Aryan papers. I lived 15 kilometres from Dubno in a village called Kordovan. This final Aktion was similar to the previous one (the elimination of the first part of the ghetto). It was carried out by Ukrainians who were sent out by the Germans, driving around with complete freedom from town to town, liquidating each ghetto, murdering the Jews who had survived the previous Aktion. During this Aktion many Jews committed suicide by hanging themselves, by swallowing poison or by jumping into the river Ikva. My cousin, Lazar Weizboim, hanged himself. The dentist, Kagan, and Dr Artmenova and others poisoned themselves. Many Jews were murdered on the spot in the ghetto. Corpses were strewn over the town's streets outside of the ghetto, where those who tried to run away fell as they were shot.

On the morning after the murder of the Jews, the looting of the last of their possessions began. The best things were taken by the soldiers, and the remainder was taken as booty by the local populace. They shared out the various implements – trade tools – among local workers and artisans of the non-Jewish populations. There was only one Polish person in the ghetto: his name was Stefan Papuzynski, the director of the high school, who had in himself enough moral honesty to refuse to accept the gifts which were his share of the Jewish goods.

While looting Jewish houses, the Ukrainians and Poles unwittingly uncovered hidden Jews, and without mercy they gave these unfortunate Jews to the Germans. The Germans understood that there were still hidden Jews. They then posted bills everywhere which called on the Jews to come out from their hiding places; these murderers promised that nothing would happen to those who came out because they were needed for work.

This attempt had repercussions. The completely cowed Jews believed that perhaps this time they would be lucky. Thus, Jews started to crawl out of their hiding places. In the period of a few days it became evident that about 150 Jews still survived in the ghetto. For a few days they were taken to work in the town in order to deceive more Jews. All those naive Jews were shot on 23 October 1942.

In this way there were no more Jews left alive in the Dubno ghetto, and thus the whole Jewish population of Volyn stopped breathing! Jews, whose families had been citizens for hundreds of years in the Ukraine, White Russia and other Eastern areas, were rooted out and killed.

*We, also survivors of the Dubno ghetto, have read Moishe Weisberg's narrative written in his own hand, and find that it is factually correct. Signed by Rachel Schreier and Asher Balaban.*

# 3

# THE TRANSPORT FROM THE DEATH CAMP BALKENHEIM

Eyewitness Account by Maurice Kraus

Collectedby the Munich Historical Commission.
Published by the Munich Historical Commission in the Journal Series
*Fun Letzten Khurben*, Vol. 3, 1946

In January 1945, approximately 800 of us were prisoners on the march from Balkenheim (near Gross-Rosen). Previously we were many more. A number were shot and even more died from starvation. Before the march the 'authorities' sapped the strength of the weaker ones. They took the strongest kapos and told them to attack the people. If one fell down, he immediately received his sentence: they poisoned the unfortunate person. While on the march we had to pull heavy wagons loaded with the possessions of the camp Kommandant, the camp Elder, and the SS men who accompanied the transport. My 15-year-old son also had to pull a wagon. We were all already exhausted and depleted. Behind our column the road was littered with the dead. Whoever could no longer walk was quickly shot on the spot. Explosive sounds continued to reverberate, and this meant that again someone was killed. If any one fell down, he knew that the last few seconds of his life had struck. Can anyone imagine the suffering of these people?

More than once other people made an effort to lift up someone who had fallen and to carry them a little way. Unfortunately, our own strength was quickly waning, and with a heavy heart we had to leave the unfortunate ones. The sound of a shot seemed like the 'greeting' of our final fate.

At night we were driven into a barn where we stood so crushed against each other that we could not move our arms. In the darkness we continually heard voices wailing: 'I am being asphyxiated!' It was dreadful and cruel as never before. Those who held out from the beginning were taken outside. Again the weaker ones were shot. The rest received their bread ration (250 grams) and the column moved on. The route went through forests. It was slippery and bitterly cold. We had to run quickly and we continually slipped. We fell, got up, and fell again. Some were no longer able to lift themselves up. It was a terrible struggle for life.

I continued to hold onto my small son and encouraged him; in addition, I sang and laughed – everything to boost his morale and to give him hope. My heart beat quickly at the thought that, heaven forbid, my son may not be able to carry on with the march. I struggled for so long to keep him alive, and I had a goal! Every few hours when he was threatened with losing his strength, I would give him a small piece of bread. How often he would say to me: 'Father, I no longer have any strength to go on, let me sit down'. I am too weak to express in writing what my feelings were then. I remember only that my teeth would be clenched and I cried.

After a long and tragic march we arrived in Hirschberg, where they again collected more than 100 prisoners. The camp Elder placed a stronger guard around them and said explicitly: 'This is a heaven kommando'. They actually sent them to the crematoria in Hirschberg itself.

We marched again from Hirschberg; it was a terrible journey, rain and snow without a stop. Half of us were barefoot. Wet and drenched through we arrived at Reichenau. Here my son was completely exhausted and he fell down. Trembling, I quickly grabbed him and helped him to stand up. There was no shortage of beatings for this; they even stamped on me with their boots. However, I withstood all of this for love; after all, my son is still with me!

In Reichenau we were loaded onto open wagons. We travelled for six days and six nights in winter in the open without a crumb of bread and without a drop of water. No one paid any attention to us; many drank urine for their thirst. Someone who was close to death from starvation even tried to cut out a piece of breast from a corpse and to eat it. To what sort of state had the SS personnel brought us! The corpses in the wagons served as pillows for our tired heads. In every wagon there were 20 to 30 in the same state. Even now I still do not understand how my son and I withstood all of this; 144 hours without bread and without water in the freezing winter nights in open wagons!

At the end of February, after the gruesome journey, we arrived at Buchenwald half dead. Almost everyone had frozen feet and other parts of their bodies. Many developed lung diseases, including my son. All of this is not one hundredth of what my son and I went through.

Central Historical Commission, File No 53/1

# 4

# THE LAST ROAD FOR TWELVE HUNDRED BIALYSTOK CHILDREN

Eyewitness Account by H. Shprung-Levkowitz

Published by the Munich Historical Commission in the Journal Series
*Fun Letzten Khurben*, Vol. 7, 1948

It was the end of July 1943. A feeling of unrest hovered in the air. The faces of people were lined and worried. It is no wonder that people were again talking about an Aktion in the ghetto. The nature of an Aktion was still fresh in the minds of the ghetto residents who had survived a terrible pogrom five months earlier. Thousands of victims were shot in the streets of the ghetto, tens of children asphyxiated in the cellars and bunkers; they are not erased from the human memory so quickly. 'What is the news? What have you heard?' one person asks another. Everyone's eyes reflect sorrow and fear of the storm of wrath which will come anew. The children arouse a different sort of pity as they feel, precisely, the ever-present anxiety of the adults.

'Papa', the six-year-old Mirele says to her father, 'why are you so afraid? You have work, the Germans won't touch you. They take away only small children who are not yet able to work.' Twelve-year-old Chayele stands in front of the mirror on tiptoe to see if, perhaps, she is big enough to be accepted in a factory and to receive a work permit just like an adult. The really young children play contentedly in the courtyard. Generally speaking, what do they play at? Building bunkers, running away and hiding from the Gestapo, shooting their make-believe guns. They play at everything that took place in front of them five months earlier.

Finally the black hour arrived. One night in mid-August 1943, the ghetto was suddenly surrounded. The Gestapo occupied the factories in the ghetto. An order was issued: by nine in the morning all Jews must assemble at a certain point. Bialystok is to become 'Judenrein' [Free of Jewish inhabitants]. The initial order from the armed hordes and the sharpness of the Aktion became clear: hiding in the prepared bunkers would this time be pointless. All the Jews must gather in the street carrying their baggage in their hands. It must be noted that amongst them the majority are young people who run around angrily with red faces and nervous glances. They are running to their previously arranged meeting points. In their hands they carry parcels, not only of clothing. Whoever understands the youth is aware that previously organised guns lie amongst the rags [for later use], and at the proper moment they will serve to redeem Jewish honour.

At about nine o'clock the streets are already full of people. The mass moves forward, accompanied on all sides by armed, black-clad, wild Ukrainians all of whom will take part in terrible cruelties on the open road. The murderers in the lead beat the people in the front and push them back with their rifle butts, and murderers who are at the back push them forward. This results in tumult and confusion amongst the unfortunate victims who are being led to their death. People tread on other people. This creates a crush of people and forms one mass. The cries and the shrieks all mix together with the wails of children, and then a vicious voice: 'Forward!' Hundreds of the elderly and the children remain lying on the spot, asphyxiated and trampled. In such a cruel way, the others are brought to the railway line.

A crowded mass of humanity lies on the ground of the open square not far from the railway station. Tens of thousands of old people, young women, men and children. During the heat of the day, without a drop of water, and at night under beating rain – without protection over their heads, exactly like a herd of calves and cows driven together before they are slaughtered. The lack of pity on the part of our torturers surpasses human understanding. A woman asked a Ukrainian guard for a little water for her small child, giving the guard a little gold watch for his trouble, the last thing which she possessed; he went away and brought a glass of water, then in front of the mother he poured it out. Two days passed in such suffering until 'redemption' came. The cattle trucks arrived and the people were loaded onto them; men separate from the elderly, from the women and the children. It was unknown in which direction the men were being sent. It was said to be Lublin, but the direction of the train in which the elderly, the women and the children were travelling was clear to everyone. Treblinka was waiting for them. With German thoroughness everything was made ready for the journey. Thousands of people had already been sent off and the remainder waited for their turn to be sent away.

Suddenly, a command: a separate transport was being organised for children from the ages of six to fourteen. They would be accompanied by 30 carers such as teachers, health personnel and a doctor as head of the group. I too was among the teachers. Three families with their children had travel permits for Palestine – they were also on this transport. The three families had long enjoyed special protection from the Gestapo in the ghetto. Where the transport was going was not revealed, but the wily Gestapo whispered into someone's ear that it was fortunate for the group, that this was their best chance of survival. The group would be exchanged for Germans from abroad. Children from the orphanage would be taken with the first group. Some of the parents would be allowed to write to their children, even when they personally could not go with this transport. All better than Treblinka.

The children, and those accompanying them, were removed from the train and taken to a special house outside the ghetto. There they were guarded by the Gestapo until the transport left. As soon as the children were taken from the assembly place, the sickest fantasy in the minds of people was played out; they created all sorts of illusions. They began to give the children the addresses of relatives in lands overseas, and agreed to meet each other again if they remained alive.

A few days later, when the ghetto was already liquidated, the children were loaded onto a special train for the transport of humans (not animals). We were not accustomed to living without beatings and with no shouting. The transport was supplied with bread and water, and in the compartments it was almost silent. At the back of the train, in a separate wagon, were the Nazi guards, but they were not at all interested in the children; it was as if they had forgotten about them. The whole journey really seemed like an excursion.

During the three days, which was the time the journey took, the children gradually forgot the tragic experiences of the last few days. Among themselves they chattered, talked about relatives whom they had overseas, and would perhaps soon see. However, from time to time, some of the older children whose faces reflected deep anxiety managed to ask their attendants: 'What do you think, should we jump from the train?' It was a difficult problem. We had already seen the people who managed to spring from the train during the previous Aktion. Bleeding, hungry and exhausted, in torn clothing, barefoot, they barely succeeded in returning 'home' – to the walls of the strongly guarded ghetto. And now the ghetto no longer existed. We knew the way which led to Treblinka. We started to go over a little geography. Here is North, South, East and West, and we advised the children: 'when the train, moving from Malkinia Junction, goes south and it goes along only one rail line, it is a sign that the train is going to Treblinka. At such a moment our fate is sealed, then all must jump.' With great tension we all focused on the moment. After leaving Malkinia Junction, the train moved eastwards in the direction of Warsaw, and we breathed a little more freely. We travelled for three days through fields, forests and over rivers, not knowing our destination.

Nature was full of beauty and life. The laughter of children playing outdoors, freely, in natural surroundings, penetrated deep into the hearts of our unfortunate children in the wagons, and left them in a dejected mood.

We crossed over the Polish border, via Silesia, Saxon, and the Czechoslovakian border. In the deep of night we arrived in Theresienstadt. There was an order from the Gestapo: the attendants must move aside and go to another train. Those who were accompanied by their own children must take them with them. The three families, citizens of Palestine, go with the attendants. That means that the children remained alone!

At that moment a decision is taken: Yocheved, the youngest attendant, very young in appearance, is hastily taken from the wagon in darkness and thrust into a new role – an apron and two plaits – at the most a 15 or 16 year old girl. She remains with the children in the train. She will at least see what is happening and will understand what it means, and will be able to help with advice.

The youngest of the children was Raizele, the four-year-old, a blonde little girl. Her mother, with tears in her eyes, begged for her child to be included in the adult's transport, although she is not yet six years old. Raizele, this little bird, who longed so for her mother, was fed, put to sleep, comforted. What can be done now with this little one? Fearful of leaving her alone, she is not yet six years old. And again a new decision is made: I will take Raizele with me as my own child. If her mother would have been here, she would certainly have taken her with her. So it will be the same for her as for the other children who are here with their mothers.

We follow new Gestapo guards, and we move to another train. Again, clean light regular wagons, first class, typical German pedantry. The allocated travel arrangements, and the almost free movement, evoke from us more illusions and hopes. In order to gas them, one does not have to take children on a journey to Czechoslovakia for so many days, and to use so much heating fuel. And how is it that we go to many places and travel for so long with the condemned, as we have seen with our own eyes, in order to be sent to the crematoria? And we travel truly as if we were on an excursion. The Gestapo personnel are really friendly, they allow us to talk to them, we are even allowed to ask a question: 'Where are we being sent'? We hear something completely new: we are going to camps where they are building children's homes. We are supposedly skilled manpower. And the children in Theriesenstadt, will they remain there? No, in time they will also join us. We have to prepare everything first. They will come when everything is prepared. We travel day and night, night and day, through wonderful blooming fields, through forests, and we pass by rivers. Nature is filled with warmth and light from the summer sun; people are in the water, swimming, rowing. The entire war and our experiences are like a bad dream. It is difficult to grasp what reality is like: is whatever we see with our own eyes, through the window, what we have in our memories and in our hearts?

Our train continues, the wheels make a monotonous sound, where to, where to? We travel along the same route that we took on our way here. We cut across the border of Czechoslovakia, travel through Silesia, we cross the Polish border and are travelling in the direction of Katowice. We become melancholy; Auschwitz is somewhere here. Our two wagons are detached from the train, the doors and windows are tightly shut; outside where we move freely, our fate is sealed: quietly, peacefully, without a word, we advance to Auschwitz. Everything starts according to a familiar pattern: women and children to one side, men and women without children on the other side. I and little Raizele, holding my hand, are amongst other women and children. Suddenly, one of the cleaners from our transport springs towards me and shouts: 'You are crazy, why do you cause your own death?' And he says to the Gestapo man in charge, 'Sergeant, this woman is here alone, this child is not hers'. And, as if with one voice, everyone else starts to shout the same thing. The child is torn from me, and I am placed with the other group. I still make a last desperate effort to save Raizele. When the SS man turned around, I tried to create a miracle, and took the little one by the hand and attempted to hide her amongst the adults. I thought that if I succeeded in smuggling her into the camp, they would allow her to remain with us. Such a beautiful blond child, perhaps they would take pity on her. But at that moment I felt a hard blow to my head, with a stick or a gun butt; I don't know what happened after that.

When I regained consciousness, I saw in the distance a truck, and on the truck were mothers and children, with them the crying Raizele. During the terribly bitter nights in the camp, sleepless from hunger, need and cold, the thought of Raizele made me even more bitter. And if a miracle occurs, and I survive, how can I live with the thought that I was the cause of Raizele's death? How will I look her mother in the eye, in the event that she might survive? Because of my pity I caused the death of the child who could now have been amongst the living in Theriesenstadt. It was hard to continue living and I did not have a moment's peace.

A few weeks passed. Those who arrived in the camp together with me are no longer alive. Of all of those women, only two of us are still living. New transports arrive, day in and day out, from various towns and villages including Theriesenstadt. Even whole families with children come to the camp. With a thumping heart I ask: 'A few weeks ago, did you see a large number of children, more than a 1,000, arrive in Theriesenstadt?' They reply, 'Yes, they did arrive. They were placed in a different camp; they are not too badly off, even alright; they have educators, but we were not allowed to see them, we don't know why.' I am happy but still I feel a stab of pain in my heart. Raizele, if I had not taken her with me, would have been alive with the others. Another two or three weeks pass. Again transports arrive. Some go straight to the gas chambers, but others go into the camp for the time being. One transport arrived, and went without exception to the gas chambers. That was the transport from Theriesenstadt with the 1,200 children from Bialystok.

# IN RADUN

### Eyewitness Account by Leib Levine

Collected by the Munich Historical Commission.
Published by the Munich Historical Commission in the Journal Series
*Fun Letzten Khurben*, Vol. 4, 1947

Radun, a small town in Lida Circle (now known as Lida District), not far from Vilna, was famous for its revered man, a genius, the 'Chofetz-Chaim', and also for its famous yeshiva. [A Jewish Orthodox college or seminary for the study of mainly Torah and Talmud, Jewish religious texts] On 16 Nov 1941, the Germans formed a ghetto for the Jews of the town, and also for the Jews of the surrounding areas, such as Netze, Batumi, Daleszyce. Many Jews who had survived the massacres of Eishyshok, Oron and Olkieniki also came here.

On 8, 9, and 10 May 1942, a massacre took place in the Radun ghetto. Almost all of the Jews there, approximately 2,000 people, were exterminated during this time.

On the eve of the slaughter the ghetto was surrounded by a heavy guard of SS men and Polish police. In the darkness of night and under constant shooting, quite a few Jews managed to escape from the town. During the three nights of the siege about 150 Jewish escapees were killed. Around 300 struggled through and lived. Those who were saved made their way to the forests and to Christian acquaintances in the towns and in the countryside (various villages). Most of the younger ones made their way to the 'Russian forest.' This is a large forest with many swamps in it which stretches from Lida to Grodno up to Bialystok. The Jewish escapees from

Radun were individually concentrated in the section which is known by the name 'Netze-forest', nearby the town of Netze, 11 kilometres from Radun. Previously there was a 'minyan' (a quorum) of Jews living there. The few young people of Radun, who were also amongst the escapees, immediately took to organising a partisan unit. They quickly produced guns which they had bought for gold from Christians whom they knew, as well as boots, clothes and watches. A number of Russians joined them; they were among the scores of workers who were brought in shortly before by the Soviets to build Netze Airport. The Germans transported all these workers to Germany, and only a few ran away; they wandered into the forests. The Jews accepted them into the otriad (partisan detachment) and the young men began their tasks. The leaders were the four brothers Asner from Netze. Their father was called Itzik, and the Christians called them 'Itzkutzi' – the brothers Itzkutzi. In addition to these four there was also Arke Berkowitz, a young man from Radun who was called 'Arke the Kirghiz' because of his rapid marching.

The otriad grew from day to day. Many Russian prisoner-of-war escapees joined them. A large number of young Jewish men and women ran from the massacres, and from the ghettos in Lida, Vilna, Grodno and so on. The Jewish group, after long marches to the East, came into contact with parachutists from Moscow, who were to be found in the larger otriads around Minsk in the White Russian forests. Among the Muscovite parachutists there was a Jewish captain, Davidov.

The Germans were attacked and their guns taken from them. The otriad acquired the name 'Leninsky Komsomol'. They destroyed many bridges, and they annihilated German police stations in the towns of the area. In the same region of Lida-Vilna they also derailed tens of trains near Oron, Olkieniki, Martzinkantz and Batumi. A Jewish partisan from Dovidov's otriad, Isaac Levo, derailed 14 trains on his own. On 4 July 1944, seven days before the arrival of the Red Army, while he was derailing the 15th train, not far from the Oron station, he was struck down by a German bullet.

The Jewish youth from the 'Leninsky Komsomol' brigade in the Netze forest went on the toughest possible missions. They were also the central-supply depot for guns. They paid with their own money or with leather or sewn articles. For the most part, Arke the Kirghiz and the four Itzkutski bothers were outstanding. They would lead the otriad away from all the hazards and from the police raids which the Germans would carry out against them.

I and my wife and cousin, Chaia Rogovska, were given the assignment to continue with espionage for the otriad. We would mix with Christians in the small towns for two to three months, remaining with a Christian close by the forest, and regularly passing on to the otriad all the information that we would glean about the occupying Germans. The news, which we would obtain in every town for payment, would be delivered to us by our allied Christians. The Polish Christians had to maintain their silence and keep quiet about us because they were afraid of revenge that might be exacted by the otriad. We remained thus for a period of about two years in more or less secure places. For the whole of the last 15 months we remained with the Christian Voyitzik Shafkowski in the town of Puzel, two kilometres from Pushtshe.

On the eve of Yom Kippur, 8 October 1943, we were visited by eight Jewish armed partisans from the Katowski otriad (Katowski – a White Russian revolutionary hero). Together with them we decided to fast on Yom Kippur. Our guests brought with them a couple of hens. Our hostess baked a few 'challah' loaves. Before nightfall all 11 of us ate the meal before the fast, some even recited the blessings after the meal. Later, just before going to bed, we suddenly heard the farmer's dogs barking loudly. We all ran to the window and saw, in the semi-darkness, armed people coming from all sides, jumping over the fence, and running towards us in the house. We understood that they were White Poles[34] who sought out and murdered the few remaining Jews. They greatly outnumbered us. We immediately opened the hiding place under the floor which we had prepared long before for any emergency that might arise. All 11 of us, with all our arms, crawled into the hiding place. The house owner's son barely managed to close us in and to cover the hole with boards. The house was soon full of Poles. They started to search everywhere. We heard how they passed over our heads, how they shouted and threatened the inhabitants of the house, told them to give up the Jews who were with them. They tried by both good and by bad means. However, it did not help; all the inhabitants vehemently denied everything. 'We have no Jews here', the housewife maintained. 'If someone saw Jews here, he made a mistake because my sister slightly resembles a Jewess,

---

34  The Red Army was the Bolshevik force which took part in the Russian Revolution of 1917 and toppled the monarchy. The opponents of Communist ideology came to be called White Russians. They identified with the antisemitic stance of the monarchy, and hoped to restablish the Russian monarchy in time. During World War II, communist Russia treated the Poles brutally and the division between the Red and White Polish forces deepened.

and she was a guest here for a week.' We were sure that the house inmates would not betray us, because our otriad was present only a few kilometres from Puzel, and they were able to exact revenge.

The White Poles remained in our peasant's house for three days and also guarded the whole town. They were waiting for someone from the Reds in the forest to come here. They were apparently told that during the night Jewish partisans would often visit here. However, they waited in vain; they captured no one. During the three days in the 'malina' (hide-out), 'thank God' that we were not asphyxiated. The place was too small for 11 people. We were unable to enlarge the opening through which we received air because next to the small air-hole there was a guard. Our clever hostess placed a crate filled with chickens there which she fed all day: while bringing food for the chickens, she would let down bags of cooked peas and pieces of dry cheese, and also bottles of water through the air-hole. Along with this she would seemingly talk to the chickens. But we understood what she meant: 'Everything is alright and they will probably leave very soon'. After a three day occupation the Poles left. Our guests, the eight men, also immediately left the dark hiding place. Lying in hiding affected them very badly because they were accustomed to moving around in the free forests, fighting battles, not lying concealed with their guns. Now we waited in the house for an order telling us what to do and where to go. We did not expect that the Polish bandits would come searching for us anew. And yet it happened. A few days had barely passed when again the gang of White Poles came; they went by the name 'Krisies Odziel', a fighting unit bearing the name of their leader, Krisie. This time, however, they did not come looking for us, but to expropriate the peasant's house for their conspiratorial purposes. Here they established their headquarters.

We remained like mice in a trap, unable to go and unable to stay. All around stood guards, day and night. Again we lay in the bunker, and the housewife fed us from outside together with the chickens. For our clever housewife, it isn't difficult to wriggle out of the most complicated situation. She pours fat over the stove. The house is filled with charcoal fumes. The gentiles who were sitting there all ran out of the house into the street. Meanwhile she makes use of the moment, grabs us out of the hiding place and packs us into the storeroom off the vestibule. After a few minutes she calls them back into the house and at night, in the darkness, she takes the three of us out through a hole in the foundation, which she made by removing a rock from it, and puts us into the attic of a stable. Guards are always in place around the stable, near the forest. It is not possible to get to the otriad in the forest. It also impossible for the otriad to come to us.

The people in our otriad had decided to communicate with us. Their plan was to first rescue us from the peasant's house, and afterwards to blow up the whole group there. However, this did not happen. The Polish watch noticed them. Shooting from both sides flared up. The Poles also used machine guns and rockets. In the encounter, about 100 metres from our stable, Arke Chizik, the youngest of the four brothers 'Itzkotzi', was killed. For those of us in the stable there remained no way out except to wait for a miracle.

We slept quite peacefully in the stable, we were even able to snore, because the lower level of the stable was full of cows, horses, sheep, pigs and they made more noise than anything. The owner also boarded up and concealed the attic on all sides. Only one small plank could be moved, through which we would receive the food which they would bring to us together with the food for the cows. The attic was full of hay and straw in which we made a good burrow for ourselves, and would lie there day and night. We allowed ourselves to talk to one another, but only in whispers, because below us the White Poles would often come in to tend their horses, and a human voice would reveal our presence. The courtyard was full of Polish freedom fighters, whose main 'battle' was to freely murder Jews. They murdered many Jewish children who had had a place amongst Christians as shepherds, or who had wandered around between the bush and the forests, and from time to time they had slipped into a town to beg for a piece of bread. The Polish 'freedom fighters' would keep an eye on the Red partisans when they would return exhausted after a march which included derailing a train or destroying a German garrison. Then the Poles would lie in wait for the real combatants – partisans. They seldom harmed a German. During such clashes many heroic Jewish partisans lost their young lives, the best fighters of Leninski Komsomol brigade, such as Yankelovitsh from Vilna, Potshter from Vasilishak, Leibe Chofetz from Ishishok, Shlomo Kurlanski from Oron, Leib Katz from Olkieniki and many more good young people. The White Polish thugs tore the guns out of the hands of the Jews, but a German soldier, the real enemy of their people, would seldom be touched by them.

In the attic we were not cold that winter. The winter of 1943/44 was mild, and in addition we put in a lot of hay and had cushions. We had enough food to eat, because our householders were fairly wealthy, and also they were not bad people. Perhaps more shrewd than good. They knew that we belonged to an otriad which would finally be the victors, and they had to look to the future with clear vision.

Looking out of the attic we would see how the people of 'Krisies Odziel' would drill. Many of them would sleep outdoors. All day we would hear their discussions about the routes of the marches and their stories. They never stopped talking about the 'Jews'. On one occasion just before night, on 27 October 1943, we heard the sound of shooting in the distance, in the town of Rokitzenishok, about five kilometres away from us. The next day, through the small opening in the roof, we recognised the red boots that had belonged to Arke the Kirghiz on the feet of one of the Polish thugs. A second Pole wore his leather coat. Later we found out that during a clash with the Polish murderers, Arke Merkovitz from Radun, the best and bravest Jewish partisan in Netze forest, lost his 20-year-old life. From our attic we frequently noticed fires nearby. Again, it was the White Poles who caused them when they discovered Jews. They would burn down the house or barn together with the Jews. Once, after such a fire, we heard a discussion amongst the thugs in the courtyard; 'But who could have imagined that Jukevitz from Liovkishok would keep Jews living in his barn?' The Jews gave themselves up right away. But one of them, Hirsch Karklinski, the watchmaker from Oron, had with him a rifle and he fought until the end … then he shot himself with his last bullet. He would not allow himself to be taken alive!

We were becoming settled in the attic, but once, while we were looking out at the courtyard, we saw how several soldiers sat on the grass and were sharing out reels of thread. From their chatting about it, we understood that they had killed Yudele Koppelman from Radun. Yudele Koppelman the tailor and his wife and two very young children and a sister-in-law had saved themselves from the Radun massacre. For months and then years they hid amongst peasant friends of theirs and in the various forests. On several occasions they were saved from German encampments and from Polish police. The small, weak, little tailor often used to meet us at night during our excursions, while he would drag himself through the mud in the dark, cold, rainy nights with a little flask of milk, a small loaf of bread, and a small sack of potatoes, which he had exchanged with his gentile acquaintances who, at one time, had ordered tailoring from him in Radun. He would venture forth with reels of cotton in his pockets; he would go and exchange the reels of cotton for food. He looked dark and emaciated from his never-ending pain. Still, he provided for his whole family, and with all his strength he fought for their lives. For the last while, he paid a great deal for a permanent place with a Christian. And still, the Christian, his good, long-standing friend, could not resist the temptation of Yudel's bag of reels of thread and brought the White Poles who purportedly searched for, and discovered, the cellar under the bread-kneading trough. They took the whole Koppelman family out of there and shot them. This was only a few months before liberation! Now, the White Poles [see footnote number 34] sit and divide up the reels of thread from the bag. They tell their friends the whole story: how they lifted up the trough and lit up a lamp; how they saw the terrified faces of the little Jews; how they (the Jews) fell to their feet and started to beg. 'We said to them: good, we will let you go free, go, you will remain alive. But with their first steps, the wretched ones still looked back at us, untrustingly. When they had walked about 15 or 20 steps, we opened fire and exterminated all of them.' Every soldier who participated is entitled to two reels of black thread, as black as the hearts and souls of the Polish freedom-fighters. And to three white reels – white and pure as the souls and hearts of Yudel Koppelman's family, who were murdered near the town of Postawy.

On 1 June 1944, during the night we heard the thud of some commotion, as if the horses in the stable were kicking the walls. But why are they kicking all night without cessation? We could not understand it. The second night was the same. Could it be from the front? We talked it over amongst ourselves, but we immediately laughed at ourselves for the foolish notion. We also do not understand why we hear the banging only at night and not during the day. We ask our housewife about it. She tells us that it is not the horses that are banging, but the Germans who are carrying out large roundups of the Red partisans in Rudniki forest. The movement carries on day and night. During the day one hears the shooting only faintly, but at night it sounds louder. On the third day the housewife comes running with a message for us: the Soviets have penetrated the front at Orsha and they are moving forward! The White Poles are also leaving; there is chaos amongst them, they don't know where to go or what to do. The front will pass by our house, and then we will again have to put up with the thugs. Later the housewife actually came to us and advised us to remain for a while in the garret. 'All around us there are still White Poles', she says; 'if they see you here, I will suffer, and they can still murder you in all the chaos.' We follow her advice and again wait for several days, days full of fear and pain. We have lived to see our liberation, but how many of us have survived? This thought tortures us so much and tests us, robs us of sleep and stops us from eating. In addition it is so hard for liberated people to remain hidden. The days stretch on for so long. We again see the White thugs, how they all prepare together for their march route. Their heads are already bowed. They certainly must already have thrown away Koppelman's reels of cotton because they make their packs easier to carry. Now they are not going to murder Red partisans and Jews; they are marching to the front to help the Red army to take Vilna. We see them off with the 'blessing': 'May they not arrive there, not remain along the way, and not be able to return'. And our wish was almost granted.

At about nightfall on the Sabbath we got rid of the White Polish murderers who had killed several hundred Jews in the region, the last group from Radun ghetto. They had carried out murder everywhere, in the various forests, in the towns and territories, everywhere that they had come across or captured Jews. They exterminated the last ones who had saved themselves from so many German attacks and had miraculously survived so many different experiences. For years people had to suffer, lie around in bunkers dependent on Christians, in stables, in forests; they already had diseased itchy skin, and they were covered with lice, starving, wandering around barefoot and naked, and still they lived and hoped for salvation from Haman's [35] downfall. And yet they, the Polish 'freedom fighters', murdered them all!

After eight months of constantly remaining in the attic, on Saturday night we went into the housewife's home. On Sunday morning at sunrise we 'freed ourselves', and went of our own free will to Radun!

Central Historical Commission, File No.667/564

---

35  According to biblical sources, Haman was the chief antagonist in the Book of Esther. As the king's vizier he had considerable power and he plotted to kill all the Jews in ancient Persia. He was eventually punished by the king who had him killed by impaling him.

# 6

# A CHAPTER ABOUT SIEDLICE

Eyewitness Account by Getzl Weisberg

Collected by the Munich Historical Commission.
Published by the Munich Historical Commission in the Journal Series
*Fun Letzten Khurben*, Vol. 3, 1946

By the end of October 1942, after the various Aktions and deportations in Siedlice and the surrounding districts, there remained alive only about 12,000 Jewish people. On 1 November 1942, the Germans issued a decree to the Jews of the Siedlice district (in the Masovian district of East Central Poland) demanding that on 28 November they should all gather in Siedlice ghetto at the meeting point 'Genshi Dolek' – it was called that in the decree – and there they would take those fit for work to their forced labour, and the others would remain in the ghetto.

On 27 November at four o'clock in the morning, our camp Sarnak, with all its 150 labourers, was surrounded by Gestapo personnel, Ukrainian troops, and Polish police. In five minutes they lined us up in the courtyard in rows. Whoever was not ready that minute received severe beatings from the murderers. Three men who had hidden themselves were found and shot on the spot.

All 150 men were sent to the railway station Ploterow, and there we were loaded into one wagon, and travelled a whole day without food or drink. For a little bit of water which a Christian brought us, unnoticed by the SS, we had to pay 500 zlotys. In the evening we were unloaded at the railway station Siedlice. The SS handed us over to the Polish police who were to bring us to the ghetto to hand us over to the Jewish police. They led us so heavily guarded that we could only imagine the worst. They placed us, however, in a relatively free ghetto. There were three blocks there – two for Jews and one for Gypsies. The blocks were surrounded by barbed wire but not guarded. However, that 'freedom' did not last for long. Twenty-four hours after our arrival on 30 November at three in the morning we were surrounded by Polish police. Thinking that they were to be sent to Treblinka, panic spread amongst the people in the ghetto. Six heroic young men who had revolvers wanted to organise an attack on the police. They wanted to shoot at the police in order to create confusion so that the Jews could in the meantime escape into the fields and save themselves. However, the Jewish police reacted and did not allow it to happen. They thought that it would cause an even greater disaster and we would all be slaughtered. They assumed that as policemen they would be allowed to live. The Polish police, noticing that there was turmoil and noise amongst the Jews, telephoned for help. Ukrainians and German gendarmes armed with machine guns immediately arrived in several trucks, and the border around the ghetto became more strongly guarded. Thereafter we had no hope of being able to get away. We were forbidden to move from one block to another. Anyone who tried to test this was shot on the spot.

We remained like this in the block until eight in the morning. Then several SS personnel arrived in the ghetto. The chief of the Jewish police was ordered to walk in front of them. Meanwhile they fired seven bullets into his back and killed him. After this, they told all of us to go out into the fields adjoining the ghetto, for eight to ten men to line up in rows and to remain standing in this way. In addition the Ukrainians beat us with sticks. First Lieutenant Feivish arrived in a small car and informed the guards that today there would not be a transport and that we should be allowed to return to the blocks. Again they beat us all severely and allowed the people to enter only one block. Anyone who wanted to find or to meet with family members had to dig holes in the walls because the corridors were so full that it became impossible to open the doors. The people had not received any food for two to three days. We survived the day with potato peel or a spoonful of red millet, but not all were able to acquire even this for themselves.

Because of hunger and the struggle to stay alive, some ignored the increased guard, and threw themselves onto the wires, trying to get through them to escape. Actually, many did manage to escape, but there were also 200 victims along with them. The shot ones lay in the courtyard near the blocks. At midday 20 men were taken to dig a grave where the shot victims were to be buried. After this the same people had to dig a second trench, this time for themselves. They were lined up alongside the grave, shot, and thrown into it. The guards then took another two Jews to cover the 20 corpses with soil. These two, however, were allowed back into the block after they were brutally beaten. They (the Germans) wanted to instil fear into the remaining Jews with all these events, so that they would not dare to attempt to escape anymore.

In this way we remained packed together tightly, waiting for death. The next day we were again ordered to line up in the same place as the day before. While we were running to the spot, we received a hail of blows. Whoever had the luck to avoid a blow was ordered to turn back so that he should receive his share.

We were led to the railway station. On the way we met a group of Jews led by SS personnel. They were then attached to our column. At the station all of us had to sit in the snow. Whoever did not sit was ruthlessly beaten. The Ukrainians and the SS personnel wandered around amongst us and robbed us of money, watches, rings and other valuables. The Jewish policemen threw away their police hats, wanting to mix in with the other people. However, the SS personnel did not allow this and told them to stand apart. A separate wagon was set aside for them. We were loaded into the train, 120 people per wagon. I heard a Jew saying that he had on him a small hatchet, saw and drill. I kept close to him. When the transport was moved to a side line we thought that we were being taken to Treblinka right away. The Jewish man immediately started to drill a hole [to facilitate an attempt at escape]. While walking between the wagons an SS man noticed the hole which was ready, and a second one in the making. He called together his companions and they started to shoot into the wagon. In this way a few men fell and others were wounded. The SS personnel were not satisfied with this. They tore open the door of the wagon and started to hit people on the head with their rifle butts in order to make room for another 20 men who until then were standing outside. The deliberate pushing of these men into our wagon was done with the intention of making it impossible for those of us in the wagon to move at all and to manage to drill holes. They guarded the wagon rigorously.

As soon as the train moved away the Jews began to jump out of the small windows. Inside the wagon people began to shove and make noise, and panic reigned. Each one wanted to get to the window first. When the train was moving at its greatest speed, people sprang from the wagons. I was amongst them.

On the way, lying between the rims of the wheels on the railway tracks, there were people with severed hands and feet, some already dead. Many screamed: 'Save me!' I had nothing with which to save them and I continued on my way. While en route I met a cousin of mine, Natan Goldberg from Sarnak, and a friend, Gedaliah Montzosch. We stayed together, but later my cousin went into a small town near Sarnak to have a shave and to ask a non-Jew whom he knew for a piece of bread. Gentiles noticed him and reported him to the Polish police. When they found him, he started to run. They fired at him and he fell from the seventh bullet.

My friend parted from me near the town of Sarnak. A gentile told him to come to him, alone, without other Jews, and if he did so the Pole would find him a hiding place. After I was liberated I made enquiries from the Pole about my friend. He told me that my friend was hiding in a potato storage hole in the ground where he had been for about two months. But he was seen and was denounced to the Polish police. The police found him half-dead, his hands and feet frozen; they shot him.

After I left my friend I was alone and depressed, left to continue on my way by myself. I approached a Pole whom I knew to ask for some bread and a hiding place for two days. As soon as the door opened, he shouted out at me: 'Get away from here, I have a wife and children, I want to stay alive!' 'Pavel', I called him by his name, 'give me a piece of bread'. 'I am no longer called that, and I don't know you; what do you want?' I asked him again for bread, and he threw a piece of bread at me as if I were a dog, and I hastily left him. On the same day, the SS shot two Jewish women with their children, and a Polish woman who had given them bread was arrested. A great panic took hold of the Poles and they protected themselves from Jews as if they were the devil.

I left the Pole and went into the fields. I approached a barn and overheard a quiet conversation. I immediately hid myself, and in fear I listened in. It was Yiddish! I knocked and asked to be allowed in. They opened up for me and I remained together with them for four or five days. The Poles, however, found out about us and informed the Gestapo. At midday the police raided us. They ordered us to get out of the barn. We hid ourselves in the straw. They began to tear at the doors of the barn and fired inside at the Jews. In great fear I opened the door a little and began to run. They shot at me with weapons of different calibres, but missed me. When the other six men saw me running away, they also left the barn. While running across the field, three men were shot. One of them fell wounded, and a Polish policeman hit him with his gun butt. Two out of the six succeeded in escaping. Two days later one of the escapees was shot. The second one was with me in the forest. On 15 November 1942, during an attack, he too was shot.

At night I went to a peasant who lived in a hovel. There I dug out a trench two metres long, one and a half metres wide, and ninety centimetres deep. I camouflaged my bunker so that it should not be visible. There I hid for about four months until 21 March 1943, and then I left for the forest. There I met 25 Jews and we remained together. On 25 May 1943, Polish police carried out a raid in our forest. Six Jews from Sarnak were shot: Gabriel Tsuker, 33 years old; Shmuel Ribovski, 27 years old; Motel Rozenberg, 18 years old; Moshe Rudszki, 35 years old; Yitzkhak Vladover, 18 years old; and Velvel Vladover, 22 years old. During an attack by the Gestapo, together with the Polish police, on 15 November 1943, another three men were killed: Yidel Ribovski, 29 years old; Herschel Ribovski, 20 years old, and Uriel Mantshoz, 22 years old.

In this way, from day to day our group became smaller and fewer in number. We carried on until 30 June 1944, when a small number of Jews from Sarnak were liberated by the Red Army.

Central Historical Commission, File No. 111/258

# 7

# THE SLAUGHTER AT THE EDGE OF THE SEA

Eyewitness Account by Miriam Zweig

Collected by the Historical Commission of Neu Freimann.
Published by the Munich Historical Commission in the Journal Series
*Fun Letzten Khurben*, Vol. 3, Oct/Nov 1946

On 27 August we were brought from Lodz ghetto to Auschwitz by rail in sealed wagons. As soon as we arrived in Auschwitz, a selection of people between those who were fit to work and those who were not took place, and I was separated from my mother, whom I lost forever. I was ordered to go to the right, amongst those fit to work, and my mother was ordered to the left amongst those unfit for work. They were destined for the gas ovens and the crematoria. My father had already perished in the Lodz ghetto from a heart attack while observing an Aktion. My father was left out of that particular Aktion because he had presented himself as a worker in a bakery. His heart, however, was unable to withstand it all and it failed.

As soon as the selection in Auschwitz was over I, together with the fit-to-work women and men, following a great deal of distress and wandering, arrived at Stutthoff. Here I again survived a selection. The healthy, fit ones were placed separately, and the weak and sick went right away to the gas chamber. After all my suffering I was still designated as healthy, and together with others, like cattle in sealed freight wagons, we were brought from Stutthoff to Jezowe, 16 kilometres from Konigsberg. This was in October 1944. The place was an aerodrome which was to be enlarged by further clearing of the forest. For two weeks I worked with a hatchet and saw, chopped and sawed down trees, and on my own I dragged them away, with the daily portion of food being only 150 grams of bread, a watery soup, plus 20 grams of margarine a week to sustain me. We slept in cold barracks on hard planks.

At the end of December 1944, when the first attacks on Konigsberg by the Red Army began, all the camps in East Friesland were evacuated into Konigsberg. In accordance with an SS personnel decision we were supposed to be sent from there to Denmark. This did not happen. After eight days of waiting in Konigsberg, all the healthy men and women were removed from the barracks – in general anyone who could still walk. The sick and the weak remained in the barracks which were set alight with the people in them. We, the selected ones, were sent to Palmnicken in the district of East Prussia. On the way more than 3,000 people died from German bullets and beatings. Out of about 10,000 men and women, only about 7,000 arrived in Palmnicken. There the Germans drove us to an amber mine[36] where we lay on straw for four days without food or water. On the fourth day, when we were let out, each one received three potatoes.

On 31 January 1945, 7,000 men were taken out of the barracks. Under the pretext that we were being sent to Denmark, they sent us to East Zeeland, that is to say, near the Baltic Sea. There ships were supposed to arrive to take us to Denmark. Not one of us thought of starting to resist. We were fully aware that we were truly at the edge of the sea. We were taken to the sea in the following order: first, the women went, the men after them. For the entire time that we were marching we heard shooting and it became a calamity. The Germans told us that the Russians were shooting at us. Later, it became apparent that the Germans themselves had shot all the men who were behind us.

The shooting of the men came about in this way: as we approached closer to the edge of the sea, the 'Vilosovtzes' [Russians in the German army] grabbed the men, and divided them into groups of 50. From the closely guarded groups they would remove 10 or 15 men, dupe them into going into the sea and then shoot them. The men threw themselves at the guards, and began to resist, but they were too weak against the murderers, and all of the approximately 2,000 were killed.

The women who walked close to the men and who saw what was going on tried to escape. Only then did we, the women who were in the more distant front rows, understand the meaning of the shooting [the sound

---

36  Palmnicken is the world's largest supplier of amber.

of] which somehow reached us. It became clear to us that we were going to our deaths and not to Denmark. Panic overtook all the women. They began to run. The SS personnel started to shoot. Every group of 50 women was encircled by SS men and compelled to remain standing in one spot. Meanwhile the guards took five women at a time, pushed them into the sea and shot them. When all the women were already lying on the ice in the shallows of the sea the SS personnel shouted to the shot victims: 'Stand up!'. Whoever lifted her head and showed signs of life immediately received another bullet. The Aktion lasted all night until daybreak. All the murdered ones remained lying on the ice of the Baltic Sea.

During all these Aktions which I had until then survived, my instinct always dictated that I should twist and manoeuvre so that I should remain amongst the last. Also during the Aktion I made an effort to be amongst those at the back of my group. I kept together with four friends (Tsila Moskovitz and Weinberg from Lodz who now live in Friesland, Silesia; the other two friends were drowned in the Aktion).

When our group of 50 women formed the last row, the guards had already taken five to be led to the sea, and we, the five friends, attempted to attach ourselves to the women in the back row. We started to struggle with the SS men, who beat us on our heads with their rifle butts and drew a great deal of blood. However, we succeeded in forcing our way to the second group of women, who were not yet in the row of people who were to be shot. Our camp Kommandant, the SS man Shtock, noticed this. He captured us and ordered that we be taken immediately into the sea and shot. We parted from the rest, kissed each other, and were then hurled into the sea. They shot at us. However, fate decreed that the bullets would not hit all of us. Each one fell in a different spot. Two us were hit by bullets and three of us remained alive. We lay on the ice all night together with the dead. The following morning, 1 February 1945, bleeding, we managed to push ourselves from under the dead promising them that we would avenge them for their young lives which the murderers had cut short.

We made our way into the Palmnicken forest near the town of Zurgena. There we were successful in obtaining papers which showed that we were Germans. We were liberated on 20 April by the Soviets. Together with the German woman with whom we had lived, we were interned by the Red Army in a German camp. When a Jewish Captain in the Red Army (he questioned us about the Jewish High Holy days such as Pesach and Yom Kippur) established that we were definitely not German, but Jewish, we were removed from the camp, and transferred to Kranz, a small town in

East Friesland where there was a camp specially for foreigners. Here we met with another seven young women and three men from our transport who also, due to a miracle like ours, were saved.

Central Historical Commission, File No. 200/314

# 8

# IN THE BRASLAV REGION

Eyewitness Account by Moshe Treister

Collected by the Historical Commission In Bad Reichenhall.
Published by the Munich Historical Commission in the Journal Series
*Fun Letzten Khurben*, Vol. 4, 1947

Until the outbreak of the German–Polish war, about 300 Jews resided in our village (at the crossroad of Braslav and Vilna). During the third week of the war the Red Army marched into our village, which was situated 40 kilometres from the old Polish–Russian border. From then onwards the whole area around Neu-Pohost, including our village, became Soviet territory.

With the outbreak of the Soviet–German war, on 22 June 1941, the Soviets decided to desert our town at the end of June. The local White Russians immediately turned on us. They looted all the warehouses which the Russians had left; then they organised an attack on the Jews in order to steal their belongings. The Jews were driven from their houses, and the White Russians removed everything from Jewish homes. On this occasion there were no murders. The attack was organised by a woman, Karlowitz, and someone by the name of Beinarowitz. Then the White Russians formed a police force among themslves, which was identified by a white band [on their arms?]. The organiser of the police force was the same woman, Karlowitz. Beinarowitz was appointed as Kommandant of the police. On 12 July 1941, the Germans entered our town. I approached the German Wehrmacht and put myself forward as a German language interpreter. They did not realise that I was a Jew. They immediately began to question me about the identity of those who had plundered the town, including the warehouses and the homes. Outside, there were large numbers of White Russians assembled, waiting for a signal from the Germans to 'put the Jews in order'. I then addressed the whole crowd with the words: 'The German army demands that the robbers are handed over to them'. Everyone was shocked and they begged that no one's identity should be disclosed. I then informed the Germans that the Soviets had taken everything when they left our village.

Making myself more familiar to the German army, I attempted to chat with them about the Jews. I asked: 'What rights do the Jews have under the present regime? Is it justified to attack them and to rob them?' They answered that Jews still do have rights, albeit limited. No one has the right to do anything like robbing or murdering them. Then I declared to them that I was a Jew. Precisely at that moment, all the White Russians from the town again assembled and wanted to reveal the Jews 'for what they really were'. I requested that the Germans order the whole crowd to disperse. One of the Germans let loose with a few sharp words publicly and stated that the leader demands that everyone should work. The National Socialists forbid theft. Everyone must disperse.

In time, terrible pogroms against the Jews began in the neighbouring towns. In the nearby town of Mior, which is situated 20 kilometres from us, White Russian hooligans murdered Rabbi Pianko and his wife. In Braslav, also close by, all the Jews of the town were forced out to the edge of the town to the marshy lake Minutshitza, and were held there for several hours. Prior to this the White Russians in the town had stolen everything from the Jewish houses. While the White Russians and one SS man were driving the Jews out, two Jews, Milotshin and S. Bloch, were shot on the way. This event immediately became known in all the neighbouring towns. Our White Russians became even wilder. During the night they stuck large placards on all the walls: 'There will be no punishment for killing a Jew' and 'rob and kill Jews'.

On 4 July 1941, an order was given by the White Russian police Kommandant in Nyavizh that all Jews who had run away from the town must return within a few days, and on every Jewish house there must be written: 'A Jew lives here'. In this same decree, Jews were forbidden to walk on the sidewalk, and were forbidden to go further away than three kilometres from the town. Anyone who disobeyed these regulations would be shot immediately.

An order was issued on 17 July 1941, that on the following day at six in the morning all Jews in the town must congregate in the marketplace.

At six o'clock all the Jews were assembled there. The whole of the town's White Russian police force was assembled together with their commander, Beinarowitz. He announced that within half an hour all Jews must put in place two yellow patches, one on the left side of the chest, and the second on the right side of the back. From then on Jews were forced to do all the dirtiest work in the town.

On 23 July 1941, the Braslav Junction together with our town were included in the Dvinsk district, which was under the Kommandant of the Dvinsk fortress. The town's Elder, Kowalski, also had authority there. An order came from him to have the Jewish teacher, Volshtein, arrested because at one time he had blasphemed the Christian God. Volshtein was arrested and incarcerated in jail. After a great effort was made, by giving gifts of gold to him (Kowalski), the Jews of the town had Volshtein freed.

On 30 July 1941, a Jewish committee was created by us with an Elder, Fagin, at the head. On 2 August the first 'contribution' was imposed on the Jews. In the space of three days until 5 August 1941, the Jews had to contribute 20,000 roubles to the Elder, Starowski. With great difficulty the sum was gathered. On 17 August 1941, a second contribution was demanded from the Jews of the town, this time 12 pairs of boots, 25 furs, 80 kilograms of bacon, and 25 kilograms of honey. The Gestapo together with the White Russian police came to take the contribution. They became violent and beat up hundreds of Jews. The White Russian police attacked Jewish households and pillaged them. The Jew Sher was a victim.

An order came from the police on 30 September 1941 that Jews had to give up all their valuable possessions, like gold, silver, copperware and so forth. This was handed over to the District Commissioner from Glubokoe. On 20 October 1941, the White Russian police went from house to house and took from the Jews all of their livestock such as cows, horses, poultry and so forth. Thus the Jewish economy was completely destroyed. The whole of the Jewish population was enveloped in a dark fog. The Jewish inhabitants became apathetic. There was only despair and desolation weighing them down.

On 5 November 1941, an order arrived from the District Commissioner addressed to the city police, saying that on 7 November 1941 all Jews must gather in the neighbouring town of Sharkawshchyna, which was 18 kilometres distant from us. There a ghetto would be created for the Jews from the nearby towns. All the Jews from our town went there. The Jews from the nearby towns of Bildyugi and Germanovitz were herded together in Sharkawshchyna. A closed ghetto was created for all of these Jews, a total of 19,000. 'Our friends' situated the ghetto in the worst area. The region was called Yozshefke. Formerly only criminals and thieves lived there. We had no water there, so we had to go to the River Disenke. We were permitted only one hour in the day, from three to four in the afternoon, to obtain water. The ghetto itself was divided into two sections. One section was assigned for those fit for work or who were useful, and the other was for those unfit for work or 'unnecessary'. A Judenrat was formed and an Elder, Mindel, was appointed. Also a Jewish Security Service was organised with Itzik Deutsch as the Elder. Our Judenrat was under the control of the Judenrat from Glubokoe with their Jewish Elder, Lederman. The SS man in Sharkawshchyna, who took care of the administration of the regional towns, was called Sonderfuhrer Weimann (Specialist Leader). The Sharkawshchnya Kommandant was a White Russian, Daniletzki.

During the first few days in the ghetto Daniletzki accomplished what he wanted to do. From the outset his hands were dipped in Jewish blood. On 10 November 1941 he took 10 Jews out of the ghetto and shot them. Two Jews from our town were amongst them, the brothers Eliahu Gershon and Woolf Ishachar Levinson.

With the creation of the ghetto all political and social activity stopped. However, it was different with religious life. All the rabbis from the dispersed towns were here. They would often gather the community together, teach them and give them courage, saying that God would help them; Hitler must lose the war, and we Jews would be helped! These exact words were expressed by Rabbi Rabinowitz from Sharkawshchyna. The Rabbis also listened to complaints of the people, twice a week, on Mondays and on Thursdays.

When we were ordered to enter the ghetto, every Jewish family was allowed to take with them 30 kg. Later, the Kommandant, Daniletzki, announced to the Judenrat that he would be coming to conduct a search in order to see how much food the Jews still had. He had to be bribed with a sum of 300 roubles in gold.

There was a small town 15 kilometres from Sharkawshchyna, Iodi, which had a ghetto containing about 1,000 Jews. The bloodiest slaughter of Jews took place there. The slaughter was carried out by the local SS personnel together with the SS man Vymann, from Sharkawshchna. A very small number of Jews managed to save themselves, approximately 50 men.

On 30 March 1942, factories were built in our ghetto for tailoring, bootmaking, blacksmithing and so forth. The ghetto inmates worked for the White Russian population in the town. We did not pay any special taxes, but the Judenrat imposed 10 roubles on every bread ration card to be used to help those who did not have the money to buy their quota of bread. The income from the planned production went to the council which handed it over to the District Commander of Glubokoe every month.

Housing conditions in the ghetto were appalling, with 20 people in one small room. Obviously sanitation could not be good. Various diseases appeared among the ghetto population. Medical help was in short supply. In addition, it is noteworthy that in the town Germanovitz, while the Jews were being forced into the ghetto, the Jewish chemist Sosnoviak was left behind. There was no one there who could take over the pharmacy and prepare medications for the White Russian population. In Pohost too, a Jewish chemist, M. Klar, remained behind. Thanks to them many Jews were rescued from death. They supplied the ghetto with many types of medication and life-saving products.

In this way we continued for a while. But then the liquidation of the ghetto in Sharkawshchnya took place. On 20 May 1942, the District Commissioner of Glubokoe imposed a contribution of 400 roubles in gold, and 50,000 roubles in paper money on the Jews. Soon after this the District Commissioner of Glubokoe, Vitvitsky, began to liquidate all the ghettos in the surrounding areas. The first one to be earmarked for liquidation was Luzhki, whose ghetto population numbered 1,200 Jews. The Aktion took place from Sunday to Monday, June 1942. The second slaughter was in the Myori ghetto on 2 June 1942 which numbered 1,100 Jews. The third liquidation was that of the ghetto in Disne on 15 June 1942, where the total number of Jews was 1,700. The fourth liquidation, on 17 June 1942, was the ghetto of Drawskoe where the Jewish population numbered 1,900. Also in Braslav the ghetto was liquidated on 3 June 1942, and 1,900 Jews were killed. The turn for our ghetto in Sharkawshchyna also came. We were very anxious about the news concerning the neighbouring ghettos. During the night of 18 June 1942, the Jews were too nervous to sleep, as they were aware of the roving figures of the SS men. At the same time individual houses in the ghetto began to burn. The Jews became panic-stricken. People ran frantically everywhere, Jews tore through the wire fence and ran into the forest and the fields. The SS personnel together with the District Kommisar, Vitvitsky, opened fire with various types of firearms, and our people were shot down in the fields. Those who were captured alive met their deaths in a bestial way. While running, my family too were annihilated in the hail of bullets. Only I was successful in saving myself. I escaped to the forest Caronka.

On 19 July 1942, an Aktion took place in Glubokoe: 2,000 Jews were murdered there and 3,000 remained. This was ostensibly because the 'necessary' ones were left there to work. On 20 August 1942, the District Commisar, Vitvitzky, issued an order which the Kommandant of the gendarmes, Keven, passed on; that all Jews who were hiding in the forest should present themselves in the ghetto of Glubokoe, that from now onwards it was illegal to be outside. Those who remain in hiding will be considered partisans! Approximately 1,000 Jewish souls emerged from the forest and went to the Glubokoe ghetto. Jewish police drove around all over the forest, the fields and the towns, and apprehended the Jews who were then moved to the ghetto. They guaranteed that the Jewish lives would be spared; however, I did not go and remained in the forest. I also wandered amongst the Christians in the town.

On 15 Septembr 1942, the SS personnel launched an expeditionary force to enter the forest, and at the same time they burnt down large numbers of towns and villages around the forests of Myori and Braslav districts. Those peasants who were suspected of having links with the partisans were shot. They decimated towns like Bahn and Zamoscze, which were around the forests of Braslav, and famous under the name of 'Novaya Moskva'. The partisans were driven away from there. For the Christians in the small towns it became extremely difficult to sustain themselves. The few Jews who were still hidden there were often betrayed by the Christians who handed them over to the Gestapo. For a small reward, such as one pud (16.38 kg) of salt, they would give up even the closest Jewish friend, who had paid all that he had for concealment in a stable. On my own, I was unable to find a place for myself in the town because all the Christians with whom I was acquainted told me that they were afraid of their neighbours; they would definitely denounce them, and they would pay with their lives. Thus I wandered for a long time in the fields in the rye. At sunset I would often grab a piece of bread in the town. It was very difficult to conceal myself in the rye. Frequently the Gestapo would carry out a raid. Whoever they caught would be shot on the spot. Since the expedition into the forest on 15 September 1942, the partisans had been displaced from their position, and because of the arrival of winter and the frost, it was very difficult for them to re-unify themselves. The greatest obstacle for them was that there was a shortage of guns.

That winter I went to the colony of Kuptshelov where I knew a Christian, Baron. I had handed over to her all my household valuables, and for this she had concealed me in a stable. For the whole of winter until 10 May 1943 I did not see the light of day. Lying hidden in the stable I would often feel terribly dejected. I would be overcome with regret that I did not go to Glubokoe ghetto. From afar rumours circulated that there it was good, and here I lie, having nothing and going hungry; darkness reigns around me always. No improvement can be hoped for, and where should I go now? Every path is now closed to me! And now an even worse period is looming. Spring is on the way; the Christians are going out to work in the fields. My Christian is beginning to feel that her life is in danger. Then she worked out a plan. This was on 18 May 1943, and early in the morning a Christian from Biruki (near Braslav) drove here. During the day I was put in a large wagon which had straw in it. This did not evoke any suspicion from the police, who were present in the nearby little towns where they controlled the traffic strictly. Lying well hidden in the straw I was successful in passing through the 12 kilometres as far as the Kolonia Biruki. There the Christian settled me in a stable. It was very difficult for me here. The Christian was extremely poor and on many days I starved. The Christian would go to the forest to harvest mushrooms and cook them. She also fed me with them. To acquire bread was extremely difficult. For five gold roubles one received a little bit of rye. The peasant was unable to buy rye with gold; this would have caused suspicion amongst the other Christians. Under such conditions and enduring severe hunger, I lived in the stable until September 1943.

Previously the last liquidation of the Glubokoe ghetto took place. It was on Shabbat, 21 August 1943. The liquidation was linked with a former Colonel of the Red Army, an important Soviet hero by the name of Radionov. In the year 1941, he was captured by the Germans. He then went to the German army with a plan to establish a new Russian army under the name 'Holy Russia' comprising all the prisoners-of-war. The new army would do battle against the shady trading of Jews. Such an army was created under the command of Radionov. Leaflets were distributed among the soldiers declaring the following: 'Pay attention to the words of Colonel Radionov – we are going to fight Stalin together with his friends, the Jews!' There they had listed Stalin, Mechlis, Kaganovitz, Finkelstein and so forth; the new program was to eradicate the Russian Government and to establish a Holy Russia without thieves and without the Czar. The army numbered approximately 8,000 men and it immediately initiated the battle. The first thing it did was to launch attacks in the forests where the partisans hid in the areas of Miechow, Lublin, Biale-Podlask, Bielovich. Pulkovnik Radionov's army was motorised, using the most modern German technology. Radionov received the highest German award for his heroic [possibly ironic] fight.

In May 1943, Pulkovnik Radionov's army was defeated in the Vilna region, as well as in the area of Podbrodzie as far as Vilna. A large number of partisans lived in the huge Bezdan forests. Here the Colonel was supposedly going to increase the Aktion. At the railway junction of the station of Krulevstshinkina (about 20 kilometres from Glubokoe) he suddenly began to play another role. There he joined up with the partisans, and together with them he took part in the struggle against the Germans. At the beginning the Germans knew nothing about this. Radionov carried out his first task exceptionally well. He invited the regional Kommisar of Glubokoe and his whole staff to visit him to view a parade. The Regional Kommisar was unable to attend, so he sent the Police Chief Keron as his representative with a retinue of 80 people, all of them SS personnel. At the station of Krulevstshinkina, Colonel Radionov had prepared a chain of partisans, and the guests were greeted by a hail of bullets. Not a single one of them remained alive. Then the partisans destroyed the Krulevstshinkina-Glubokoe railway line, and prepared for battle against the Germans.

Colonel Radionov's act made the Germans very fearful that the partisans might attack the ghetto in Glubokoe and set the Jews there free. For 20 days in the Hebrew month of 'Av' (August) 1943, the Glubokoe Regional Kommissar, Vitvitzky, with a group of soldiers and SS men besieged the ghetto.

They began to burn down the houses and to fire with machine guns from all sides. Whoever had hidden themselves in the bunkers were killed by hand grenades which had been thrown into the ghetto, and from fire and smoke. Only 10 Jews saved themselves and joined Radionov's partisans. The Colonel once again proposed his plans to the partisans, but unexpectedly he was caught in a German blockade in the region of Vetrisk, in the district of Polotzk. There he was killed together with most of his partisans.

At the beginning of September 1943, the assassination of the Regional Kommissar of White Russia, Wilhelm Kuba, occurred by means of a bomb in his bed, and he was torn to pieces. The assassination was splendidly carried out by a Jewish partisan disguised as a village girl who worked for the Regional Kommissar as a domestic servant. The situation in White Russia deteriorated considerably, and a German order was issued to exterminate the partisans in the forests and to liquidate the Minsk ghetto, which at that time contained 70,000 to 80,000 Jews. The liquidation of the ghetto took place in the most appalling way. The Gestapo, together with the White Russian police, created a blockade of the forests where partisans were holed up. It lasted from 17 September to 2 October. They burned and destroyed towns over a distance of hundreds of kilometres. In the forests, too, it was abominable. For six days there was continuous bombing from large aircraft.

A large number of Christians from the towns were removed to an unknown destination, but those guilty of having links with the partisans met their death immediately.

Tararaka, the Christian man at whose home I was hidden, dug a trench for me in his stable and put me in there, then covered it with hay. I lay there for three days without any food at all. On the fourth day I received just enough to keep my soul alive. However, he saw that the situation was very bad. Everything was burning and they [the Germans] were carrying out searches from house to house. He then left for the forest. When the blockade was ended, and it became quieter, I left my bunker a shattered man. I was unable even to stand.

In February 1944, the Germans appointed Ostrowski as President of the White Russian Council. He immediately issued an order about mobilisation of men from 20 to 40 years old. In all the towns and villages, under the leadership of the Germans, military units with the name S.Ch. were formed. The mobilisation was carried out in greater Masshtab. In all the towns and villages parts of this army were integrated. However, the partisans simultaneously mounted a counter mobilisation. They went from town to town recruiting farmers to become partisans. I joined the Fourth White Russian brigade. They assigned me to the economics section.

On 2 June 1944, a month before liberation, we were attacked by four German divisions. They surrounded the Polotzk area from the river Disna as far as the large forests of Minukhi. The attackers descended upon us with an enormous army of tanks and aircraft. We were encircled for three days. Forty per cent of our partisans were killed, 30 Jews amongst them. The Commander of the White Russian Fourth Brigade, Yarmak, a Russian, also fell in battle. On the fourth day, we broke through the encirclement and got out of the forest. We destroyed and burned the vehicles and the whole town of Stare Pohost where the Germans were ensconced. Emerging from the mire our unit numbered only 3,000 men.

On 1 July 1944, the Red Army arrived and liberated us. Each one of us left to search for his home.

Central Historical Commission, File No. 483/545

/ 9 /

# SOBIBOR

Eyewitness Account by Yekheskel (Chaskiel) Menche

Collected by the Regional Historical Commission in Regensberg.
Published by the Munich Historical Commission in the Journal Series
*Fun Letzten Khurben*, Vol. 6, 1947

I lived in Kolo, near Kalisz, together with my close family members, as many as 200 people.

On Hannukah, in December 1940, a transport took place, and I was amongst those who were sent to Izbica near the river Wieprz. The assembly place was where transports brought Jewish people from all over Poland, Czechoslovakia, Holland, Hungary and France. We lived in Izbica for about a year and a half in the region set aside for the Jews. The younger ones had to work in kommandos. From 15 April 1942, continuous transports of Jews were sent from Izbica to Sobibor, an extermination camp near Wlodawa in the district of Lublin. The camp had existed since the beginning of 1942. I too landed in one of the transports together with my closest family members numbering 20 persons. I will describe here my additional experiences in this extermination camp.

The transport in which I travelled comprised approximately 6,000 Jews. The Germans pushed from 120 to 140 people into a wagon weighing 15 to 20 tons. Upon arriving in Sobibor we were immediately faced with a tragic reception. A Jewish Kommando called the 'Train Company' unloaded the 'goods'. All the children and the aged and those who were in poor condition were thrown onto lorries and taken somewhere. As we found out later, they were taken to the graves to 'enjoy themselves'.

Then the Germans called for the healthy young men, the so-called fit workers. Some did handwork. Altogether the group which had been selected consisted of about 40 Jews. I and another two Jews were assigned to the tailoring factory, two Jews were added to the carpentry factory and the remaining 35 Jews were sent to do menial work such as that of bath attendants, tending the gas ovens, sorting clothes and at the same time checking every item of clothing in order to look for gold, money and other valuables. Their function was also to pull out the gold teeth from the people who had been gassed and so on. All of these labourers worked until they were tortured to death. And then, when a new transport arrived, they (the previous workers) were sent to the gas ovens, and new victims were chosen in their place. The remainder of the 6,000 Jews from the transport were gathered together by the Germans in a certain place. The Kommandant, Shtroibel, delivered a speech to them. He said: 'All of you will receive land in Ukraine where you will live and work in peace. Your clothes must be changed and before you give up the clothing, each one must write a letter to your family, saying that you have arrived safely in East Poland, that you are working and you are satisfied.' (It is worth reminding you that many dead and crushed people were removed from each wagon.) After the Kommandant's speech, the people were taken to the shower facilities and from there to the five gas ovens. The aforementioned corpses were burned in four large already prepared pits. About 300 SS men were involved in this work. According to my reckoning more than 1,500,000 people were burned in the camp.[37]

The torture in the *appel-platz* (assembly place) and the 'pieces' (German slang 'stucke' referring to Jews – dehumanising them, also refers to 'performances') specially thought out by Kommandant Weiss were indescribable. For example, every day after work the people would be arranged in a row from one to eight. One of them would be dressed as Moshe Rabeinu (Moses): a big beard, a camp robe, a Jewish hat, and a stick in his hand. He would climb onto a table and would sing together with everyone the song specially composed by the Kommandant.

> Moses! Moses! Where are your brothers in the narrow sewer?
> When the Jews will already be in there
> We will shut the trapdoor
> Then all nations will have peace.

---

[37] This number is questionable. The general concensus is that about 300,000 people were gassed and their bodies burned in the ovens.

And all those there had to fall to the ground and say: 'Amen.'
A so-called 'gypsy song' had to be sung often:

> How joyous our life is
> We are given food
> Tralala, tralala!
> In the green forest,
> Where everything makes us content
> It is certainly better
> Than in our home.
> Tralala tralala!

In summer we suffered additional discomfort. In the month of May Kommandant Weiss ordered that every worker had to collect a specific number of beetles, the so-called may-bug.[38] Anyone who did not collect the specific number received 25 lashes. Therefore each one drove himself to meet the required number of beetles; this led to fights among the workers themselves, and the Kommandant took additional pleasure from this.

On 25 June 1943, a transport from Vilna, carrying more than 2,000 Jews arrived. The people arrived stark naked. In each wagon weighing 20 to 50 tons, 200 to 250 people had been jammed. When the wagons were unloaded we saw terrible scenes. More than half of those transported were dead. The half-alive people who remained were sitting on the corpses; Obersharfuhrer Frentzel, who was present at the unloading, called out: 'Oh, how beautiful this picture is'.

In October 1943, thoughts of resistance began to surface. We realised that finally the same death awaited us all. We began to organise resistance according to a worked-out plan. Forty Jews were members of the resistance group. It is noteworthy that the officers would specially send people from various countries to the work places, so that they would not be able to understand one another because of their different languages.

The day chosen for the uprising was 14 October 1943, at exactly four minutes past noon. The work was divided between two groups, each one consisting of 20 people. One group, to which I belonged, worked in the tailoring workshops. SS personnel who came to try on, or to pick up, their orders entered many of the rooms. People from this group (the tailoring workers) undertook to kill 16 SS men by various means, and to take from

---

38  A species of European beetle known as the cockchafer, but it is colloquially called the May bug

them their uniforms and guns. After completing all this, they would meet with the second group, which consisted of 20 men who worked in the munitions workshop. The second group was to acquire more guns, and then the 40 men were supposed to get all the Jews from the camp together and to run to the neighbouring forests. One of the 40 resistance fighters was chosen to be the runner. He had the mission to keep the other factories informed about the task being carried out. The SS who had orders waiting in the factory were told in advance that they should come on 14 October at four in the afternoon to take away or to try on the tailoring work.

On Thursday, the first day of Succoth (14 October 1943) at four in the afternoon, the invited SS arrived. They always arrived punctually at the pre-arranged time. They had additional agendas: if the head of the workshop did not have the work ready, he would be sent immediately to the gas ovens. I and my friend Leon Lerner (he now lives in Bayreuth, Bavaria) killed two SS men: Sergeant Greishitz, and Corporal Klatt. We carried out the 'deed' in the following way: while they were trying on the uniforms and they turned around with their backs to us, we chopped off their heads with sharp axes which we had prepared earlier. The runner immediately ran to the other rooms of the factory to give them the information that we had succeeded. He continued to pass on the news to all the workshops. Ten minutes after four, all 16 SS men were dead.

We immediately changed into the German uniforms and with guns in our hands ran to free the rest of the work kommandos who were already waiting for us. We had all discussed meeting in the *appel-platz*. When we came there, we shouted out to the Ukrainian guards: 'Hurray gentlemen, Vania is here!' ('Comrades, the war is over!' [Vania was the nickname for the Soviets]. The German guards who protected the gate also became confused. This lasted for only a short while. A few minutes later the Germans worked out what was happening and opened fire on us. Because of the comparatively small number of people on our side it was impossible to start a battle with the Germans. It was therefore better for us to run away from the camp. We tore through two rows of barbed wire fences and a water-filled canal. Many of our people were killed by the mines which were spread out in the canal. The group which worked in the munitions magazine was captured. They did not succeed in coming to the *appel-platz* at the arranged time. Out of the whole number of 600 workers, about 100 Jews escaped to the Parczew forests, which are found on the way to Lublin-Zamoscz.

In the forest we organised a partisan group. We had enough guns from the camp. We fought back against many attacks which were initiated by the Germans and the Ukrainians. We suffered a great deal from the Armia Krojowa bands [A.K., the army of the Polish Nationalists]. They supposedly wanted to carry out work together with us. In reality, they just sought ways and means of deceiving and killing us. Once, they did the following 'trick': together, we were going to launch an attack on the German guards. The A.K. units told us to go first, but when we were in place in front, the A.K. units opened fire on us. We quickly became aware of what was happening and we ran away. Sadly, eight of our people, our little family, died during this incident.

The almost 100 who succeeded in escaping from Sobibor during the uprising became spread out over various places. After liberation we got together, a total of 20 people.

It is worth reminding people about the two heroes who led the uprising in the camp, and thereafter also commanded the partisan group. One of the Jews was from the Minsk transport under the pseudonym 'Soshke'. We do not know his real name, and according to current gossip he is no longer alive. The second one was Leibel Felhendler from Nilkovke, in the district of Lublin. He was killed in Lublin by an A.K. murderer in 1945, just after liberation.

Central Historical Commission, File No. 651

# 10

# THROUGH GHETTOS AND CONCENTRATION CAMPS

## Nemencine, Ozmiana, Czeczmer, Kovno, Ponevezh and Eastern Prussia

### Eyewitness Account by Leah Rudovshevski

Collected by the Bad Zaltzshlirf Historical Commission.
Published by the Munich Historical Commission in the Journal Series
*Fun Letzten Khurben*, Vol. 6, 1947

We lived in the town of Nemencine near Vilna. In June 1941, a few days after the outbreak of the Russian–German war, my husband went to Russia. Because of my two small children I could not run and I remained behind 'on the spot'. At the end of June, a week after the outbreak of the war, the German army arrived. There was an immediate order that all Jewish women whose husbands had gone to Russia were to be arrested. I succeeded in keeping [the secret of] my husband's departure from them. Quickly a second decree was declared: Jews had to wear white armbands with a yellow Star of David on their sleeves, Jews were forbidden to walk on the sidewalks, Jews were not allowed to greet Christians, and many more rules. All these orders affected the Jewish population so much that we shut ourselves in our houses and showed ourselves in the streets as little as possible, in order to avoid coming face-to-face with the cruel reality. One day when I wanted to buy something for my children to eat from a Christian woman in the marketplace, a Gestapo man gave me such a hard slap that I fell and fainted, and remained lying there for a few minutes. Beaten and humiliated I barely managed to drag myself home.

A yeshiva boy who had escaped from Mezritcz arrived in our town. The evil ones would organise various spectacles using the boys from the yeshiva for the fun of large crowds of passersby. One day they took a group of boys fully dressed and drove them into the river Vilna up to their necks. On another occasion they brought together a group of rabbis, spread them out in the courtyard off the kitchen for Lithuanian workers, on Legion Street, and ripped out their beards and beat them savagely. The screams of the tortured reached the heavens. Most of the ones who organised these events were Lithuanians. Approximately two weeks after the occupation of our district, one Friday a vehicle with Gestapo personnel was driven to the House of Study. They threw the synagogue's prayer books and Torahs out into the courtyard and set them alight. They ordered the yeshiva boys to dance around the fire and to sing in Polish: 'Moses is burning, Moses is burning'. News constantly came in about the mass slaughter of Jews. We suffered through several months in a permanent state of deadly fear. One day on a Friday shortly before Rosh Hashana, 19 September 1941, at around three o'clock in the afternoon, a truck drove up to the police sector carrying a number of Lithuanian sharpshooters. They unloaded machine guns, rifles and ammunition belts.

A terrible panic gripped the Jewish population. A delegation from the Judenrat went to see the Lithuanian mayor, Tcherkuskos. Using this opportunity he extorted a large sum of money from the Jews, assuring them that no harm would befall them. The Jews calmed down a little. At about 10 at night a truck with about 30 sharpshooters drove up to the house of one of the town's Christians, Rutshkowski, who was a virulent anti-Semite. That night I dreamed that around me there were rivers of blood flowing, Germans were chasing after me and wanted to shoot me, but I got away. I woke up and told my friend Hanna Liobelski about my dream. At that moment we heard knocking on the window. It was already five o'clock in the morning. Orienting myself to what was happening, we ran out of a second door to the courtyard and took off for the back of the town. I gave up my four-and-a-half-year-old little daughter to a Christian woman neighbour who promised me that she would take care of her. (Later I found out that on the same day of the slaughter my neighbour herself took away the child and handed her over to the murderers.) After running two kilometres with my older son and my friend we arrived at the place of a Jew, Berel Grod. He was the owner of a tar works and was sure that, because of the important work which he did, he would be allowed to live. But knowing that the Christians from the nearby villages had been sent out to go and dig graves, he sent his family into the forest.

Soon the Christians informed us that the police had already come there looking for Jews. We ran away to the forest and from there we made enquiries from a friendly Christian. Already knowing what was happening in the town, he took us to a swampy forest where no people ever came. It was quiet for a few hours. At about 12 o'clock in the day, the sound of a lot of shooting could be heard, mixed with heart-rending screams. The slaughter was then in full force.

Night fell. Suddenly we heard footsteps close by in the forest. We remained in a state of waiting for a minute. It was the Christian with a Jewish girl, Sheinka Zor, who also came to him to be hidden. She described to us the course of the extermination that day. The murderers gathered about 1,000 Jews in the synagogue, later taking them to the prepared graves and murdering them.

We remained in the forest for another few days until the peasant came and told us to leave because the police were moving around there looking for Jews. These same police had offered him a big reward for disclosing runaway Jews. We left the forest going in a different direction. On the way we came across a small empty house; it was a bath house. We decided to go up into the attic and to hide there. The attic was so low that one could only lie there. At the time we were happy with even that hiding place. However, we were quickly discovered in the attic by a Christian who told us that we must leave the place immediately, otherwise he would hand us over to the Germans. Again we started on an unknown road and reached a monastery. The monks refused to hide us. We requested that they show us the way to White Russia. We left and took the road that they had indicated and arrived in Nemencine. By taking side roads we avoided the village. After a few days of walking, on exactly the Eve of Yom Kippur, we arrived in my birth place, Ozmiana. The Jews of Ozmiana were in complete disbelief about what we told them concerning the Jews in Nemencine. They could not imagine that such things could happen. The Aktions in that area came a little later.

A few days after our arrival in Ozmiana an order was issued instructing Jews to go into a ghetto. There were almost no men here because, right after occupying Ozmiana, the Germans deceived about 1,000 Jewish men supposedly to give them work, but they were later killed.

On Simchat Torah [a Jewish holiday] again a disaster occurred. The German gendarmes found a photograph of three Jewish women in a Soviet parade. They then carried out a search throughout the ghetto. They recognised two of the women and arrested them, but they did not find the third. While taking away the two arrested women, they noticed a Jewish girl, Liba Persky (a cousin of mine, a beauty) who happened to leave the house without the Jewish insignia. They arrested her too and murdered all three in the ghetto. A short while later another incident occurred. The head of the German gendarmes and ghetto chief, Keil, an infamous killer, noticed a Jewish woman buying two kilos of grain from a farmer. Immediately, he took the woman and her small child and, in addition, another 10 well known activists from the Judenrat, among them the beloved activist, Mrs Solotura, and led them to the cemetery. On the way, the child, who understood that they were going to be shot, continually shouted: 'Mama, mama, I still want to live!' All of them were shot.

There were still about 300 Jews in the Ozmiana ghetto. They were from Ozmiana and the nearby villages like Smorgon, Alshen and Zuprany from which they had been gathered and packed into the ghetto.

At the beginning of 1942 there again took place a mass slaughter of the Jews. I was a road labourer. One day when we were already arranged in lines to go to work, we saw from a distance how Jewish policemen with rubber truncheons and whips in their hands chased all the Jews out of their houses and sent them to an assembly point. The largest number of policemen, about 60, had been brought from the Vilna ghetto for this purpose, and the rest of the policemen, about 20, were from Ozmiana ghetto. At the assembly point the policemen divided all the Jews into two groups. One group of 1,000 men was handed over to the police who were already standing there, prepared to act. The people were sent three kilometres from the town to Zelianka, and there they were pushed into a barn. At night two people (a man and a woman) dug under the foundation of the barn and escaped. All the rest were murdered the next day. A young man from Ozmiana, a road worker, wanting to help his father, went in the direction of the barn. On the way, he encountered the Vilna District Commissioner, Murer, an infamous murderer, who shot him. About 2,000 Jews still remained in the ghetto. Every day, escapees from Vilna would arrive, running from the Ponary[39] slaughter but the gendarmes shot them all.

The yeast manufacturer, Avraham Strugotsh, was charged by a local Christian with having donated a large sum of money for an aircraft to the

---

39  Ponary was a village situated near Vilna. The Ponary massacre was carried out by German Einsatzgruppen and their Lithuanian collaborators. 100,000 victims were murdered by the Germans

Polish Republic. He and his wife were stripped naked (winter in 1942 was extremely cold) and were forced to go in this state to the cemetery where they were horribly tortured and later murdered. The ghetto Kommandant, Kyle, would frequently demand large contributions from the Jews and always made an effort to persecute them.

Three weeks before Pesach, [the Jewish holiday of Passover] 1942, an order was issued stating that the Ozmiana ghetto had to be liquidated. The Judenrat was ordered to register all the Jews in the ghetto who would be taken to other camps, each one in accordance with his own choice. I went with a group of 800 people to Mielagenai, a village near Czeczmer (Lithuania). In Mielagenai the camp was already overcrowded, so we were sent close by to Vievis. Later we heard that the Jews who were registered to go to Kovno were sent immediately to Ponar where they were murdered. We numbered about 200 Jews in Vievis, men, women and children. There we worked at various jobs for two months. Parents registered their children as older than they really were so that they should be considered to be fit for work. Thus the children had to carry out the most difficult tasks as equals with the adults, including my 11-year-old son, Shloimele, who was then still with me; this was his fate. Two weeks after Shavuot we were taken to Czeczmer, 50 kilometres from Kovno, to a camp which was surrounded by barbed wire and strongly guarded by Lithuanians. Here, we at first worked on the roads, split rocks, pushed wheelbarrows full of sand, and sorted.

Once, on a summer's day while we were at work, the work foreman (Zelinger) who was a man of about 60, came to us and reported that we must gather in the camp. We were overwhelmed by a deathly fear because we already knew what this 'smelled' of. In the camp square after we were arranged in columns, 50 men were selected and driven away. There was a boy of 13 among the 50 men. He had a mother and a sister in the camp. We were certain that they were being taken away to be murdered. We later found out about the fate of the 50 men. Three months later, while we were at work, a Christian man came to us and called for the 13-year-old's sister. Her little brother was waiting for her behind the bushes. He looked appalling: shabby, dark and in rags. He told us that the 50 men were taken to Ponary, near Vilna. There they were kept in a cave in chains, and worked at blacksmithing every day; they were lowered by rope into a tunnel where they had to lay out the dead (who had been brought there) on logs, pour petrol over them and set them alight. Among the 50 men there was a Jewish engineer from Russia. He organised a group of 21 men who dug out an underground exit from the cave. They would take the earth in their pockets to their work in the tunnel, and there they would throw it out. Within three months the exit was completed, and the 21 men succeeded in escaping. The 13-year-old boy was also among them. We were afraid to keep him in the camp, so he went away to a friendly Christian.

In 1944, two weeks before Pesach, the slaughter of the children took place. I broke a foot on my way to work and I was taken to the camp hospital. One day at twilight while I was lying there a great tumult began. The doctor, Gordonovitz from Vilna, came to us with the nurse, Hile Baran from Ozmiana, and announced that an order had been given that anyone who was able to walk had to go to work the following day; they could not remain in the camp. At five o'clock in the morning, at dawn, the camp was surrounded. The official scribe received an order to compile a list of all the children and those who were unfit to work. For every person who might hide himself, 10 people would be taken in his place. According to the compiled list, 10 children were missing as their mothers had hidden them. The Germans shot anyone they got hold of in their place. During this slaughter my 11-year-old son, Shloimele, was also murdered. He left me a farewell letter: 'My wish to see my father was not fulfilled. I am being taken to my death. You, mama, must remain strong to survive the war and perhaps one day you will be able to take revenge for our blood.'

I was told how my Shloimele begged the murderers: 'You are going to murder me, but have pity on my mother, she will not be able to bear it.' To this, the murderer answered: 'Your mother too will not live'. More than 200 souls were murdered, children and older people, among them many mothers who died together with their children rather than give them up. The extermination was carried out by Keitel, the man who had liquidated the Jews in Lithuania.

Shortly after the Aktion, on a Friday, SS personnel surrounded the camp and assembled all 300 Jews in the square. We were all sure that this was our end. After a few hours of holding us in the square, they took us in trucks to Kovno, to a prison camp where we worked near an aerodrome in a meat factory, sawing wood and doing various other sorts of hard labour. After a few weeks of work we were taken to a forest next to Ponevezh where they were building an aerodrome. Aside from the thousands of Jews who were brought there from two separate camps, there were also large numbers of people of different nationalities who worked there. We did not work in that place for long. In July we were moved to Stutthof concentration camp near Danzig. On the way many people who wanted to save themselves leapt from the train. There were numerous victims. We arrived in the camp at 12 o'clock at night. We were immediately arranged in rows of five under a strong guard of the SS with machine guns, and were led one row at a time into a large building. In the morning the men were taken to the baths one group at a time. A few hours passed, and the men were brought back in prison clothes. In the baths they searched us and took away every little thing. We received old, torn clothing; everyone's clothing had a red cross insignia on it. There were 1,000 people in our group, among them also the children who had been hidden during the children's Aktion.

On 15 August 1944, 500 of our women were assembled in the *appelplatz*. A terrible panic came over us. Then the Polish Camp Kapo, Max, an infamous killer, attacked us with iron rods and killed many women. The remainder of the assembled women were taken by ship to a village, Steinort, not far from Danzig, and from there to a camp 15 kilometres from Neumark Pommern. [Pommern is a historical region of the southern shore of the Baltic Sea] We were there for five months and worked hard at ditch digging and lived in the worst conditions. A large number of our women died from starvation and cold. Then the Russian offensive started in Eastern Prussia. The Germans left region after region. We were forced to walk for six weeks, barefoot, naked and hungry. Many of us fell along the way; many also ran away. We were taken to a village, Rzeplin, near Bitow, where we were liberated four weeks later by the Russian Army.

Central Historical Commission, File No.531

# 11

# TREBLINKA

Eyewitness Account by H. Shperling

Collected by the Historical Commission in Tirschenreuth.
Published by the Munich Historical Commission in the Journal Series
*Fun Letzten Khurben*, Vol. 6, 1947

In September 1942, there began – what we had already begun to feel weeks earlier – the destruction of the Czestochowa Jews. The city is surrounded by SS units. Wild shooting, people screaming and wailing, and a roar from vehicles, wake us at dawn from our deep sleep. We take a peek at the street and see how SS personnel violently break into the houses and chase the people into the street under the beatings of their gun butts. We see how they sort out the people with unnecessary force into work units; only a small number of them are specifically assigned work, the remainder are transported en masse. Somehow a premonition tells us that this is the road to death, and we decide to conceal ourselves in the bunker which we had previously prepared. More elderly Jews come to us, and we lie together hidden in the bunker, locked away from the world and talking about our appalling situation. During the day we dare not go out. At night, however, we sneak out to the fields and together we search for something to eat: there is cabbage, a leafy vegetable called rape and other greens. We gather them and cook them on the electric cooker. At night when it is dark we go into the houses of the murdered and search through the empty rooms.

Almost at the end of the evacuation our bunker was discovered. Whether this was treason or just by chance we do not know. The leader of the evacuation Aktion, Regenhardt, personally 'honoured' us by demanding that we all leave the bunker. We all emerge because we know that if we are discovered during a second search, we will be sending ourselves to immediate death. We are led along Pshemishlower Street which was evacuated last. Of the 7,000 Jews whom they rounded up there, 300 men and 10 women were assigned to a work-kommando in Czestochowa. The remainder are driven into a large factory yard. They are headed for the gas ovens in Treblinka. On the day we were transported, before leaving each one was given a loaf of bread for one zloty. This is a previously planned measure by the Germans: according to the number of zloty collected, they were able to assess the total number of persons being transported, how many train wagons they needed for all the people, and also how many people they could fit into a wagon. The next day at 4.00 a.m. the transport begins. Everyone has to place themselves in a line. All have to remove their shoes, tie them together and hang them over their shoulders. Then begins the barefoot and silent march to extermination. A container was placed at the exit from the factory yard. Under the threat of a death sentence every person must throw their valuables into the container. Few do so. Fear grows as the march continues. People start to reconsider, and, from all sides, valuables start to fall, money, foreign currency and so on. Jewish possessions are strewn on the road of the death march.

As we arrive at the train the SS drive the Jews into the wagons, 80 to 100 people in each one. Lime is thickly spread in each wagon. Each full wagon receives three loaves of bread and a little water. Then the doors are closed, locked and sealed. Ukrainian and Lithuanian SS stand guard on the steps of the wagons. We are locked in like cattle, pressed together tightly. Only a little bit of air gets to us in the wagon through a tiny barred window, barely enough for us to breathe. The lime helps little and in the wagon an unbearable smell increases. Women collapse from weakness, others vomit. The natural functions also have to be carried out in the wagon. Everything becomes much worse. In addition we are tortured by a deadly thirst. We hold out until we are desperate and we continually ask the SS guards to bring us water. For some time they allow themselves to be begged. Finally, they agree to give us water but only for money. We gather together a sum of several thousand zloty and we give it to the guards. The SS take the money but we don't see any water. In this manner we drag ourselves along slowly, with pain and suffering, until we arrive in Warsaw. There our train is moved to a siding. First thing on the morning of the following day we travel as far as Malkinia junction. Seven kilometres from Treblinka we notice Polish people working in the fields and we attempt to communicate with them.

We want to know from them at least something about our fate. But they look up from their work infrequently and then they shout to us only one word: 'death'. Horror envelopes us. We are unable to understand this and our thoughts do not want to accept it. Is there really no way for us to be saved? One person talks about us being burned, a second talks about being shot, a third tells us about gassing, another talks about inhuman and unbelievable torture. We are all overcome by a terrible anxiety which causes a number of cases of hysteria. We do not have enough time to think about it. A special locomotive detaches 20 of the 60 wagons from our train. About five minutes later, it returns and takes another 20 wagons. A woman next to me mutters and groans: 'Already killed, we are dead, dead, dead … my God why do we deserve this?' A cold shock overcomes me. I close my fists helplessly. And now they take the last 20 wagons. I am in one of them. At first we travel slowly. It can be clearly seen that here the forest has recently been cleared. Fearfully we travel towards a very big gate which is guarded by a large number of SS men with machine guns. The train comes to a halt and the whole reception kommando receives an order to stand and remain standing. Then the gate opens and the locomotive pushes all the wagons into the camp and remains alone on the outside. The gate locks behind us. The wagons move slowly towards the large ramp. All around there are SS guards, ready to greet us with hand grenades, rubber batons and loaded rifles. Now they tear open the wagon doors and they drive us almost fainting out onto the ramp. We can barely stand upright and take deeper and deeper breaths of fresh air. A terrible wailing noise, shrieks and cries arise. Children look for their parents, the sick and weak ask for help, desperate women tear out their hair, but immediately the SS falls upon us and chases everyone further. Old people, weak and sick people, and small children without parents are taken out on stretchers by a kommando with Red Cross bands, while others are held under the arm. They take all of them into a large building, into the so-called hospital. A fire burns there in the centre. On one side there is a long bench. The old, the sick and the children must undress completely, supposedly for a medical examination. Then they have to sit on the bench, one next to the other, facing the fire. In answer to their questions, they are told that the fire is to keep the room warm, so that none of the sick will catch a chill. Behind them there appears a kommando with machine guns. You hear a short sound of popping – and they all fall into the burning fire as they are shot in the head. Immediately another kommando arrives and places new branches of wood onto the corpses, while new victims already await their own extermination.

In the meantime the drunken SS wielding their batons drive the remaining men and women from the ramp and chase them through a gate which leads to a large square. The square is encircled by barbed wire which is carefully camouflaged with green branches. On the right there is a large open barrack, the women's barrack. On the left there is a second barrack open for the men. Then an order comes over the loudspeaker: women to the right, men to the left! Indescribable, heartbreaking scenes of parting take place, but the SS separate everyone. The frightened children hang on to their mothers. Finally the people are divided into two groups. An order is given: to undress ourselves and to put our things in a bundle, the shoes to be bound together in pairs. However, all in the huge camp seem to be waiting, but the drunken SS let loose with their batons and force the people to undress. Slowly or quickly, more or few, ashamed, undress themselves, men and women, and discard their clothes. Others attempt to talk a little with the Jews who are in the work kommando to try at least to find out about their future fate. They tell us the terrible truth: no one comes out of this camp alive. Also, there can be no talk about escape; our death is here. But we simply cannot believe this. People are too attached to life even when, a thousand times, everyone is informed that everything that they have been told is the truth. Finally both the men and the women are undressed. We are fainting from thirst and beg for a drink of water. But we don't get any, even though in the middle of the square there is a well, as if to spite us. Now the naked women are driven to the barrack. With their hands the women hide their breasts as well as possible. At the entrance to the barrack the haircutting kommando waits for them. The hair of every woman is hacked off with one movement and is immediately packed into prepared sacks. Then the women are put into groups, and with their hands in the air they are marched into the death camp through a back entrance. Meanwhile, the naked men have to pack together all the women's and men's clothing. Each one must carry as large a pack as possible and, running, go through a side gate into a second enormous courtyard surrounded by long barracks which are situated there. The bundles of clothes have to be placed in these barracks. Then everyone has to show himself with hands in the air, marching to the beat of striking batons back to the main courtyard. Here the men are chased, running many times around the perimeter until they are completely exhausted, because while they march to their death, they must be so tired that in the death chamber they are not able to show any resistance. Finally they are all chased into the men's barrack, and there they are driven to a door which leads to the death camp. There, in front of the door, 30 people are selected, among whom I too am included. We are divided into five groups of six men each. Each group gets a few workers. We will be in the work kommando for the camp. For the moment we are saved.

Treblinka consists of two camps: Camp One which receives the transport, takes the looted goods and prepares the way for death; then, Camp Two, the so-called 'death camp' where a systematic and quick extermination of the arriving transports takes place. I was in Camp One where the work is carried out through a number of kommandos. Kommando 'Blue' can be found here. The members of the group wear blue armbands and take over the newly arrived transport at the ramp. The kommando has to clean up the corpses, the garbage and the excrement in the newly arrived wagons as quickly as possible. The kommando work with brooms. Each two workers must clean a wagon in a period of 10 minutes. Then comes Kommando 'Red' – the men with Red Cross symbols. Their duty is to bring stretchers or to lead the old people by the arm from the ramp, as well as the sick, and children up to the age of six years, also children who have lost their parents. All must go into the death hospital. In addition to this there are separate Transport Kommandos, Train Kommandos, Sorter Kommandos, Camouflage and Barrack-building Kommandos, as well as kommandos of carpenters, tailors, shoemakers and so forth. A kapo under the Camp Elder is appointed over all the kommandos. I belong to the Sorter Kommandos who have to sort the discarded clothing into better and worse, and place them in the relevant piles in the barracks. Every specific piece of clothing must be searched in case there are valuables sewn into or hidden in them. Everything must be very carefully opened and the patch with the Magen David [six pointed star symbolising the Jewish religion], the Star of David, must be ripped off, so that it will not be seen to have belonged to a Jew.

Every box of shoe polish, every table lamp, every belt is cut apart to find anything that might have some value. The watches are placed separately, the gold is separate. Diamonds, rings, gold roubles, gold dollars and so forth are also separately organised. Collecting and sorting photographs is particularly strictly watched. A Jew received a death sentence for taking a photograph for himself. Mass shootings took place simply because one of the Jews hid a photograph of his wife and closest relatives on himself. In every tied up package the Jewish sorters have to put a note with their names on it, so that it would be obvious which person needs to be punished for the smallest mistake in his sorting. I still see now the punishment of a 19-year-old boy who forgot to remove a patch with the Magen David from a piece of clothing. He was shot in the courtyard in front of the lined-up kommandos.

He had to look right into the barrel of the gun. Before he could even move his head he was given two terribly cruel blows to the face. A few seconds later he fell down, his head crushed, and was immediately taken away.

With each order for clothing, the looted objects, beautifully packed and properly sorted, are sent away. Most of it goes on very large transports carrying one type of article, a second transport goes with only women's silk underwear, a third one with shoes, and so forth. Gold gets loaded on to trucks and is separately sent. The SS become incredibly wealthy. For the inhuman work in the camp they receive four weeks leave and always travel dressed in civilian clothing. Each one is accompanied by many suitcases. They take the best clothing, the most expensive and beautiful gold and diamond objects to their families.

Between Camp One and Camp Two three enormous digging machines work day and night heaping up huge piles of earth. The acrid smoke of the burnt corpses is there day and night reaching the heavens, and can be seen for kilometres in every direction. When the wind blows in the direction of our camp, there is such a terrible stench that we cannot begin doing anything. At first, when the wind changes direction, we are able to continue with our work. It is strictly forbidden to cross over from one camp to the other. At the beginning the food carriers would come to us from Camp Two and would tell us about the latest news of the gruesome events that take place over there. It sticks in our throats, it screams feverishly in the brain. It often takes hours until we are even able to continue with our work. Our flowing tears are not able to ease our powerless fury and our burning pain. They tell us how the road to the death camp passes through a garden. Close by the death shower stands a booth where everyone for the last time is urged to give up money and gold, always with the threat of the death sentence; for the spirit of Nazism does not allow anything, even an object of the smallest worth, to be lost. A Magen David hangs over the entrance to the death showers, and there the victims are prodded with bayonets and are driven by bayonet thrusts into the showers. During the time that the men come into the shower rooms, more or less composed, the women enact a different part in terrible scenes. Regardless of anything else, the SS know how to control the women with their rifle butts and bayonets. When all the unfortunate ones have already been driven into the rooms, the doors are hermetically sealed. After a few seconds unholy and shocking screams can be heard through the walls, screams that find their way to the heavens calling for revenge. The screams become weaker and die out. Finally it becomes completely silent. Then the doors are opened and the dead bodies are taken and thrown into enormous mass graves which hold from 60,000 to 70,000 people. When there is no longer any room for fresh victims in the mass graves, a new order comes to burn the corpses. A deep trench is dug and old boxes, wood and similar items are thrown into them. All this is set alight, and a layer of corpses is thrown on top, and then again branches, and on them more dead and so on, layer after layer. Later there is an order to dig up the corpses from the older mass grave and to burn them. When digging up the dead who are already decomposing, one finds still more money and valuables in the stomach and intestines. This shows that even at the moment of death, the Jews still believe in life. The smell of blood, the stench of decomposing bodies, and the smell of burnt flesh is blown by the wind onto all the workers of the death Kommando. Nobody lasts here for more than a few weeks. Even the SS Kommando is changed every two weeks and immediately sent on leave; the murderers themselves are unable to stand this devilish work.

Later it became forbidden for the kommandos to have any contact between the two camps. Even while exchanging shoes or clothes with the kommando of Camp Two, our people are not allowed to approach them closer than the border of the camp. The workers in the death camp would give us the foul and bloody clothes of the murdered in exchange for our rags.

At one time a serious epidemic of typhus broke out in death Camp Two. In order to control the epidemic, the sick were separated from the others and left naked, with each one allowed a blanket to wrap around themselves. They were chased outdoors and driven to the high piles of earth outside the chambers. Here they were shot, the dead falling into the fires which were already burning at the bottom of the mass grave. Shortly after this, barbed wire fences were erected between both camps. This work was done by the kommandos from each camp. We again [they had previously been together] had the opportunity to pour out our heartbreaking anguish to one another, and to mourn our bitter fate.

Fresh transports continued to arrive at Treblinka. Sometimes there was a small interval of a few days. Generally, however, every day 10,000 people were murdered in Treblinka. One day the human transport brought in up to 24,000! The Polish Jews, who were the first to be sent to Treblinka, foresaw their fate. They immediately understood that Treblinka meant their end. It seemed to them as though they were cattle to be slaughtered. While they were driven from the wagons, and while they were herded off the ramp, and also as they were undressing before going to their death, they were beaten.

Resistance took place amongst them only once, when there was an opportunity for a few Jews from the Warsaw ghetto to take the chance to gather some revolvers and hand grenades. The success of this was not exceptional. There were only a few wounded SS. The punishment for these people was immediately very severe. The Kommandant, Franz, deliberately left the attackers alive and had them severely beaten and tortured, until death released them. Suicides took place mainly among doctors and their family members; secretly they would bring cyanide with them.

The transports of the German and Czechoslovakian Jews are received with all sorts of tricks and ploys to deceive them. On the platform direction signs are installed – to Bialystok, to Kovisk. Also place names: Railway Station 1, Exit to the toilets, and so on. The people are not beaten upon their arrival. Even orders are given in a polite and friendly manner. A woman who had brought with her many containers of possessions, and did not want to go into the hospital, was assured that her packages would soon be sent to her. However, she would not accept this. She had worked all her life to accumulate her possessions and would not entrust them to anyone. The officer in charge, Sepp, finally lost his 'patience', and could not resist using his riding crop. Then she let go of her suitcases and went, lamenting, with a man from the Red Kommando to the 'hospital'. On the way she told him that she hoped to have a long rest there in order to regain her strength once more. The SS are even more cautious with the Bulgarian Jews. They arrive here in fine passenger trains, and attached to their trains are more passenger wagons stacked with wine, bread, fruit and other groceries for the SS who consume all these products in a real feast. The Bulgarian Jews go, without a care, to their death. They receive soap and towels and, waving their towels and whistling, they go cheerfully to the death camp.

The gypsies are not brought here in train wagons but in small groups on horse wagons. They are also not sent to the death camp. They are taken to the 'hospital' where they are shot and burned.

Only once did Jews manage to leave the camp alive. The German men at the front wanted women. One-hundred and ten of the most beautiful Jewish young women were chosen and were sent there under the care of a Jewish doctor. In the camp which was so full of horror there were a few SS who rewarded themselves with their own 'specialities'. For instance, the chief officer, Sepp, would regularly seek out small children from newly arrived transports and, as a trick, he would split open their heads with a shovel. Every day officer Franz Kurt – the commanding officer of the Camp Kommando – would look for people from the Work Kommando, and under the guise of different, invented complaints (working too slowly; someone gave a hostile look and so on) he would order them to undress completely and then he would whip them with his riding-crop until he had killed them. The devil of our camp is Corporal Mitter. He has to have several victims every day. He goes randomly to the first person he sees and searches his pockets. If he finds something, he gives him murderous blows until he falls dead. If he finds nothing on people, he looks them in the eye for a moment and says: 'You look poorly, you certainly think too much; therefore you are dangerous and must die'. After this statement, he beats the victim for so long until he no longer shows any signs of life. Corporal Suchamil, the barracks cook, was particularly involved with the 'gold-Jews'. They were the Jews who sorted the gold and the valuables. Suchamil would regularly send home gold and other valuable items without limit, and the 'gold-Jews' who knew about his thievery were naturally not allowed to live for long.

Only once in Treblinka did I meet an SS man who was repelled by the inhumane actions. Already on the first day of his arrival everything looked unbelievable to him; it seemed like a miracle that he took a Jew from the work kommando to the side, and asked him to tell him the whole truth. 'Impossible, impossible!' he muttered, and accompanied his words with slow shakes of the head. After a few days we no longer saw him.

Our lives are always filled with fear and pain. Often we envy those for whom everything is behind them. We always have death facing us. Food is scarce, and we have to use any means to steal a lifesaving morsel, like bread, potatoes and the like from the new transports. We steal even though we know that a terrible death awaits us for theft. One is shot for smoking. Someone was killed when, from cold, he covered himself with a torn old fur and lay down on the pile of clothes. For him they invented a special death: he was torn to pieces by the dog, Barry, which was specially trained for such purposes. No one could ever have imagined that Corporal Kurt Franz would give him one blow to his face which finally killed him on the spot. Our work time was from six o'clock in the morning until six in the evening, one hour break at midday. In the evening when we are already dead-tired, we must sing different songs to the accompaniment of an orchestra. The first is the 'Treblinka March', and after that a Polish song that describes the fate of a mother who sells her child in order to avoid starvation from hunger.

At the beginning, Jews would escape from Treblinka almost daily. Then the controls were made much tighter. When escapees were caught they would be hung by the feet on a high pole until they breathed out their souls in terrible torture. At one time two Jews were hung up in this way. While hanging they shouted to us: 'Run, run, Jews, because in the end this death awaits you. Don't take into account what you have to eat – our fate will be yours tomorrow.' To state that you are sick is almost impossible. In the hospital they will only accept those who have a temperature of more than 40C; if someone is sick for more than six days he is shot. In any case shootings became a daily occurrence. The shot Jews are placed together with the bodies of the newly arrived Jews from the latest transport.

Our situation becomes more deadly every day. Day and night we think about avoiding our bitter fate. In this respect, an unexpected occurrence comes to our aid. There was a Jewish doctor in the camp, Karanschitski, who used to treat the SS. One day Corporal Kurt comes to him for a medical examination. He immediately notices the doctor's full briefcase. As an answer to the corporal's question about the contents of the briefcase, the doctor grabs a surgical knife out of the briefcase and plunges it into the body of Corporal Franz. Franz runs out into the courtyard. The doctor chases after him with the knife. At once Ukrainians come from all sides and throw themselves upon the doctor. However, he manages to swallow poison. Immediately, all the doctors in the camp are summoned. By pumping Dr Karanschitski's stomach, all efforts are made to keep him alive. When all of this doesn't help, Kurt takes out his riding-crop and whips Dr Karanschitski until he is dead. The next day the Jewish kapo is searched and a bag of gold is found on him. He is shot on the spot. Tension grows daily. We Jews see that it is now a question of life or death. At some point in the past we buried money and valuables knowing that without some financial means we cannot even think about escaping. We also accumulated a few guns. Now is the time for us to get organised. Engineer Golevski, the camp Elder, the new kapo, Kurland, and Moniek, the kapo of the courtyard-Jews (who worked in the courtyard of the camp), are the leaders of the uprising. A 14-year-old Jewish youngster steals into the Ukrainian watch-house at night and takes arms and ammunition – bullets and machine guns. The arms are distributed and it is decided on which day to begin an uprising. As I remember, it fell on a day in summer 1943.[40] On that day the dreaded chief

---

40  On 2 August 1943, prisoners quietly seized weapons from the camp armory, but were discovered before they could take over the camp. Hundreds of prisoners stormed the main gate in an attempt to escape. Many were killed by machine-gun fire. More than 300 did escape – though two-thirds of those who escaped were eventually tracked down and killed by German SS and police as well as military units. Acting under orders from Lublin, German SS and police personnel supervised the surviving prisoners, who were forced to dismantle the camp. After completion of this job, the German SS and police authorities shot the surviving prisoners. The Germans had ordered that Treblinka II be

officer, Franz, together with 40 Ukrainians, went off to swim. At six in the morning, a signal shot had to go off as a sign for the uprising to begin. A terrible tension oppresses the Jews.

At four in the morning, the Jews are made aware that our plan might fall through. Staff-Sergeant Kuttner arrested 20 Jews on whom he found gold. Finding gold or valuables on Jews indicated to the SS that they were preparing to escape, and it was assumed that that is why the Jews had prepared themselves with valuables, in order to sustain life should they escape. In this instance the SS immediately launched a search among all the Jews in the camp.

It does not take long before we see the SS leading the 20 Jews to the 'hospital' in order to murder them there. At a short meeting we decide: this is the minute to start the uprising! Right away a hand grenade is thrown at the chief officer, Franz. The signal to rebel is given, the Ukrainian SS open fire wildly. The Jews gather together, throwing hand grenades and firing their machine guns at the guards. Several Ukrainians fall, and the approximate 1,000 Jews in the camp begin to tear through the fence. Beyond the fence the path leads to the forest.

The Ukrainians shoot at the escapees with a barrage of bullets. Some are hit, but the majority manage to reach the forest safely. Desperate activity begins. All the telephone wires are cut; vehicles are vandalised so that they cannot be driven. Any gasoline which we find is spilled and set alight; the death camp Treblinka begins to burn. Pillars of fire rise up to the heavens. The SS shoot chaotically into the fire.

Appalling punishment begins. The Jews divide themselves into small groups. I remain together with three others. There is from now onwards only one watchword: forward, forward, forward. We succeed in covering 12 kilometres from Treblinka. We can still see behind us the fires from the burning Treblinka. During the day it is important not to travel. We can still be noticed. We hide ourselves in inaccessible places. At night fear drives us on. But hunger begins to torment us.

---

dismantled in the fall of 1943. From July 1942 through November 1943, the Germans killed between 870,000 and 925,000 Jews at the killing centre. Treblinka I, the forced-labour camp, continued operations until late July 1944. While the killing centre was in operation, some of the arriving Jews were selected and transferred to Treblinka I, while Jews too weak to work at Treblinka I were periodically sent to Treblinka II to be killed. During late July 1944, with Soviet troops moving into the area, the camp authorities and the Trawniki-trained guards shot the remaining Jewish prisoners, between 300 and 700, and hastily dismantled and evacuated the camp. Soviet troops overran the site of both labour camp and killing centre during the last week of July 1944. Source: http://www.holocaustresearchproject.org/ar/treblinka/revolt.html.

We deliberate with one another about whether or not we still have a chance to live, or whether it is not easier to take our own lives. Someone talks about hanging himself but the will to live is stronger. As the best speaker of Polish, I sneak into the nearest town in order to bring back some food. Slowly and cautiously, uncertainly and with a hammering heart, I emerge from the forest and I approach a peasant's house which stands free and separate. It is about 30 kilometres from Treblinka. With a prayer and a glance toward heaven, I step onto the threshold of the house. With my first glimpse of the woman, I understand that she recognises me [as an escapee from Treblinka] 'You have certainly escaped from Treblinka,' she calls out to me. My condition, my clothing and, most of all, the desperate expression on my face exposes me. But the woman calms me down immediately and says that I need not be at all afraid, that she will help me as much as possible. However, she cannot hide me. The SS is searching and hunting in all the surrounding little towns. And she does not want to put herself and her family in mortal danger. She gives me bread and milk, and tells me to return at 11 at night. At the arranged time all three of us come to her house. This time her husband and daughter are present. We consult each other, and we decide that the best thing would be to go to a particular spot and to jump onto a moving train. At that particular spot the train travels at no more than 10 kilometres per hour. We have no other way out, and we decide to try this. They give us a satisfying dinner and they give us also bread and eggs for the way. As an expression of our thanks, we leave 20 gold dollars. Under cover of the night's darkness we take to the road. We arrive at the appointed place, but we decide not to jump onto the moving train; we might fall under the train itself. We continue on foot. We arrive in Rembertov. From there we want to travel on the train, but we don't have any Polish money. We exchange a diamond ring worth 20,000 zloty with a peasant and receive only 500 zloty in return. In great fear we buy our tickets and arrive safely in Warsaw.

Out of all the escapees a large proportion were killed immediately or captured. The road of suffering for the rest was still long and deadly. Only a small number of the escapees from Treblinka, about 20 men, lived until liberation. I personally met some of them later in the American Zone in Germany. They are: Reizmann Shmuel from Vengrov; Kodlik from Czestochowa; Schneidermann who is now living in Foehrenwald; Turovsky who now lives in Berchtesgaden.

Central Historical Commission, File No. 525

# 12

# IN THE WHITE RUSSIAN FORESTS

Eyewitness Account by Moshe Meyerson

Collected by the Historical Commission in Bad-Salzchlirf.
Published by the Munich Historical Commission in the Journal Series
*Fun Letzten Khurben*, Vol. 4, 1947

I was born in the year 1896 in Volozhin, a town famous for its Yeshiva, and located on the road between Vilna and Minsk. I lived in Horodok, also a small town in the same area. On 25 June 1941, the Germans occupied Horodok. Right away on the first day of their rule they issued an order that all men, both Jews and Christians from the age of 10 and older, should assemble in the marketplace. If this order were not obeyed, then the town would be destroyed and its inhabitants exterminated. In the marketplace the Germans divided the men into two groups – Jews and Christians. Everyone had to sit on the ground. Two Christians who arrived a little late were shot in the street. This event caused a terrible panic. The Germans searched all the assembled people. They confiscated everything from the Jews but not from the Christians. A large number of Jews who thought that they would be taken to work had brought with them packets of food. The Germans confiscated these from the Jews and apportioned them among the Christians. After sitting around for five or six hours the Christians were freed. An hour later the Jews also were released. On 26 June, the day after the occupation began, a tank entered the town and this incident caused deadly fear amongst the Jewish residents. One of the tank crew immediately shot a Jewish youth, Yaacov Eidelman, and also wounded a Jewish woman who died two days later. Another Jewish youth was lightly wounded in the hand. The murderers then cut off his hand in front of everyone.

Eight days later an order was issued which required 12 Jews to present themselves at the Kommandant's headquarters. They were the wealthiest in the town and had been pointed out by the Christians. In the Kommandant's headquarters they received an order that within 15 minutes the Jews should gather together all their valuables. If this were not done, then all the local Jews would be murdered. Ten of the assembled Jews left the Germans in order to announce this to the Judenrat and two people – the brothers Shapira, Arieh and Reuven – were held by the Germans as hostages. The order was carried out, but they did not release the Shapira brothers. They were taken away to the town of Radoszkowicze. They were freed only after a required sum of money, 500,000 roubles, and a large quantity of manufactured goods and leather were paid for the brothers. Every day we were forcibly sent to work, everyone without exception – men, women and even children. While at work we were terribly tortured. The local police in particular stood out in this respect – White Russians and Poles. They would attach six men to a cart loaded with a weight of six tons to take to the mill which was located far behind the town. When the people would stop for a second because of the weight, the police would beat them with vicious blows using their rifle butts and iron bars. Blood flowed but the police did not let up. The cargo had to be unloaded at the designated place.

After some time the Germans took 12 hostages and again forced the Jews to give up their possessions. We lived under really difficult conditions until the Germans created the ghetto in the first days of the month of Adar (end of February 1942). Approximately 1,500 Jews were crowded into eight houses. To enlarge the ghetto another four houses were included in it. In the ghetto, although we had previously given up our possessions, the Germans again started to seize our money and various articles. The Judenrat deliberately began to resist carrying out decrees, and they called on every Jew, each separately, to demand that he take an oath through the rabbi (Rabbi Galperin from Rakovi, who was also a member of our Judenrat) to inform them about what he still possessed; either to bury it or to hide it, or to keep it available for immediate use.

At the beginning of the month of Sivan (mid-May 1942) the Germans removed 100 youths from our ghetto and sent them to work in nearby Krasnoe. My two children were amongst the 100, a daughter of 19 years and a son of 17 years. On Sundays they were allowed to come home. The

Judenrat had the right to choose any worker and to replace him with another. My children remained there for the whole period.

In a few weeks time we received news of the slaughter of Jews in the villages close by: Rakovi, Radoszkowcze, Volozhin and others. It became clear to everyone that the danger was great. People started to look for some means by which to save themselves. Everyone resolutely took to the task: building for oneself a hiding place, a shelter. Once on Shabbat morning, at the beginning of the month of Av (in the middle of July 1942), we heard the sound of engines. The Jewish 'watch' immediately informed us that the ghetto was surrounded. In great fear we began to run to the shelters. The Gestapo, together with the police – Poles and White Russians – attacked the ghetto. They ran from house to house and chased out the Jews while beating them with iron bars. In the streets they sorted the people into groups. Anyone who was bleeding was chased into the synagogue, which was a central meeting point. Those who were not bleeding were arranged in columns, and later they were sent in trucks to work in Krasnoe. The number of those sent away was 400 young men and also women. As well as those who were sent to Krasnoe, there were also approximately 200 Jews assembled in the house of study. The Germans calculated that 900 Jews were missing. They then made an announcement to the labourers that all the hidden tradesmen should present themselves, and that no harm would come to them. Many workers emerged from their hiding places willingly. But many were also discovered later in their bunkers. All these Jews were beaten and forcibly driven together into the synagogue where they found the other 200 Jews.

In one house, at a certain Zuckerman's, the Germans encountered people just emerging from their hiding place. They immediately took her two-month-old baby from Mrs Zuckerman, and threw it into a stream next to the Study House. The two older children, having seen the bitter fate of their little brother, started to cry piteously and begged their mother to save them. Their mother did not desert the children, but later went together with them to their death. Before then, however, the murderers ordered the mother to leave the children, and she alone was freed and allowed to return to the ghetto.

The assembled people in the synagogue were taken a kilometre away from the town and driven into a barn where they were burned alive. A number of people who were still concealed in the ghetto came out of hiding during the night thinking that the 'storm' was over. However, the German bullets did not make a distinction; all of them were shot and then buried in the ghetto. Altogether about 900 Jews died during the slaughter.

In the middle of the night about another 200 men emerged from their hiding places. They all arrived safely in groups in Krassnoe. Among the last of them were my wife, my 13-year-old daughter and myself. Eight men from this group went straight from Horodok and joined the partisans. Another 12 men from the group were a doctor, three tanners with their wives and a few more tradesmen. They were left by the Germans in Horodok and survived for another six months.

On the way to Krassnoe we met our ritual slaughterer, Reb Hirsch Eidelmann, with one of his sons. He told us that his wife, his daughter-in-law and two little grandchildren were killed in his home by the murderers. He and his son hid in the attic among boxes and by chance were overlooked. Lying in the attic they saw through the cracks how the Germans led a Jewish family out of their house. They immediately shot the father of the family, and the mother and children were forced to drink his warm, flowing blood.

The supervisors of the slaughter were Schmidt and Gendel, the infamous SS murderers in our area.

All the legal and the illegal survivors from the slaughter in the small towns – Volozin, Ivia, Radon and Horodok – were concentrated in Krassnoe which was full of Jewish youth who were sent here previously for work. Altogether there were about 12,000 Jews. In Krassnoe itself a ghetto was formed, and a kilometre behind the town, a labour camp. In the ghetto there were about 4,000 people, and in the camp approximately 4,000 men. The Kommandant of both the camp and ghetto was Gestapo Agent Kundt. The Jews from both the ghetto and the camp worked in the arms depot (Feltzug Park) loading and unloading ammunition and in construction (building work), also on the railway lines, in the sawmills, and at various other forms of hard labour. My wife and son and younger daughter were in the ghetto and worked in the munitions depot. I and my older daughter were in the labour camp where we worked in construction.

Most of the young people, particularly those who had already lost their families, and who continuously heard the tragic news concerning the small towns around us, decided to run away to the forest, and to take revenge on the enemy with guns in their hands. While organising themselves they began to acquire arms which they stole from the gun depot, hiding them in their trousers or in among the wood which was delivered for heating, and then smuggling them into the ghetto where the arms were cached in a secret place. About four weeks after the battle in Horodok the first group escaped to the forest. The 10 men were: the two brothers Rogovin, Zelig and Arieh, a third Rogovin, their cousin, Shklinkt Herschel, Shklinkt Moshe, Goll Isaac, Manne Mendel, two brothers Shpringer and Elterman Chone. In the middle of the day, one of the Shpringer brothers, whose job was that of work-advisor, removed the sign 'Building Advisor' from the wall and escaped to the forest. After him the rest of the group also left.

In the forest the 10 partisans learned from Christians whom they knew that very soon several policemen from Horodok would be driving to Molodezhnaya to acquire food. This small group, with little experience, but heroic partisans, then worked out a particular plan of attack on the policemen. They went onto the highway and waited for the enemy in a camouflaged place. The attack was a success. They shot six policemen, managed to take their guns away from them, and at the right time they retreated. After this, thanks to the guns which were obtained with such difficulty, they took another six men out of the ghetto. The partisan group now consisted of 16 men.

One day the partisan group heard from close by a persistent sound of shooting. They became aware that this must be other partisans doing battle. Led by their commander, Chone Elterman, they went to assist. When they arrived at the place, the partisans had already retreated because the attack was unsuccessful. They came across only one wounded partisan, the Brigade Commander of Tchkolovska Brigade (Gribanov) who was left behind by his comrades during the turmoil. He asked them to take him to the Fersheier forest where his brigade was. They did so and, because of his recommendation, they were all accepted by the 'otriad' (platoon) 'Kuznietzove' from the same brigade. Our 16 partisans, however, were unable to rest without taking revenge on their enemy. They continually put pressure upon their commander to allow their platoon to go to Horodok. They were successful in getting their way. At the end of Autumn 1942, on a pre-arranged evening, they left for Horodok. The platoon at the time consisted of 300 men, and in Horodok, the enemy troops, Germans and policemen, consisted of close to 200 men. After an eight hour battle, the platoon was forced to retreat in the early dawn, managing to take with them the wounded and the dead. Among the fallen there were two Jews.

After returning to the forest Chone Elterman, with the permission of the commander, went to Krassnoe with the purpose of setting up links between the camp and the ghetto, so as to be able to regularly lead armed groups out of there into the forest. As if nothing had ever happened he, Chone, went daily into Krassnoe to his work. He explained to the work-overseer, who was very fond of him, that during the time that he had not appeared at work he was ill. Meanwhile, on the quiet, he organised groups of workers who, on a daily basis, would take arms out of the munitions depot. On a specific night, together with a group of 30 men, he again escaped to the forest. It was easy to remove any traces of the escapees. Daily eight to ten men would die from infectious diseases and poor living conditions. Also, after the 30 men had escaped, a secret Jewish organisation which had connections with those in the forest and who regularly delivered arms to Jewish partisan groups remained behind.

Life in Krassnoe became very difficult for the Jews and we had to carry out the most strenuous work daily under the batons of the Gestapo and policemen. They would put 12 girls, still young children, to work carrying a log 16 metres in length; they struggled until they died, unable to move the log from the spot. If any of the men attempted to help them, they would be beaten by the murderers until helpless. We felt as if we were dying, and the majority of us decided to escape to the forest.

When the Judenrat heard that escapes were taking place in massive proportions, they insisted that escapes should stop because this would bring about the destruction of the few remaining Jews in Krassnoe. At one point, when the Judenrat received information that, at night, Jews were going to run to the forest from a designated place in the ghetto, a granary, they sent two Jewish militia men, Leibe Baranovitz and Lieberman, to disrupt the group's plans. The group would not allow the militia men into the barn, but they tore open the door and entered. One of the group, Malkin from Volozhin, out of great anger ran to one of the militia men and hit him very hard so that he had blood pouring from him. The two militia men informed the Judenrat of these events. Meanwhile, a group of 10 men left the ghetto, swam over the Berezina River, and arrived in the forest to join the 'Tshkolovsker' Partisan Brigade.

The Jewish partisans again worked together planning an attack on Horodok, this time on a larger scale. On a night at the beginning of the Sabbath (January 1943), the whole of the Tshkolovsker Brigade, 3,000 men, left for Horodok. Cutting off all roads to the local German garrison with men lying in wait, they surrounded the town and Chone Elterman sneaked in and threw a grenade into the German police department. This was the signal to open fire. The Germans together with the police, in great confusion, began to leave the town, but everywhere they met with partisans. There were many victims on their side, but among the partisans only a few, including two Jews. The partisans entered the town and confiscated livestock and other necessities. Several places in the town were set alight. Here the partisans met the 12 Jewish tradesmen who had been left behind after the slaughter in Horodok. The partisans suggested that they join them in the forest. The Jews did not accept their proposal and as a result, on the day following the attack, the 12 men were transferred to Rodoszkowicze where they were killed two days later by the Germans during the great slaughter which took place there.

Hearing about the killings in Rodoszkowicze, we in Krassnoe were overcome by a deadly fear. We felt that our turn would come shortly. One day before Purim (March 1943), I was sitting with my family together with the family Gelfer from Horodok, talking about our bitter fate. I suggested to them that we escape to the forest. None of them agreed with me. They decided to remain and to leave it to fate. That same evening a peasant (Starzkevitz) whom I knew came and offered me work. However, at the same time, he said that no one must know about it. I did not place any importance on his words, as I thought that he was afraid that someone might find out that he has contact with Jews. The next day at five o'clock in the morning I stole out of the camp and went to the peasant's hut. At seven thirty, when I was already at work, the peasant passed on to me the news that half an hour ago the ghetto and the camp were surrounded by Germans, and even the town was guarded. I was drenched in a cold sweat. Half crazy, at that moment I felt a strong desire to be with my family. The peasant, however, stopped me, saying that it was foolish on my part to attempt this because I would not be able to find out anything about them, and I would expose myself to certain death.

I changed into peasant clothing, and, heavily burdened by my silent suffering and pain, I arrived at the back of the town half an hour later. (The peasant farmer made it possible for me to leave by taking me out through his garden.) Without a particular goal for myself, I went straight to the middle of the highway without thinking about the great danger of walking along such a route. After walking a few kilometres I instinctively climbed up a nearby hill. A thought quickly entered my head: perhaps I could see something from there! At that moment I climbed up the hill and glanced towards Krassnoe. Tongues of flame with pillars of smoke reached up to the heavens in a huge display.

I stood on the hill for a long time until I collected my thoughts, steadied myself and once again walked in the middle of the highway to Horodok. Later, just before nightfall I met another peasant who was coming from Krassnoe. From him I learned the details about the slaughter. After surrounding the ghetto and the camp, the police, together with the Germans, began to order the Jews into barracks which were not far from the ghetto, with the pretext that over there they would be sprayed against typhus. Even those who had gone to work were turned around and driven into the barracks. Those who were forcibly gathered together were later ordered to undress completely, and about 20 men were driven by truck to a barn not far from the town. As the 20 men dismounted from the truck, the murderers shot them with machine guns and after that everyone – the dead, the half-dead and even the lightly wounded – were thrown like garbage into the barn. When the barn was full the murderers set it alight. The groups of Jews who were brought next were thrown into a second barn, and when this one was full, it too was set alight. And this is how the 'work' progressed, until all of the Jews were dead. During the slaughter my wife and my three children were killed. All 8,000 Jews, from very young to adults, underwent the same process to their deaths. Only eight men survived.

In the evening I arrived in Horodok. I entered my own house in which a peasant now lived. There was no police station in the town because the partisans had recently dispersed them. At night partisans knocked at the door, and we were asked whether there were any strangers there. My house was situated on the side of the town and it was accessible from the fields. I went out to them, and there were 10 Jewish partisans from Staritzke's otriad, all of them from Horodok. I filled them in about the slaughter in Horodok, giving them all the details. With the agreement of the otriad commander, I joined them. The commander then sent us to the mayor, Produkhe, to put into force a death sentence. We left, taking the mayor from his house, and the Jewish partisan, Rogovin, delivered a bullet to his head. A Russian, left behind by the Russian army in 1941, was the mayor's servant. He informed us where the mayor had buried looted Jewish possessions. We dug up everything and took with us the most important items, loading them up in six wagons. The Russian servant joined our partisan unit.

That same night we drove to the otriad in Fersheier forest. There we met more Jewish partisans with whom we were acquainted. After a long talk all of us together decided that we should take greater revenge on the enemy. Chone Elterman was in charge of implementing this. The whole district feared him. He used to find out by whom and where Jews were being harmed, and he would immediately punish the perpetrators. He would shoot the guilty ones and confiscate their belongings. The Germans wanted to capture him at any cost and they put a price of 25,000 marks on his head. Five partisans from our platoon, with them Elterman who went to Rayon to carry out an operation, stayed at a peasant's hut during the night.

Exhausted, they did not set up a watch, and while they slept, their host betrayed them. At daybreak, they found themselves trapped by Germans together with militia men armed with machine guns; they had surrounded the house. Then the house became engulfed in flames. Elterman smashed the door, and through the thick smoke he ran into the street. He grabbed a horse and escaped while still shooting. He paid no attention to the hail of bullets which were aimed at him, and he managed to extricate himself from the dangerous situation. The other four partisans were unable to save themselves. A rumour that Elterman had been killed circulated among the Christians. However, Elterman was energetic and strong; not even taking a rest, together with the brothers Rogovin and Lidsky, he regularly embarked on a 'zshelezke' (sabotage). They tore up railway lines, destroyed trains, and burned bridges. He always emerged from all the danger hale and hearty. In the month of Av (August 1943), the Germans placed a full blockade around the forest. They brought an army of 120,000 [this number is difficult to substantiate] German inhabitants of Vlasov, and policemen from the district. The blockade had been in place for five days when we stormed our way through and again went over to Rayon. During the battle 20 partisans from our brigade were killed, among them six Jews.

At the end of 1943 we launched another attack against Horodok. We took away what we needed and then set the city alight. In March 1944, before the heavy offensive against the White Russian front took place, a blockade was once again organised by the Germans. They then started to mobilise the town's youth. To counter this move, we the partisans were ordered to start mobilising the youth for the partisan groups. About 800 men from our brigade left to carry out the order. They divided themselves into two groups of 400 men each. One group, in which Yaacov Eidelman was a participant, discovered that not far from there a German division was pursuing their own goal of mobilising the town's youth. The partisans went out to confront them and they began a battle. Yaacov Eidelman (a cousin of the Yaacov Eidelman who was killed by a member of a tank unit in the early days of the occupation) noticed that a German was aiming a machine gun at them, so he ran towards the man and began to struggle with him until he managed to get hold of his gun, strangled him and brought the machine gun to the partisans. After a six hour battle the Germans were forced to retreat, leaving about 50 dead and a lot of ammunition. After the battle the commander of Marozofsky brigade addressed the partisans, and he publically thanked and praised Yaacov Eidelman for his heroism. In his talk the commander stated: 'People say that the Jews are cowards, but look at this: in front of you stands the great hero Yaacov Eidelman, a Jew; learn from him!'

Four weeks later 12 partisans, among them one Jew, this same Eidelman, went to reconnoitre the ambush area. They sent four men to scout around in order to check whether they could get through the German line. The Germans deliberately let them through in order to be able to attack the whole group. The 12 men came under heavy fire, but in the beginning they put up a fierce battle. However, later they realised that the Germans, because of their superior numbers and better position, could overrun them, so they retreated and continued shooting while they did so. The second-in-charge assisting Yaacov Eidelman threw down his rifle and ran away, so the only one who remained surrounded by the Germans was Eidelman. When the commander saw that Eidelman was missing from the group which had retreated, he became very angry. He called the second-in-charge who should have covered Eidelman, and publically stated to him that if, in the course of the day, Eidelman did not return, he would pay with his head for his shameful behaviour. Two hours later Eidelman arrived in good health and cheerful, carrying the machine gun and the rifle which the partisan had thrown down. Uninjured he had managed to break free of the surrounding Germans while shooting a few of them. For his bravery, Eidelman received a commendation, and his military rank was raised to that of 'Captain'.

A massive battle was being prepared for us by the Germans. Already troops were standing by prepared for this purpose, but the offensive on the White Russian front destroyed the German plans. The Soviet armies celebrated one victory after another, and the front continually moved closer to us.

When the front moved very close to us and the Germans were retreating, Chone Elterman asked the commander for permission to take his company to cut off the German retreat. At first the commander did not agree to this. However, Elterman would not give up his plan and pestered the commander until he agreed. Elterman and his company set out for the Ivanitz–Baksht–Ivia–Lida highway and hid while waiting for the Nazi troops to pass by. They engaged a large number of German soldiers in battle, but the small number of partisans was forced back. A few of them were killed and the rest returned to the otriad. When the commander saw that Elterman was not present, he gave an order that, even if Elterman were no longer alive, they must bring his corpse back to the otriad. They brought a severely wounded Elterman back to the partisan otriad. That same night they flew him in an aircraft to Moscow. After spending 11 months in a hospital there, he returned to Horodok, a physically weak and broken person. A few months later, he died in Minsk. On 13 July 1944, we, the liberated, went to Minsk with our whole brigade. A week later, a group of 20 of us, Jews from Horodok, went back to our destroyed or severely damaged homes.

Central Historical Commission, File No. 722/864

Poland: Jewish partisans, led by Jechiel Grinszpan in the Partshev forests (1943).
Donated by the Historical Commission in Eschwege.

Germans hang partisans. Donated by Z. Knall, Munich.

SS-man on the way to Poland to execute 'actions' on Jews.
Donated by the Regional Historical Commission, Regensburg.

Human heads on stone statues from a concentration camp in Germany.

The Warsaw cemetery during a deportation action. Donated by Z. Knall.

After a deportation action. Donated by M.F. Galicia.

Ukraine: A Jew on the gallows. Donated by A. Kowalski.

Crematory in Bergen-Belsen Concentration Camp. Donated by Historical Commission Stuttgart.

Bergen-Belsen concentration camp . Donated by Regional Historical Commission Stuttgart.

Bergen-Belsen concentration camp. Donated by Regional Historical Commission Stuttgart.

Salzburg. A group of Concentration camp inmates at liberation. Donated by Joseph Grunwald.

Lodz ghetto. Looking for food among the refuse on Dworska 6. Donated by G. Maizler.

Viennese Jewish intellectuals locked up behind bars. Donated by Y. Weisman.

Gogolin, Silesia. Polish Jews in labor camp.

Siedlce, Poland. The first deportation, August, 1942.

Jewish woman shot during the deportation.

Siedlce, Poland. A whole family is occupied with pulling the drum of 'gold' in Lodz ghetto (the so-called faecalists). Donated by Pinchas Schwarz.

A group of children from Lodz ghetto have been rounded up and are waiting to be transported on the cattle trucks.

Abandoned children in Warsaw ghetto. Donated by M.Kurlik.

In camp. Pulling the wagon with the soup vessel.

# 13

# IN CAMP KALDYCHEVA

Eyewitness Account by Yudel Samsonovitz

Collected by the Historical Commission in Neu Freimann.
Published by the Munich Historical Commission in the Journal Series
*Fun Letzten Khurben*, Vol. 6, 1947

After the slaughter in Baranovich, during which 3,500 Jews died, 350 men from the existing ghetto were transported in trucks during the period of Channukah [Jewish holiday], 1942. The Jews were crowded into a camp near Kaldycheva. Around October 1943, after the High Holy days, another 120 Jews were sent here from Baranovich. I was included in the group. Shortly before our arrival a massacre took place in the camp. In their excitement the Germans regarded this as a show. They shot 250 Jews and threw them into an oven which was hastily erected for this purpose. The Security Service and the police looked on at this picture with great enjoyment. The head of 'Distribution' was the kommandant of the camp, Yorn, a tall and heavy man of about 40 years of age. His superior, Lieutenant Amelung from Riga, was an ethnic German from Latvia, short and thin; Corporal Otto was a tall, dark German of about 38 years of age; and the Security Service man, Shefler, short and blond, was also a German. With them was a police kommandant, Babke, himself a White Russian from Baranovich, who was in charge of the White Russian police. His deputy was Stefanuk, also a White Russian. Amongst these high ranking police officers there was also a Lithuanian, Dira. He was a brutal murderer and a specialist at torturing Jews.

In the camp we found 100 Jews who lived in horse stables. There, together with them, we spent the night. Early in the morning they were driven out to go to work and we were taken to a square in the camp. Security Service personnel and policemen ordered us to immediately surrender any money which we had and anything of value. They warned us that we were not to hide anything. If, after a search, they should find anything, we would be shot. After a thorough search they took everything away from us. White Russian police surrounded the whole camp. Immediately we noticed that the 100 Jews who were sent to work that morning were being brought back into the camp. One of the Jews was covered in blood; he had attempted to escape when the White Russian police had beaten him savagely.

Our 20 men were lined up together with the 100 others and they began to sort us. Out of the total, 92 of the healthier ones and the skilled tradesmen were chosen. The remainder were immediately beaten with iron implements and clubs and the police dogs were set upon them. They were chased with clubs to the trucks. Notwithstanding the beatings and the bites from the vicious dogs, the prisoners shouted to us: 'Take revenge on the murderers for our innocent blood and pain!' They were driven to the police station. There they had to undress and were told to lie down in the trucks; again they were given deadly blows with clubs. One of the Jews had a good pair of boots. Not wanting the murderers to use them, he cut the boot-leg with a knife. The policemen noticed this and attacked him. One policeman chopped both the Jew's legs off with blows from an axe. Subsequently, the Jews were transported by trucks two kilometres from the camp, to the Berezovka forest by Shoreditch, and there they were shot.

After this Aktion the Kommandant of the camp, Yorn, gave a speech to the inmates. We would be subjected to a special Aktion, he said: 'For as long as we are here, you too will be here. After that we will finish you off.' Then the Kommandant approached us, tore off from each of us our *Magen David*, and attached white patches to our chests and shoulders.

We worked in the camp at various trades: shoemaking, carpentry, watchmaking, tanning and millinery, and meanwhile we began to build a jail there at great speed. We immediately understood that this is for us. We started planning how to escape from the camp. We formulated various plans. One plan was to set alight the stables, and to run away during the moments of panic. But this was cancelled because a fire would light up the area and it could be very detrimental to us. We decided to make a hole in the wall of the stable and to escape through it to freedom. Escaping was very risky because the stable was always locked and guarded by policemen with machine guns. Therefore, each one of us was provided with poison which the chemist, Bore Neifeld from Baranovich, had himself prepared. (Neifeld is presently in Poland.) In the event that we should fall into murderous hands while we were escaping, we would not hand ourselves over to them alive.

Subsequently, when we had jointly decided on the night for the escape, two of the men ruined the plan. They worked in the tailoring section and several nights before the selected time, they of their own will escaped from their factory one night. The police began to chase them, shooting at them and shooting flares towards them. They managed, however, to save themselves and escaped into the forest. There, they joined up with partisans. The wrath of the Germans overwhelmed all of us in the camp. The guards watching over us immediately became harsher. In addition, the police started to torment us with various drills. One of us, in the meantime, broke the little container of poison and accidently burnt his foot just when we were ready to break out that very night. Not wishing to leave our friend we postponed the date. However, new threats would occur all the time. Here, someone would develop a temperature; there, other problems would arise. In this manner we had to keep on postponing our escape. Finally, however, the day arrived. In order that there should be no noise while we were breaking out, and that the plan should go ahead safely, we chose by number who should emerge first, then second, and so on. Taking into account that I was born in Horovitch not far from the camp, I was well acquainted with the district. I gave the desperate ones courage by undertaking to show all of them the way. Because of this my wife and I were given the privilege of leaving first instead of leaving in 36th place, according to the number drawn. I was given a revolver with four bullets. Over a period of time we learned how to prepare for our escape from the camp. We would do exercises in the barrack, crawling on our hands and feet in order that we would learn to move quietly so that the police would not become aware of us. For each one of us a Jew from Sverzhen prepared knives which would allow us to defend ourselves in the event that we were discovered. Among the 90 Jews there were nine women who worked in the laundry. Only two of them remained alive: my wife, Meta Samsonovitch, who hailed from Baranovich. The second is called Louisa Movsovitz, born in Danzig.

One of the Polish policemen from Stolpce helped us with our escape. He gave us three hand grenades. He became aware that we planned to escape on a particular night, but he gave us a signal that we should not do so because on that same day there was to be a police search in the area. We followed his advice and didn't leave.

We managed to create an exit hole in the wall within two weeks. The carpenters smuggled building materials and a saw and so forth from their factory. The hole led into a room of one of the factories. On the final night, in the room we left a friend who would help us open the exit hole from the opposite side. We wanted to avoid additional hammering while doing this. Nearby detained Christians slept. We were very much afraid that they might become aware of the hammering on the last section of the hole in the wall.

At the end of March 1944, we decided to leave during a dark and stormy night. We quietly opened the hole in the wall, and 100 men laid down quilts and coats next to it so that our footsteps should not be heard. We took with us watches, underwear and shoes that we had made for the Germans. In general our escape was successful, but one of us remained in the camp stable. He was asleep at the time and no one noticed him. It was a great help to us that we had poisoned all the camp dogs a week before we escaped.

Later we heard exactly what happened after our escape. The following morning, when they opened the door of the barrack, the guards saw that there was no one there. Great consternation followed. They immediately ordered a pursuit and a search of the surrounding forests and fields. Twenty-six of our people became lost and remained lying in a trench exhausted. Suddenly they heard the noise of vehicles. One of them quickly shouted out that they should run. The others remained sitting and the police saw them. Amongst them was Kushner, the main organiser of the plan to escape. He came from an area near Slonim and was a shoemaker by trade. In the Polish army he was awarded the honour of a medal – 'Virtuti Militari' (for Military Virtue). As soon as the police attacked him in the trench he shot himself with a revolver. The remaining 23 Jews were taken alive by the police back to the camp. Amongst them were three women. In the camp they were horribly punished by terrible torture until they dropped dead. The detained Christians were forced to march by the rows of the dead so that they should see the punishment which is meted out for an attempt to escape.

One woman was tortured appallingly and she was forced to write a letter, written in Yiddish, to the escapees, telling them to return and saying that they would not be punished. We were informed about all this by partisans.

Arriving in the Naliboki forest (the Nalibotzke glade), we the escapees came across a Jewish family camp of partisans, 1,200 Jews with women and children. The camp was called 'Kalinin' and its leader was Bielski, from the Novogrod area. (He is now in Israel.) We affiliated with the camp members. Here in the forest we took revenge on the Germans for our suffering.

Central Historical Commission, File No. 129

# 14

# THE LAST RESISTANCE FIGHTERS IN BIALYSTOK GHETTO

Eyewitness Account by Rabbi A. Burstin

Published by the Munich Historical Commission in the Journal Series
*Fun Letzten Khurben*, Vol. 7, 1948

The history of resistance in the Bialystok ghetto has already been written about to a greater or lesser extent. I do not want to repeat the details of the ghetto struggles; I want to pass on only the information about the final heroic moments of the last 72 sacred martyrs which I personally witnessed. Until now I have not come across any description of those moments. Perhaps there are almost no more people still living who were there, so I believe that is my Holy duty to describe what I saw and heard.

It was Friday on 23 August 1943. The greater majority of the last remaining inhabitants in the Bialystok ghetto had already been sent out. The Jewish resistance force had previously been neutralised. German and Ukrainian bands went wild while searching for, and discovering, the last of the Jews hidden in bunkers and other concealment places. A Ukrainian gang seized me in Podliash Street from an attic in a house right by the ghetto fence where I had hidden myself since Sunday, 15 August 1943. Below, on the first floor of the same house, 25 men lay dead; they were Resistance fighters who shot at the Germans during the time of the Resistance battles. Hand grenades, which the Germans had thrown into the house from outside the ghetto, killed them all. The Ukrainians handed me over to a German officer who told me to face the wall so that he could shoot me. The Ukrainians who were supposed to carry out the sentence suddenly heard voices from a nearby burning house. They immediately turned towards the house. In the meantime, I secretly handed to the officer a silver box and a little watch which had remained in my pocket.

The officer softened a little and ordered that I was to be taken to join the Jews who were supposedly going to the transport. A number of Germans took me to the assembly point in Yorovietzke Street, corner Kupyetzke, and there I came across several Jews who were sitting on the paved footpath surrounded by a large number of guards. From time to time the murderous thugs brought more individual Jews whom they had discovered in their hiding places. The heat burned viciously. A woman who was sitting near me, a mother of a two-year-old child, fainted and fell unconscious. It was heartbreaking to see how the child tore at his mother's head and screamed frightfully. The cruel murderers did not want to hear our pleas, and would not under any circumstances allow us to bring a little water with which to revive the woman. At about 10 o'clock in the morning we noticed a lot of movement amongst the murderous bands. Right away we saw coming from nearby Tshepele Street a group of about 70 Jewish men, and also 20 Jewish women, all of whom were being brought here. The whole group marched with heads held high, quiet and proud, as if in a victory march. The fact that most of them were barefoot and wearing ragged clothes was irrelevant; from everyone's eyes there radiated courage, resoluteness and heroism. During all my wanderings through various camps I never again came across such an exalted appearance amongst Jews. The Germans led them to the location of the Judenrat in Kupyetzke Street where on that day the extermination personnel sat, with the chief murderer, Fridel, as their head. I heard various shouts of derision against the German killers, and calls for the honour of the Jewish nation from the Jews who were standing there. Presumably that is where their sentence was to be carried out. They were brought back to Yorovietzke Street and were organised into a long row at a certain distance from us. The Germans brought out a little table from a nearby Jewish house and placed upon it a machine gun aimed at the group of Jews. I was not a resident of Bialystok and I did not know any of the people there. Out of the whole group I was acquainted with only one person. His trade was reel making. He was the son-in-law of the ritual slaughterer of Tikocim. I had seen his wife, the ritual slaughterer's daughter, the previous Sunday, the day of the first transport, wandering about with her two very young children in her arms. She was looking for her husband who had left her alone with her two babes at such a horrible time while she wept bitterly. At the time I did not understand how a man could leave his wife alone at such a terrible moment with one of the children only three months old! Only then did it become clear to me. The spool-maker from Tikocim went to defend Jewish honour.

The young man from Tikocim recognised me and smiled at me. The Germans began to carry out the sentence. They took five men from the first row, led them to a nearby wall not far from a soda water factory, and shot them. Then the Germans took the second row. While walking, one of the five shouted out: 'Down with the murderers! Our blood will take revenge!' and also added a revolutionary maxim. A bullet from a Lithuanian felled him before he even reached the wall.

When the Germans had regrouped, and went to take the third row, something completely unexpected happened. The whole group suddenly tore away from their places and pounced upon the Germans and the Ukrainians. They threw over the table with the machine gun and started to strangle the Germans. There ensued hellish chaos.

Hundreds of Germans ran there from the surrounding streets. The personnel from the transport groups immediately took up positions, like a fiery wall between us and the those who were resisting. All the Germans shot at the people with their rifles, pistols and machine guns. The struggle lasted for 10 minutes. When the shooting stopped, there was a blood-curdling picture in front of my eyes. Yorovietzke Street was red from blood. The sacred martyrs lay in various horrifying positions. A few people from our transport group were also shot dead by stray bullets. The Germans began a shocking bacchanalian revelry against the half-dead prisoners. One Jewish fighter, in his death throes, sat up. A tall, corpulent German went over to him, removed his hat and said to him, 'Good morning, Sir! How are you?' and then kicked him in the face. Other Germans, laughing sadistically, shot the still surviving heroes. Two men from the group remained untouched. The Germans took one of them into a yard and spoke to him. We saw how he shook his head. Then they beat him with spades. The second one could not bear the test and went away with a German. He presumably gave away some information.

Jewish carters arrived. They loaded the sacred martyrs onto wagons and took them to the Bialystok cemetery. Several cartloads of sand were spread over the blood to cover the evidence of the last fighters. Stealthily my eyes looked into a psalm book which I had on me, and they searched for the words: 'God of revenge'.

# 15

# EXPERIENCES OF A JEWISH ARYAN

Eyewitness Account by Anna Holtzman

Collected by the Munich Historical Commission.
Published by the Munich Historical Commission in the Journal Series
*Fun Letzten Khurben*, Vol. 7, 1948

I was formerly a Christian, born to Aryan parents. In 1924, at the request of my Jewish husband, I converted to the Jewish faith. I have never regretted taking this step. I never gave up my Jewish faith even after my husband died in 1935 and left me with two small children.

I would like to convey to you my experiences in Munich during the Nazi period when they treated me as a 'full Jew'. Until 1938 it was still bearable although even then we had to put up with various abuses. These, however, came mostly from the general public, from neighbours; I was often insulted, spat upon. I had to swallow all this; we were helpless.

The extent of the frequent malevolence is reflected in the following event. Mrs Levine, who owned the building where we lived, owned a shoe business close by. One day she had a quarrel on the business premises with a certain man. She was alone, and the man attacked her and began to beat her. She ran out into the street, the man chasing her and continuing to beat her. As it happens, I arrived at that moment. She noticed me and ran towards me, then hugged me. However, Mrs Levine's maid then called out that I am also a Jewess, and the man turned towards me. We ran into the bakery. The woman owner quickly locked the shop and called the police. Two policemen arrived and broke up the gathering.

Conditions really deteriorated after 9 November 1938 (Kristallnacht). One fine day a woman came to me and said that she had been sent personally by the State Minister, Wagner, to enquire about taking over my house. She stated that my house belonged to a Jew, but she wanted to have it because she liked it. She expected me to vacate it immediately because she wanted to move in right away. Her tone infuriated me and my answer to her was: 'Please tell State Minister Wagner personally that there is a mistake here; the house is not available'.

Two days later two men from the Gestapo arrived and took me to the German Chancellery in Artzim Street to a particular government department man, Horn. He asked me whether I was the Jew Anna Holtzman. My answer was 'yes'. Then Horn began to abuse me verbally in the worst way: for what reason had I been so rude to the woman who had come to me, what was my problem? He ordered me to leave my house immediately. But I did not do so because I maintained that they had to first send me an official order concerning the house. A week later they again brought me to the same place. This time Horn was even angrier and again he grossly offended me, but this time, not because of the house, but because I was not Jewish by birth, something I had not told him. He accused me of being totally Judaicised. Finally he said to me: 'I will pass on to you a second truth; you will still hear from me'.

It didn't take long before I was again summoned to a particular Government Councillor, Shvingenstein, who greeted me with the following words: 'You are in the right place here with me. I come from Streicher's "school": do you know what that means?' I thought that in any case nothing would be different, so I answered: 'One can see that you are a real Jew hater'. A German woman sat nearby and typed every word that I uttered. Then came his question: 'Why did you not renounce Judaism, like all the others did?' 'I will not do it!' I replied. He became furious, but even so he thought it right to advise me to make a special request to the 'Leader' about allowing me once again to be part of the German people. I refused to do so. Then he advised me to separate myself from my son, to leave him to his fate with the Jews: 'He appears to be a "full Jew" and it is difficult to save him. We are on the way to finding the quickest, most radical way to solve the Jewish problem.' This conversation took place shortly before the first Jewish transports. I replied to him: 'Do you mean that I should desert my son in order to save myself? I would not have a moment's peace; no mother would do this!' 'Then you are not entirely Judaicised,' he replied, 'because every Jewish woman would have done so, just to benefit themselves. I know Jews well, I have read the Talmud.' I answered that even if I had not read the

Talmud I know the Jews better and I know that no Jewish mother would do so. 'Then you cannot be helped,' he concluded.

I again had to go to Shvingenstein after a certain period of time during the war. He had prepared a 'special request' and I was supposed to sign it. I did not do so. He became really furious and shouted out: 'We won't have any serious dealings with you. You sent your daughter to America to spy. She has Jewish blood in her, and she has connections everywhere because of her non-Jewish appearance; we know this.' I replied that his anger prevented him from thinking logically; in any case he could not possibly believe that a 14-year-old child could be sent into the world to spy. He said: she has Jewish blood in her, and Jewish children are taught from early childhood to be ready for anything; they know everything. But even in America she will be lost. America would lose the war, and then we would do the same to the Jews there as we do in Europe. We will see to it that Jews will no longer exist and the world will be freed from these parasites. You can still save yourself – sign this.'

When I again refused to sign, he wanted to know, unconditionally, why?

'I cannot overlook my feelings so lightly. When Jews experienced good times, I was together with them; now, when things are bad for them, should I turn my back on them?' I told him that I would not do this!

He replied: 'From your point of view you may be right, but I must follow through with the necessary consequences'. 'I have done so until now [not compromised my feelings of moral decency], and will do so in the future,' was my answer. I turned around to leave the office and to my amazement he accompanied me to the door.

Three weeks later I received an order to appear before the Housing Department. I was sure that I would have to move out. The official [in the office] telephoned the Gestapo in Wiedenmeier Street, the location of the Department of 'Jewish House Expropriations'. To my great surprise, after ending the conversation, he said that the order for me to leave my house had been cancelled. I actually remained in my house until it was damaged by bombings.

After this I was often called to the infamous 'Jew destroyers', Mugler, Wagner and Shrot. At one time Mugler created a terrible scene: I was informed that all those who were in the Aryan position such as me had already renounced their Judaism. I was the only one who was unwilling to do so. He shouted: 'I would willingly beat you soundly now, not taking into account that in addition I would shoot you'. I smiled directly into his eyes; however, I remember how my feet trembled, and while rushing home I felt as though I was flying.

This same Mugler once came to us to ascertain whether the 'Magen Davids' (Stars of David) were in order. It was a Sunday at about six thirty in the evening. He sent someone in to notify all the Jews who lived in the building that they had to go out onto the street with their coats on. We had to assemble in a semi-circle (we were six people), and with folded arms he stood in front of us and gave us various bits of information about all the punishments which awaited us if we were caught without the Star of David. With a pen he carried out a test to see whether the stars were tightly sewn on; heaven forbid that they should be pinned on. A German woman who was with him photographed us. Naturally, a small group of people who looked at the 'spectacle' gathered very soon and, satisfied, they laughed. Mugler would make such visits quite often; at other times he would appear in the middle of the night and pull people out of their beds.

I had to contend with various persecutions from the 'Local Branch' in Richard Wagner Street. A resident in our building, a 100 per cent Nazi, was on bad terms with the owner of the building and he wanted to spite him somehow. If one searches, one finds. He found out that the proprietor had raised my rent five marks per month without permission. I was called to the Local Branch where the Kommissar of Criminals was in charge, and they expected a signed statement from me so that they could charge Levine (the proprietor). Understandably, I would not make a statement and they berated me. I was summoned several times about this issue, and each time they attempted to hoodwink me into providing a statement. Once, after this, when I had been waiting in the cold corridor for four hours, they told me I should not dare to show myself with an Aryan man, because they would lock me up for race-defilement. I was often called to the Local Branch about such things and various other matters.

They regularly summoned me to come until I found the courage to refuse to go. Then they gave us over to a political group of 'house-administrators' which was supposed to keep watch over us, and to pass on everything to the Local Branch. They forbade me to take any of my possessions from the house to the town to protect the items from bombs. They sent reports about every parcel that I took out. They also measured our Magen Davids to check that they were the correct size and not covered. It is well known that we had to manage with their meagre rations. I and my son were the only ones in Munich who had to live on the amount given on Jewish ration cards. Everyone else had one or more people in their families who had Aryan ration cards; and they used to receive some assistance from their relatives. It was impossible to survive on Jewish rations. I had to take all my possessions to various towns to exchange them for food in order to be able to carry on during those difficult times.

My son, too, had a lot to put up with at the time. In 1942, when they closed the Jewish schools, he was 13 years old. At the time, he went to work in a nursery garden as an assistant and received the wage of an apprentice. Later our rations were decreased. Over a period of 10 months we never received any meat, eggs, milk, white bread or flour. After the 10 months they provided us with 400 grams of meat and nine bread rolls per month. We never again received eggs or milk. During the whole period of the war we were never given clothes, ration cards [other than food ration cards] or haberdashery items – only once in three months 'new-resources' for 20 pfennig.

One cold, rainy day, my son arrived soaking wet and freezing cold after a whole day working outdoors. I asked him: 'Hugo, are you not troubled by our being Jewish?' He answered: 'No, it does not bother me that I am a Jew; I am proud of it, and do not want to be anything else!' He is also the only one of mixed parentage (mischling) in Munich who did not put in a request for classification as an Aryan.

Because I did not reject my Judaism I lost the right to retain my house which my brother-in-law had given to me in 1938. The house was situated in Wiesbaden, Zeeraben Street, 13, and the gift certificate is still in my possession.

On 7 January 1945, during an aerial attack we lost everything. On 8 January, I together with all the neighbours went to the 'artsgruppe' (local branch) about a house. But they told me that, for me, they had nothing. We did not even have anything to eat, because although we were still able to buy in specific shops with our Jewish ration cards, we were unable to purchase any food with them in a restaurant. Therefore, we were forced to leave Munich in a hurry (although we were forbidden to leave the city). We went to a certain village and later the Gestapo searched for us. My son was with strangers who knew that he was a Jew. I was with another good person. That is where we remained until the Americans liberated us, and we were freed from bondage.

One thing pleases me greatly, and that is that the Nazis were unable to demean me; with all the investigations, not one of them noticed how I trembled in fear – and that is my greatest satisfaction.

Central Historical Commission File No. 80

# 16

# THE LARGE FACTORIES IN KOVNO GHETTO

Eyewitness Account by Moshe Segalson

Collected by the Munich Historical Commission.
Published by the Munich Historical Commission in the Journal Series
*Fun Letzten Khurben*, Vol. 8, 1948

During a period of four months, from the entry of the Germans into Kovno to the end of October 1941, 55 per cent of the whole Jewish population in Kovno was exterminated. At the start of the German–Soviet war, after the big Aktion, only a total of 17,000 out of 38,000 Jewish souls remained in Kovno. Of them approximately 5,500 were men, and 11,500 were women and children. It became clear that the Nazis had the intention of destroying the whole Jewish population. To this end the latest Aktions demonstrated that first of all they intended to murder those who were unable to work; from this group most of the victims were taken away in the selections.

After the main Aktion, workers came into the town: the aerodrome brigade, 3,000 men working day and night shifts; the Heeres Bau brigade had 1,000; and in other smaller brigades there were another 1,000 people. Thus about 12,000 non-working people, the women, children, elderly and the sick, remained in the ghetto every day.

The aerodrome required more and more workers, but the local work conditions – day and night outdoors in muddy soil in the cold, without suitable shoes and clothing, and poor care – were so difficult that physically, for weaker people, it meant certain death.

The ghetto was in a very difficult situation. The town Kommissar knew that there were still thousands of people there and, if this were so, the ghetto could supply more and more manpower for the aerodrome. The Jews themselves knew that the current population, weak, old and sick, could not be sent to the aerodrome or to any other hard work. The only possible solution was to find lighter work in the ghetto itself for these people; to be precise, the Elder met together with the tradespeople, mainly handworkers, to get advice, and to discuss the difficult situation which had been created. From these discussions it became apparent that the percentage of artisans amongst the non-working ghetto people was very small, because the largest number of tradesmen were working in the town brigades. Because of this fact, and also taking into account the technical possibilities, production projects were worked out to include a maximum of non-tradesmen, mostly women and old people, with a minimum of artisans. The thinking was that the work arrangements would also alleviate the poor material situation in the ghetto. The town Kommissar put together these projects. Simultaneously steps were taken to create a closer link, by means of fine gifts, to the appropriate officials and the town Kommissar who were able to control the situation. The main point was, as they saw it, that they (the Jews) encouraged the Germans to feel that they had a personal stake in the establishment and maintenance of such factories.

It was decided to create the ghetto factories at Krikshtiukeitshia Street 107, in a former Russian military barracks, which later served as a Lithuanian technical, agricultural and work school. About 100 people were immediately engaged in making the site suitable for work. By 12 January 1942, the space was ready for a tailoring factory, for glove-making, for shoemaking, and for brush manufacturing, as well as for a laundry. In reality, those were the most important sections for which the ghetto was necessary to the authorities, especially the aerodrome workers. Already, during the first 'Aktion in Riga' [unclear why the Aktion in Riga is mentioned] on 6 February 1942, about 250 workers who were at that time working in the factories, and who had come out to the square with their families, almost 750 people, were not transported. Because of this the factories were in great demand. The factories could not cope with additional workers. The workshop officials made every effort to open new departments, in particular to find work for the non-artisans, and some women.

Sections like wool shearing, toy tools (made from fabric), old clothes (sorting out different fabrics from used goods), basket weaving from willow twigs, and a feather department (plucking feathers) were created exclusively for the women. Owing to the newly opened women's department, within four months the number of workers in the factories reached 650, of whom 500 were women.

Under these conditions the mood lightened. The town Kommissar could be persuaded that the other people in the ghetto could also be employed. At the same time, the town Kommissar and his officials began to take goods from the factories for their personal use. For these high officials of the town in the Kommissariat, a special factory with different tradesmen such as tailors, bootmakers, hand knitters, fashion experts, corset makers, furriers, bag makers, and other types of handwork, was established, and they worked only for the private service of the officials. This special factory operated with the full cooperation of the workers, so that the [Jewish] leadership could develop their plans for the benefit of the ghetto.

The most significant effects from the establishment of the factories were:

1. to be able to employ as many people as possible
2. to be able to find ways of earning money by various means since the ghetto was in an extraordinarily bad economic state
3. to have the opportunity to go into the town and to develop relationships with the outside world.

In order to achieve this, one had to become involved with as much work as possible on the other side of the ghetto. As much as they were successful in garnering work, it consisted primarily of repairs and washing. There were, for example, the sorting of outer clothing, washing, cloths, shoes, boots, pullovers, sacks, saddlery, furniture, military food containers, and also other things. So we had the opportunity to increase the number of departments, and obviously to increase also the number of working Jews. The factories had as many as 44 sections. And the number of workers totalled nearly 4,600 people, which was the highest number prior to the liquidation of the ghetto.

Not only was the ghetto itself concerned with the factories creating a favourable impression on the German higher echelons. The town Kommissar, and later the SS Kommandant, also had the same interest. Without taking into consideration their own personal and material benefits, the factories provided them with a comfortable reason to avoid going to the Front.

The factories had prior knowledge about the frequent visits of the important commissions which used to come to the ghetto to determine its fate [to allow it to continue or to liquidate it], and instructions were given to the workers to: 'let the film go on!'; that is, to prepare themselves to make a positive impression so that the result of the visit should be a good one. We would pass on to the important German guests exaggerated reports about the achievements of the factories, and these would be further embellished by the town Kommissar himself, and later by the SS Kommandant.

The factories, although economically viable, were becoming a grandiose deception on a large scale. In this regard, it is worthwhile pausing for a moment: 4,600 workers in so many different sections must inevitably produce something. Yet there was not even a minimal output; in addition, genuine sabotage took place. Several examples can be given as illustrations.

Eleven hundred people were kept busy under the guise of an inner administrative apparatus, such as an accounting management, technical bureau, factory ambulance, factory kitchen, bakery, fire brigade, factory police, transport, maintenance division (inside the factories), departmental chiefs, departmental bookkeepers and others. The laundry was done with German soap and chemicals, creating the opportunity for doing the ghetto residents' washing also. The greatest saving of soap in the laundry occurred during the summer months when washing woollen covers [took place]. Instead of washing the covers in the laundry with soap, they would only be rinsed in the Vilya River which flowed past the factories.

The work of the tinsmiths and the painting departments involved repairs being done (by removing dents and by painting) and to making military food containers (aluminum drinking cups and food pots). When the section opened at the beginning of 1942, the first order to be received consisted of 4,000 drinking vessels and pots. For the three quarters of a year that the department existed, a total of 460 pieces were delivered. Most of them were used for the Jewish workers in the town-brigades and for the partisan movement; the rest remained on show for the visiting members of the commissions who used to come to inspect the work. The German management was especially proud of this department.

A good source of income for the ghetto was the tailoring sections in which 1,200 men and women worked. Their work consisted mainly in repairing old military garments. When repairing the garments, some parts could be cut up and a portion of them could be utilised for other things. This gave a great uncontrolled opportunity to use them for the needs of the ghetto. The clothes would be taken apart, dyed, and then transformed into civilian garments. The shoemaking section brought no less benefit. The better shoes were exchanged for worse ones and the unwearable shoes.

When there was nothing for which to exchange them, some of the torn ones would be surreptitiously placed back with the total number, and in this way the workshop was able to cover up the ghetto's need of shoes. The ghetto had the benefit of these and other departments.

In such 'transactions' the most difficult aspect was the checking by the Germans of the number of goods. For this purpose, the best bookkeepers in the ghetto were employed, and they really showed great skill in manipulating their work. With different combinations they managed to make their accounts tally with the real numbers. It finally went so far that the factory accountant (Rosenblatt) went into the town every month to the German work providers and on the spot he would audit their books in such a way that they matched the factory's figures so that the great deceptions should not be uncovered. It is understood that all these 'masters of something' (the German officials) were bribed, and in addition they were helped with their own bookkeeping to cover up their thefts. It is simply unbelievable that during the period of three and a half years of factory reports, and with such a gross waste of materials, the German inspectors did not succeed in uncovering this scheme. The factories were the only Jewish ghetto concerns in which the workers were organised. They had a democratically elected committee which was responsible for the mutual good of their society, and for the whole time remained in closest contact with the factory managers. Management, together with the workers committee, can be characterised in brief: the workers used all their skill to 'milk' the German goods warehouses in the factories; and the factory management expanded their efforts in order to keep the 'cow' alive.

### Great benefits which the ghetto had from the factories

1. Thousands of men and women, the elderly and the sick, the youth who, according to German understanding, could be of no use, would have been in danger of extermination, but they became a productive element in the factories.
2. Through the factories, the ghetto's need for clothing, shoes, washing, soap, wood, bread, which was baked illegally in the factory bakery, and for Pesach – matzoh – was met.
3. Through the factories, the ghetto had the opportunity to make broad contact with the outside world. Passes to go into the town on Tuesdays were given, and many individuals benefitted from this, as did the whole ghetto in general.

4. The transport from the factories, which was only lightly controlled at the gate of the ghetto, provided numerous opportunities to take out and to bring in goods and food and, most importantly, it helped to transfer children surreptitiously from the ghetto into the town [rescuing them by this means].

5. Political movements in the ghetto, with the exception of the Zionists, were concentrated in the factories. Here there was good 'soil' for such work, which required a secure place for conspiracy and secrecy. Meetings took place mostly during the night shift. The leaders of the different political parties were registered with the different departments of the factory and received the proper work documents. In reality they were free of work and could devote themselves fully to their party interests.

6. The partisan movement in Kovno ghetto emerged and developed exponentially with the full material support of the factories. When leaving the ghetto, every partisan received from the factories a full military pack, which consisted of one military coat, a uniform with trousers, three sets of underwear, boots, a pullover, warm gloves, handkerchiefs, a food bag, a hat, leather straps, a cartridge bag, food containers and so forth. Some groups even took double rations in order to meet the needs of their comrades who were already in place. As well as the different sections in the factories which used to work during the night shift to meet the needs of the partisan transports, the repair department fixed and assembled guns for them.

7. The religious Jews of the ghetto also received the fullest support from the factories. All the rabbis and almost all of the yeshiva students were involved in the factories. There the illegal Rabbinate and the illegal Study House functioned. All the rescued Torah scrolls were hidden in the factories. For the religious Jews there was also a kosher cauldron in the factory kitchen. As the official rest day for the factories was Sunday, the cleaning squads were required to make all the rooms spotlessly clean on this day. Therefore the squad did not work on Saturdays (having worked on Sundays), and in the ghetto they were called the 'Russian Christian Brigade'. Obviously only religious Jews belonged to this brigade.

8. For the Kovno ghetto the worst experience was without doubt the Aktion against children and the elderly. At the start of this Aktion hundreds of people, mainly children, as well as the elderly and the physically weak, ran into the factories to save themselves. The adults, for the moment, were taken on as workers. It was horrific for the hundreds of children. They had to be hidden in attics, in the supply warehouses, in the laundry among the dirty washing, in underground bunkers which were constructed under the factories, and in other such cramped places. With great self-sacrifice, many of the elderly and the children, separately, were saved. During the two terrible days when more than 12,000 children and elderly from the ghetto were transported or murdered, there were three to four hundred children hidden in the factories. Of those subsequently found, only two were transported.

9. The factories also played a large part in saving children by taking them out of the factories and placing them in the town. Before the children's Aktion, and separately after the Aktion, the factories made the effort to create closer contact with decent Lithuanians in the town (unfortunately these were only a few individuals) and to persuade them to take Jewish children and to hide them. With the aid of the factory transport, a large number of children were successfully taken out of the terrible conditions in the ghetto, and were hidden in the town and especially in the villages.

After the children's Aktion[41] the children's vocational schools in the ghetto could no longer function. The factories took in close to 300 students and employed them as 'tradesmen'.

As soon as the factories began to work [from the beginning], important German commissions began to visit. As time passed the visits became more frequent. It did not take long for it to become known what the intentions of these important guests were (when they came here). We knew what their

---

41  In the summer and autumn of 1943, the Vilna and Swieciany ghettos were liquidated and the ghettos in Kovno and Siauliai were converted into concentration camps. A few months later approximately 1,200 babies, children and elderly inmates were murdered in the Kovno ghetto, and many youngsters were sent from the ghetto to labour camps in Estonia: http://www.yadvashem.org/holocaust/about/final-solution-beginning/baltic-states

plans were from our own Germans in the town Commission, who were personally interested in the existence of the factories. They told us that not only the senior German authorities wanted to liquidate the ghetto, but also that the Lithuanians were exerting considerable pressure on them to destroy it. Their reasoning was that they needed the return of the houses (the ghetto area was formerly inhabited by Lithuanians). The aforementioned Germans would inform us timeously about the arrival of commissions. They would send positive reports to their superiors and the senior supervisors of the factories. The Jews, on their part, once again immediately paid great attention to the outer appearance of the factories, and always made the effort to ensure that during a visit all the machinery with its apparatus should work efficiently and thereby make a suitable impression on the important guests. All of this brought the desired result, and the factories continued to function until the final liquidation of the ghetto on 12 July 1944.

In addition, because of the factories, the Kovno ghetto (and also the Shavel ghetto which was under the same SS Kommandant) remained in existence until the actual retreat of the Germans from Lithuania.

# 17

# VOLOZHIN

Eyewitness Account by Yosef Schwartzberg

Collected by the Munich Historical Commission.
Published by the Munich Historical Commission in the Journal Series
*Fun Letzten Khurben*, Vol. 8, 1948

The 'shtetl' (village) Volozhin is to be found in the area of Vilna, Lida and Molodechno. Until 1939 the Jewish population of Volozhin numbered about 3,000; the town was at the crossroads of the Novgorod district which was well known among merchant circles because of its large export of wood, flax and seeds.

In 1803 one of the largest yeshivas in the world was established in the town. Thousands of yeshiva students from all parts of the world received their Talmudic education there. There was almost no Jewish person who had not heard of the Volozhin Yeshiva. Practically all our greatest geniuses, rabbis, leaders and writers from the last few generations, studied in this yeshiva. Chaim Nachman Bialik also studied in the Volozhin Yeshiva, and a hill near the town was known by his name.

The yeshiva functioned only minimally during the First World War, because Volozhin was very close to the front. In 1922, the yeshiva again thrived under the management of the famous genius, Rabbi Yaakov Shapira. In 1933, a certain important merchant, who had himself been a student at the yeshiva, came to Volozhin, and renovated the yeshiva at his own expense.

With the Soviet occupation of Volozhin in 1939 the existence of the yeshiva came to an end. The head of the yeshiva, Rabbi Yaakov Shapira, died before the war. His son-in-law, Rabbi Chaim Valkin (the son of the Rabbi of Pinsk), took over his position, and together with the family of Rabbi Yaacov Shapiro I secretly took them to Vilna, which at the time belonged to Lithuania. In the actual building of the yeshiva a restaurant was opened, where a number of drunks would gather. The inhabitants of the shtetl for whom the yeshiva was the main centre were really bothered by this. Unfortunately it was not easy to have the Soviet decree [unclear whether it is the decree which allowed the yeshiva premises to be used as a restaurant] abolished. Along with this it should be noted that the sentry of the restaurant in the yeshiva, Gedaliah Mordechai Vidrowitch, applied to the manager of the restaurant, Wainer, to free him from this work, because he lived every night in fear. As soon as it is midnight he hears spirits studying and singing. Wainer laughed at this, and one night he himself went to guard the restaurant. Late at night, when he himself heard the studying and singing, he ran from the area, fainted, and from then on was afraid to enter, even during the day.

The Germans entered Volozhin on 25 June 1941. Before entering, they shelled the town with artillery fire, and caused fires by dropping incendiary bombs from aeroplanes. Local inhabitants were fired upon when German tanks rolled into the town: Chaim Eliahu Persky, Alter Shimshelowitz, Pesach Moise and Alter Berman were shot. As soon as the Germans occupied the town, the local Christians immediately started to loot both the warehouses left by the Soviets and also Jewish goods. Two weeks later, according to an order from the Gestapo, a Judenrat consisting of 12 people was formed, with Yaakov Garber at its head. The work of the Judenrat consisted in carrying out the regulations of the Gestapo and the local powers. They provided workers and arranged various collections and [aided in the] Aktions when money, gold, jewellery, leather, and manufactured goods for the Gestapo and local leaders were collected. In this way two months passed until the establishment of the ghetto.

The ghetto was formed in August 1941, in the lowest section of the town, 'Aroptzu'. 3,500 people were accommodated in only 50 to 60 houses, residents of Volozhin itself as well as those people who came from the surrounding villages such as Vyshneve, Holshen, Oshmege. There were also Jews who had escaped from Vilna. All Jews had to wear yellow patches. There was no limit to the persecution of the Jews. The Jews had to do the hardest work in the fields, in the forest, cleaning the streets and so on. Handworkers and other specialists worked at their trades. The Jews received only 20 grams of bread per person, nothing more. The Jews managed to get food from local peasants with great difficulty by giving them their most precious possessions. A Security Police Force, consisting of 30 men under the leadership of the local teacher, Gliker, was also organised in the ghetto.

A certain advocate, Stanislav Tursky, who was earlier sent to Kartuz-Bereze as an extreme 'endek' [a member of the fascist, anti-Semitic Polish National Democratic Party] and also for improper use of his work, returned to the town sooner than expected. Tursky had linked up with the town's anti-Semites, with the barber Baranski, and had started ugly agitation among the peasants against the Jews. Very quickly this anti-Semite was appointed as Mayor, and he immediately put into action his bloodthirsty plans. On the second day after he took over, he arrested many Jews, among them the beloved town doctor, Avraham Tzar, his daughter Nechama, Chaim Tsirulnik, Aharon Galperin, Shimon Levitt and Lipa Tzimmerman. As a result of his intervention, all these people were shot behind the town the day after being arrested.

The town police force consisted of former criminals from the nearby towns, run by the SS and encouraged by the town's anti-Semites. They would assault the Jews and beat them mercilessly. In this way, the policeman Minkowitz (the son of a Polish policeman) who had been in Ander's army,[42] broke both the hands of the Jewish woman, Freidel Rozin, and afterwards shot her. The girl, Rosa Berman, was shot and then thrown into a latrine. Shachne Poretski too was terribly beaten and then shot.

On 28 October 1941, Moke, the SS man from the Volozhin Gestapo, demanded that the Judenrat immediately gather a large consignment of leather which they then collected within two hours.

On 4 November 1942, this same Moke came again with five SS men, and he ordered the Judenrat to call together the Jews of the ghetto for a meeting. In addition he flogged the Jewish policemen, driving them to chase greater numbers of the inhabitants with more speed [to the meeting]. When a larger number of Jews were gathered, Moke chose about 200 children and parents and sent them back. He ordered that the remaining people be chased into the town cinema, supposedly for a meeting. The hall [of the cinema] was locked and about 10 people at a time were led out to the nearby sports pavilion where they were shot. When this became known in the ghetto, the Judenrat collected a greater sum of money and goods and

---

42   Ander's army was given this name in recognition of its commander, Wladyslaw Anders who led the Polish forces in the West. The army was formed in Russia after Hitler had reneged on the Molotov - Ribbentrop non-aggression pact between the Russians and the Germans after they had divided Poland between them.

handed them to the criminal Moke, who then halted the Aktion against the remaining 150 people, who were then released to return to the ghetto. More than 200 Jews perished in this Aktion together with the chairman of the Judenrat, Yaacov Garber. At the beginning, Garber, together with other members of the Judenrat and the ghetto policemen, had helped to bring the people into the cinema hall. Becoming aware, however, that the situation was really serious, Garber kept his word about also going into the hall, and shared the fate of the other Jews of the ghetto.

After carrying out the Aktion, White Russian and Polish police, as well as the local peasants, removed the best items from the dead, the jewellery, pulled out gold teeth, and then called upon 40 Jews to bury the victims. During the Aktion the young Yaakov Finger and also Tsafin and Zacharia Kayklin succeeded in running away from the sports field, although they were wounded. They arrived in the ghetto and informed the people about what they had seen and had survived. All this caused great fear among the Jews in the ghetto, and devastated them even more.

After the slaughter, a number of families were taken to work in the adjoining village, Krasnoe, where later they too were murdered. The people who remained in the ghetto lived in terrible conditions and in deadly fear. One day SS men entered a house where Jews used to pray and they took a Torah scroll, tore out the Tree of Life, unrolled the scroll along the length of the house, and then trod on it with their filthy boots. After a few days they returned and selected 35 Jews who were made to lie on the Torah scroll before being shot.

The Winter of 1942 was extremely hard for the Jews in the ghetto, although no Aktions took place until Spring. The local anti-Semites like Advocate Krestianov, Turski and so on, did not stop their campaign against the Jews and continued to demand that they be liquidated.

At five o'clock in the morning on 10 May 1942, the ghetto was surrounded by the SS and the police. They quickly entered the ghetto and at the gate they shot two Jewish policemen, Yochanan Klein and Itzchak Narushevicz, and started to shoot into the ghetto killing many people. Then they began to chase the Jews into the forge which the Russians had built in Moshtshitzke Street not far from the lower hermitage. Here they crowded together all the captives, about 800 men. The crush was appalling, and the wails of the children were indescribable. The SS would shoot into the crowd in order to silence them.

The Rabbi of Olszak, the new Rabbi, who was also there, instructed the people to break the ovens [of the forge], each one to take a brick, a stone, an iron bar to break down the doors, attack the SS and to run. However, Israel

Lunin, a member of the Judenrat said: 'A respite is also good' and he did not allow this to be carried out [breaking down the ovens].

The Head of the SS called upon the Judenrat member, Aharon Komanetski, to clean his boots. The moment that Komanetski bent down, the SS man fired a bullet into his head. When the people saw this, they began to climb through the roof. The Germans observed this and began to fire. Despite this, several people such as Mordechai Mlot were successful in escaping. The whole community of 800 people was detained on a very hot day, in a choking atmosphere, from five in the morning until five in the evening. Then they started to assemble women, children and the elderly in groups. They were taken to the courtyard of the peasant, Bulove, close to the Jewish cemetery, and there the head of the SS shot everyone with an automatic weapon. After the people were shot, they were burned together with the peasant's house. It is worth noting that when the groups of Jews were being led to their deaths they were accompanied by the local peasants who played music. Many of the elderly went to their deaths wearing their prayer shawls and white robes [burial shrouds for male Jews].[43] The hunting of the Jews in the shtetl on this day resulted in the deaths of another 800 Jews; they were shot in attics and in other hiding places which had been uncovered. The corpses lay unburied for three days. When they were taken for burial, the peasants threw dead dogs, cats and faeces onto them.

The third extermination in which the last 450 Jews perished took place in the month of September 1942. The remaining Jews in the town numbered 15 to 20, some of whom joined the partisans and others who were sent to camps.

The young Lazar Ragozin who was awarded high commendations for destroying 19 troop formations and their supplies was among the Volozhin partisans. At the time Leibel Lieberman was also with the partisans.

Munich Historical Commission, File No. 1373

---

43  *Kittel* – a white linen robe – which serves as a burial shroud for male Jews. It is also worn on special occasions, such as Yom Kippur, the Day of Atonement, by Ashkenazi Jews.

# 18

# MYADEL AND SURROUNDINGS

Eyewitness Account by Henia Menkin

Recorded by Yaakov Fleischer. Collected by the Hasenek Historical Commission.
Published by the Munich Historical Commission in the Journal Series
*Fun Letzten Khurben*, Vol. 9, 1948

At the outbreak of the war in 1939 the Soviets took over our village, Myadel, at the crossing of Vileyka, in the Vilna voivodeship. We remained under Russian rule until the outbreak of the German–Russian war in June 1941. About 150 Jewish families lived in Myadel. We were a family of six people: my husband and myself and four children. We worked in agriculture. Just before the outbreak of war in 1939 my husband became ill and a Polish surgeon operated on him. When the Soviets were on the verge of entering the village the doctor fled; there was no one to apply the dressings, and as a result my husband died.

As soon as the German–Russian war broke out, the local White Russians and the Poles began to go wild and to entertain themselves with baiting the Jews. They showed their real faces when the Germans arrived. They beat and murdered; they also pointed out Jews to the Germans and led them to Jewish homes.

The Germans began to harass and torment the Jewish population. They forced men and women to work. They sent people to work in the fields and to do various unnecessary 'black' [the most difficult and dirty] physical labour.

During the first week of the German occupation the White Russians and the Poles, under the leadership of the Germans, assembled 25 of the finest Jewish men and tortured them. They threw the unfortunate people, while they were still alive, into a grave near a lake. Other forms of cruelty were used to torture the Rabbi. The murderers set a dog upon him, which tore him apart and pulled his intestines out. A few weeks later the Germans took Jews and ordered them to dig up the victims from their graves. Additionally, they warned that no one was to weep while removing the corpses.

We lived in terrible fear all the time. At least the Germans were not present in the old Myadel where we lived, but we were always afraid that the so-called 'punitive forays' would come. Whenever the punishment forays came there were Jewish victims. There were 15 Jewish victims from the first punishment attack. The Germans also issued an order that Jews had to wear a yellow patch; that was in August 1941. As soon as it was decreed, the Poles and White Russians had a free hand to do to the Jews whatever their hearts desired. They really exploited this decree. Every night they robbed the Jews and, in addition, beat them terribly. One night they broke into my house. There were four men. My daughter recognised a school friend, the pharmacist's son. They chased us out of the house and then they beat us mercilessly in the street. My daughter started to beg the pharmacist's son to spare our lives. They entered the house, looted all the best things, and the rest were scattered about and destroyed. After this they left for other houses. At that moment we heard shots. Such robberies took place almost every night and we didn't even have anyone to whom to complain. The Judenrat was in New Myadel which was not far from us, and they would often demand taxes from us for the various contributions which the Germans demanded from the town.

In the village we had food to eat. Most of the inhabitants worked in agriculture and had prepared themselves [with provisions]. The peasants also brought products which they would exchange for household goods and other things. However, life was made very bitter by the ever-present fear and insecurity and the ever-increasing contributions demanded from us. We understood that when the Germans finished collecting our possessions they would murder us. Because of this we constantly thought of escaping. In the nearby forests partisans had begun to form groups.

Once on the Sabbath the Germans and Poles arrived and ordered that all Jews must assemble in New Myadel. When we arrived in New Myadel the local Jews had already been driven out of their houses. Poles on horseback chased us to the lake. When we arrived at the lake they gave an order that we should all enter the water. With the help of their horses, they forced us into the water up to our necks and we had to submerge ourselves; a little later they ordered us to get out of the water. We survived such frequent experiences. One day, just before the Day of Atonement, we were informed that the Germans had imposed a huge levy on the town. They demanded 300 leather coats, 500 pairs of leather boots, another large sum [of money], together with gold and other valuables. The village was already impoverished and denuded. At the same time the partisans told us that a new slaughter was being prepared in the town, and that we should escape to the forest, but without children. We organised ourselves and decided to run away on the eve of the Day of Atonement. In the meantime the Germans arrived from Ozmiana where there was an administration site at the crossing. Jewish aides came together with them. The majority were characters who had fallen from grace, and who served their German bosses faithfully. Knowing that we were preparing to escape, they began to threaten that they would inform the Germans. We barely managed to implore them not to do so and we shook hands, promising that we would not run away. Consequently, we were not able to escape on the scheduled day. Quietly, we again started to organise ourselves, but we were unable to let everyone know. On a Friday night we, a group of 300 people, left Myadel. Most of the Jews of Old Myadel had already run away, but in the second Myadel a few hundred persons still remained.

That night it was very dark. It rained heavily and we had to walk 18 kilometres to Nievier through the forest. The route was difficult and we discarded the food which we had taken with us. We were tired, wet, and very thirsty when we arrived at Nievier at about two or three in the morning. At the swamps there, a few partisans appeared with their Commander, Yekel Segalchik, from a nearby village, Dolhinov, on the Vilna side. Segalchik handed us over to a peasant who led us deep into the forest where the swamps were. We were terribly thirsty from the journey, so we adopted the following solution for ourselves: with a foot, we scraped a little trench, and drank the green water which had collected. There we slowly got organised. We lay down under trees, and that is how we lived.

The partisans confiscated any guns that the youth had and gave them to their unit. A group of 18 people left, among them my two older daughters. Meanwhile, more small groups of Jews escaped from other towns, and joined us. We were already about 350 people in the Nievier swamps.

Just after we had escaped from Myadel, a terrible slaughter was carried out. Seventy Jews were murdered. A ghetto was then established. The partisans promised all of us that they would lead us further eastwards. After being in the Nievier swamps for several weeks, partisans approached us and said that they could not take all of us further at once, they could only do it in groups. The first group was made up of 75 people. They went in the direction of Dolhinov. When they were already in the forest next to Dolhinov, the Germans surrounded them and killed 40 people from the group. The 35 who survived ran further eastwards to the region of Oshetsk, where there were more partisans.

After a few days, when the first group left our section of the forest, Russian partisans came to us and took all those who were still left out of the swamps. It was a dark night. When we had travelled about 30 kilometres, the partisan who was leading us became lost and led us to a small town where there were Germans. A partisan led in the front, and we remained behind the town. There were also children among us, for whom the partisans had provided wagons in which to travel. Suddenly we heard shooting from the town. We understood that we had fallen into a trap and we began to run back. But the Germans thought that we had already passed through the town, so they gave chase in a forward direction. When we ran back, daylight was already appearing, and slowly it became lighter. We had to run fast. After returning, we discovered that seven people were missing, those who were unable to move fast. We entered the thick forest in the so-called Russian thicket. It was already very cold. Winter had arrived. The only thing which kept us going was wood of which we had enough. We burned wood, made fires, and kept ourselves warm. We started to dig trenches, and made mud huts. Each hut was at a distance of half to one and a half kilometres from the other. It was difficult to procure food. At night we would leave the forest and go to the peasants to ask for a piece of bread or some potatoes. I had two children with me, a boy and a girl, plus a nephew for whom I had to find food. We built a mud hut – a four-sided trench, covered over with grass; we built an oven from stones, but the smoke choked us. Thirteen persons lived in our hut where we remained until March 1942.

Often police raids would take place in the forests. The Germans would search for partisans, and after each raid there would be people missing. After one such raid in the forest, we became afraid to remain in our hut, and we ran deeper into the forest. There we settled in an abandoned hut. Because Spring had begun, and the snow was beginning to melt, a lot of water drained into our hut. We had to leave it and remain outdoors. Typhus began to spread and my children became ill. The boy soon improved, but the girl was still very ill. We remained outdoors with the children. Ironically, being outside saved our lives. Once, after Pesach, we heard a lot of shooting at dawn. Germans came running from the town, Andrijevki. Those who were in the huts did not manage to escape. My daughter was sick, so she was unable to walk, and we had to carry her in our arms. We covered many kilometres running. We eventually came to a place which was wet and had tall grasses growing there. We went into the grass and hid ourselves.

When night fell we allowed ourselves to return. But we did not know the way. However, on leaving the grassy area, we heard someone coming from a distance. Soon we met a family who had also hidden themselves in the grasses. The woman was sick and her husband carried her across his shoulders. He was already an older man and he was able to orient himself. We returned to our original place. The Germans had burned the huts which we had set up in the forest. Many of the mud huts had been destroyed and the Jews killed. There were more than 50 dead.

We remained in the forest thicket until August 1943. A partisan told us that the Germans were preparing to put a blockade around the forest, and that we must escape from the thicket. About 30 of us left the thicket. Prior to this time many of us had gone, with difficulty, further eastwards. A large number had been murdered by the Germans during the raids and, in general, the group had dispersed; each one took care only of himself, finding food, and learning how best to organise himself.

When we came to the edge of the forest we had to travel on the highway through a small town. My nephew said that he would first go and have a look and that he would come straight back. He left and when I saw that he hadn't returned, as the watchman, I went into the town. As soon as I went out, I was stopped. I soon understood that I had fallen into the hands of the Germans, because I saw in front of me soldiers in German uniforms. They apprehended me and started to ask questions: where I was coming from, where I was going, whether there were partisans there, and so on. Naturally, I denied everything and said that I knew nothing. They soon left. We later found out that they were Russian partisans disguised as Germans. My nephew, when he left the forest, also saw them, so he ran away to Nievier. Two months were to pass before I met him again. We returned to Nievier to the swamps because we were afraid that the Germans might come with their dogs which would find the mud huts. In the swamps the dogs weren't able to get near. I was unable to go with the whole group because my son had fallen ill, so I had to sustain myself on the way. I arrived there [in Nivier] only after two months when I met my nephew. There we constructed a hut and lived in it. This was in the summer of 1943. The Russian offensive was formidable and the partisans were involved in the struggle. In a short while the whole region was in the hands of the partisans. They carried out bold attacks on German transports and also attacked German posts. The Germans were afraid to come into that area, so it became easier for us. We went to work for the farmers in the fields and we immediately had food to eat. By then we had been in Nievier for a year. During the winter of 1943–1944 we built mud huts and felt generally freer. We did not suffer any raids, so the days passed by quickly.

In June 1944, when the great Russian offensives took place, we began to feel that the day of liberation was near. We saw large fires and heard loud artillery fire and bombings every night. It was not long before the Russians entered our town. After the liberation we returned to our own town, Myadel. My two daughters, who had gone away to join the partisans after a short stay in the forest, were sent together with others to Russia to bring back guns and ammunition for the partisans. However, they did not return to the partisans, but remained in Russia to work in Vladimir. I did not know where my daughters were to be found. They assumed that we were no longer alive because they had heard that the first group that left Nievier to go to Dolhinov was murdered. They sent a telegram to the Mayor of Myadel asking whether any of us were to be found there. In this way I found out about them. After many attempts, the daughters arrived in Myadel, and all of us left there.

Historical Commission of Hazene

# 19

# IN A HUNGARIAN WORK BATTALION

Eyewitness Account by Moshe Dov Taub

Recorded by Arieh Rate. Collected by the Lechfeld Historical Commission.
Published by the Munich Historical Commission in the Journal Series
*Fun Letzten Khurben*, Vol. 10, 1948

We lived in Morava [Hungarian: Muzsai] near Berek in Hungary. In July 1943, I was called up for a work battalion. For understandable reasons I had no desire to go there, so I hid myself in Budapest. I used to receive letters from my father in which he said that, because I did not present myself to the battalion, our family was being constantly harassed by the police. I therefore decided to present myself to the work battalion in order to avoid the severe punishment which awaited me for desertion. I obtained, for a large sum of money, a document which said that my delay in appearing was because the work battalion did not accept me as, ostensibly, there was no place for me. On 10 October 1943, after hiding myself for three months, I finally presented myself to the work battalion.

After a few days about 40 men out of a total of 350 were transported in a wagon to the former Rumanian town of Banie, near Satmar [Satu Mare], which was settled by Hungarians. For the journey each one of us received a 1 kg loaf of bread, and a little bit of sweet conserved [sic] coffee. The journey took four days. Immediately upon our arrival in the town, the Hungarian orderlies 'honoured' us with excessive beatings and started to treat us like the worst criminals. During the first few days they moved us 10 kilometres away from the town, and made us do really difficult gymnastic exercises;

in addition they rained deadly blows on us. As almost all of us came from religious homes we wouldn't eat food from the kitchens, but used our own money to buy food. We were all approximately the same age, 18 to 20 years old, everyone healthy and robust. On the first day we surmised that these inhuman exercises had one goal – to weaken us and torture us to death. After 14 days the Hungarians allocated to us the task of splitting rocks. They gave us an unheard-of daily quota which we could not reach under any circumstances. Because of this, after returning from work, exhausted and broken, we would again receive terrible beatings.

After we had worked for a month enduring pain and suffering we were sent over to the old Rumanian border, to Rodna near Bistrita. There we worked at digging trenches on the hill 'Retunde', 15 kilometres from a settlement. We had to perform the most difficult physical work [on a daily diet] of only 250 grams of bread and a few beans. Working like this we excavated winter trenches in the rocky mountain; we also dug out entire tunnels. Many of us became ill from the constant beans, cooked tastelessly. Ten young men who did not want to eat non-kosher food lived on bread alone.

After three months of hard labour we were sent away from there to the Polish border, to Volove, from there to Kolomyya, and from there to Vyzhnytsia. The journey took several weeks, and I am not in a condition to be able to describe what we went through. We all resembled skeletons rather than living humans. Vyzhnytsia lies between Kolomyya, Delyatin and Kumov [Kuti]. Here they sent us out into a field which lay between two lakes and which looked like an island. We slept under the open skies; food consisted of 200 grams of bread and a thin soup made from grass, full of sand. In this distressed state we had to go a distance of eight kilometres, again up incredible mountains not far from Kolomyya, and dug trenches. We used to pull up grass on the way and eat it. Passing through a forest we would find mushrooms which we would eat. Twenty young men went crazy from these same mushrooms. A few weeks later we were taken somewhere not far from Kosovo where we worked at building fortifications. This work too was unbelievably hard, and we were beaten very often. Life became so difficult that all of us wished for death.

While working there we learned that in the nearby mountains there were many partisans. The partisans in the region fought hard against the Germans. They would attack them very often, and, thanks to the thick forests and the mountains, the Germans were unable to thwart them. The partisans would simply make fun of the helplessness of the Germans. For example, they caught our overseer and after four days they returned him in a completely naked state.

Seeing that we no longer had anything to lose, a few individuals from among us escaped to the partisans. Thereafter, seeing that this escape had been successful, whole groups started to run away, up to 10 men at a time and more. After a few days there only 200 men remained. Finally the Germans found out and they guarded us with greater vigilance. One of us, Asher Shwartz from Sakmer (a son of Tuvia Vatemacher), was suspected by the Germans of wanting to flee, so they shot him. We did not receive any food for four days. The Germans received an order to divide us into groups of 10. Fortunately the Germans had to retreat so we got away with only a fright [fear of what the Germans might have been planning].

We retreated together with the German military and marched as far as Hungary. We departed barefoot and naked and did not look human. The Germans were becoming short of a younger labour pool, and seeing that we were no longer suitable for any work, they sent us for two weeks of convalescence to Koenigsfeld. There we received one and a half kilograms of bread every two days, bacon, meat and other fatty foods. Being so terribly starved, many fell sick from the food and died. In general these were happy days for us, and, receiving good food, we talked ourselves into believing that the Germans were doing penance because they had tortured us without reason. Some of us believed that the Germans might be made to feel ashamed by the Russians, who could arrive at any time. In short, we were all in good spirits and thought that the Jewish sun had again begun to shine.

The 14 days ended very quickly. They placed us behind the front and we were 'offered' the job of carrying crates of ammunition weighing 50 kilograms to the front. I cannot tell you the exact location of the work area, because we were unable to find out where we were. I knew only that the top of the mountain to which we carried the crates was called 'Tempo'. Dragging oneself with a heavy 50 kilogram crate on the shoulders took 24 hours to get there, and by the time we had survived the climb to the top of the mountain, each one of us wished for death. We were all barefoot and the stones injured our feet. Our guards beat us with their rubber truncheons and we held onto life with the last of our strength. I often imagined that very soon my life would end. However, to our misfortune, our souls refused to part with us under any circumstances. We also had to take a great deal of care not to do the wrong thing because not only did the guards lash us immediately, but also we received a serious beating at the top after offloading the crates. We would remain there for 24 hours.

We worked in this way for 14 days, but later the Germans retreated from there too. It was clear to all of us that the Germans would soon slaughter us. We therefore decided to escape; we were just waiting for an opportunity. I knew very well that, in my threadbare clothing which showed my emaciated and dirty body, it would not be easy for me to run away and hide from the Germans and the Hungarians who, when it came to killing Jews, were not so different from the Germans. But I decided that I had to get away from the terrible 'dogs'.

I almost perished from this attempt. It was a dark night, the road was crowded with people who were running as quickly as they could. Our guards went around with their revolvers in their hands, and as soon as someone stopped, or a woman tried to turn aside, they would pull the trigger and the Jew would be sent to the other world. Even taking all of this into account, I knew precisely: now or never! I took a good look around to see where my guard was, and I convinced myself that he was a few steps in front of me. I sprang to the left, and before the guard managed to look back, I disappeared into the darkness of the night.

After two hours of running I was sure that no one was chasing me, so I sat down to rest and to think about what to do next. I was terribly afraid of two things: the daytime and hunger. Oh God, I thought to myself, if You could make it dark now, or punish our enemies with blindness as in Sodom, perhaps this time I would be saved. I thought perhaps I would find food because it was October 1944, and the fruit was still hanging on the trees. When the accursed morning came, I hid in the forest, and although I was a coward even at home, here I was not afraid of any animals. My one fear, God forbid, was that I might not come across even one living person.

For eight days I hid in the forest, and at night I would walk. Finally I arrived in Mozhai, the city of my birth. I knew the district very well, and in the first moment I rejoiced, I was among my own people. But I quickly took into account that they [the Germans] probably did to the Jews here what they did in the Polish towns, and who knew whether there was still a living Jew in Mozhai. Therefore I decided to go back into the forest and to wait until the Russians would arrive. In that way I wandered around and fed myself from the fruit on the trees.

Three weeks had already passed since I took that lucky step, and I still had not seen a single person. Suddenly, while I was in the forest sitting under a tree, I saw a Christian acquaintance. It is easy to imagine how nervous I became. But I quickly calmed down and started to talk to him. I soon convinced myself that he didn't recognise me; apparently I was far from resembling my old self. The Christian told me that the Jews from our town had been liquidated and he advised me to run away from there, the quicker the better, because a few days previously they had captured someone, Abraham Schwartz, and shot him. Abraham Schwartz was from our town and I knew him well. I decided to leave that place.

A few hours had passed, and I really went into the lion's den. I noticed German artillery which had retreated; they saw me and detained me. They paired me off with another Jew, Moshe Weiss from Kloizenhalten, whom they had captured an hour earlier, and they told both of us to run in front of their vehicles. We fell after 10 kilometres. Finally they stopped and began to eat lunch. A senior officer gave an order that we should be led out to the fields to be shot. A Hungarian officer of lower rank, with a gun in his hand, took us a short distance and then ordered us to dig a grave. Both of us had spades, which we specially took with us, so that in the event that Germans might come across us, we would look like workers.

We started digging, and the junior officer continually shouted: 'Quicker, quicker!' While we were digging, we both said a prayer of repentance knowing that these were our last moments. Engrossed in our work, we did not notice a Christian woman approaching. Suddenly we heard how she asked the junior officer: 'What are these people doing?' Upon hearing that we were digging our own graves, she started to scold him roundly and said that he did not know what might happen to him and that he could not casually bring about the death of innocent people. He started to make excuses that it was not his fault, he was given the specific order to do so, and he must do his duty. 'It's not true!' she shouted, 'You must not kill them. Shoot twice in the air, and I will fill the grave, they will certainly not check to see whether or not you have shot them.'

The junior officer allowed himself to be persuaded by the woman, and he even shook hands with us and hoped we would survive. When we had walked a few steps, we heard two shots. We did not doubt that this gentle Christian woman was the prophet Eliahu [the Old Testament prophet Elijah].

From there we went to Rede, about 15 kilometres [may be inaccurate] from Berek, where the following day we were liberated by the Russians.

Historical Commission Lechfeld

# 20

# DEATH OF A RUNNER

Eyewitness Account by Cessia Shilling

Collected by the Munich Historical Commission.
Published by the Munich Historical Commission in the Journal Series
*Fun Letzten Khurben,* Vol. 10, 1949

One day in August 1944, when we had just turned around from work, we were suddenly distracted by the siren alarm. It was still long before the regular time for the evening rollcall. We immediately understood that something of great importance had occurred in the camp. At once we heard whispers in the ranks: 'It is certain that whoever had escaped, good luck to that person, may God help her and protect her'. We immediately became happy that the 'runner' had disappeared from the women's camp.

She was well-known throughout the women's camp. She was a sweet darling girl in her early twenties. In the summer of 1943 she had been brought to Auschwitz in a Belgian transport of Jews. Her beauty and charm prevented even the murderers from killing her. They even found a light form of work for her. She became known to the SS as the 'runner' (the role of a 'runner' was to pass on the orders of the SS officer to the block and room Elders). As a runner she had the opportunity to come into contact with prisoners in the individual camps which were separated by electrified wire fences, and no ordinary prisoner could pass from one camp to another. In this way Mala became the link between one camp and another, this being of great help – like passing news from one family member to another, or from friends, which was then very significant. And so those black days and years in Auschwitz passed. Mala was more and more loved by the prisoners and was trusted even by the SS men who employed her. Feeling that the trust in her was very strong, she decided to make use of it at the right moment when it would help the resistance movement in the camp. However, every prisoner in Auschwitz knew the catchword of the SS: 'No one must leave the camp alive'. But one wants to live. The news spread that the Soviet Army had conquered Hitlerism [sic] and had come closer to Auschwitz. This was after the great offensive of the summer of 1944 when the Soviets had invaded Poland and had gone as far as the Vistula River. At the time the question of saving the camp from total destruction became really urgent. Mala took upon herself the task of making contact with the outside world, especially with the partisans of their area. In addition, she was helped by a certain Edek, a Pole, who was very friendly with Mala and who was one of the oldest prisoners in the camp. Edek had been in touch with the Polish partisans even earlier, and together with Mala he now decided that he should break out of the camp and propose to the partisans that they should attack the camp and, by this means, save the people from annihilation.

But one can say only the following: to get oneself out of Auschwitz was not the easiest thing. Of help here was the strong belief of the SS men in Mala. Godel Silver, one of the leaders of the resistance movement, provided uniforms for Mala and Edek. The uniforms and other necessary clothing for an escape were hidden by Yekel Rozensweig in Block 8 of Camp D. Dressed as SS personnel they succeeded in getting out of the camp.

For about two weeks Mala was free. But fate intervened and she suddenly became ill. Not having any place to go, she went to the German hospital in Myslowitz and remained there until she was well. Edek came daily to visit her and to keep her informed about the current situation.

One day, when Mala had started to feel better and Edek was sitting by her bedside as he did every day, the hospital was surrounded by SS men and gendarmes, who were specially placed there in order to search for the two escapees from Auschwitz. While carrying out searches in the whole area they also searched the hospital. Here the tattooed Auschwitz numbers [on the arms of Mala and Edek] were revealed. Mala and Edek were arrested and brought back to Auschwitz.

Difficult and painful days began for Mala. She was locked in a cellar, standing half-submerged in water, without food, and regularly tortured in different ways so that she should reveal who had helped her to escape. It was clear to everyone that someone from the German camp personnel must have assisted her. But Mala would not disclose who had helped her. All the different proposals promising that she would be freed if she would only disclose who it was that had helped her were rejected. All the torture was for naught. Mala did not disclose anything. After seven such painful days sentence was passed: Mala was to be hanged.

With great ceremony the murderers prepared for the execution. They decreed that a gallows was to be set up alongside the 'Farnia' (the main road of the camp which led from one camp to another), and in the evening, when the prisoners were returning from work, the execution would be carried out in front of everyone!

The day was beautiful. But in the evening, while we were returning exhausted from work, we saw how red the sunset was as if all of heaven were burning. And we thought: if only the sun would pour all its heat into Auschwitz and burn everyone and everything. But this miracle did not happen. Awaiting us was the awful picture of the innocent Mala being killed for her only sin – wanting to save herself from death.

Everything was ready as we stood in the 'five rows' [lines of five people] on the camp main road, as it was decreed that every camp prisoner must see the execution in detail. After standing about for a long period, a murmur was heard: 'They are leading her …' We thought that on her way to the noose she would be full of sorrow with tears in her eyes. But Mala was a heroine, and she wanted to die as one. Along the whole route Mala did not stop rebuking and reviling the destroyers. She argued that they should not believe that all their deeds would go unpunished. 'Your grey day is already close, and the end will be ugly – and you will not hang me'.

Hearing her last words, the camp Kommandant and the 'shit-selector' [the person who helped with the selection of the Jews] laughed heartily, and at that moment Mala took the opportunity to tear herself out of their strong hands. The camp Kommandant gave her such a mighty blow in the face that he became covered in her blood and fell down. Then she speedily pulled out a dagger which she had hidden in her shoe, and quickly cut the veins in her hand. Other murderers came running and rapidly brought her to an ambulance in order to stop the haemorrhaging of blood, so she could be brought alive to the gallows.

Pale and exhausted, with only weak signs of life, she was led from the ambulance and was brought to the gallows. When the ropes were about to be put around her delicate neck, Mala gave up her soul. With heads hanging down and eyes full of tears, the mass of prisoners dispersed. Throughout the whole evening in the blocks the same message went from mouth to mouth: 'Mala, you still live amongst us, all honour to your memory!'

# 21

# IN AUSCHWITZ
# WITH TWO SMALL CHILDREN

Eyewitness Account by Esther Weiss

Published by the Munich Historical Commission in the Journal Series
*Fun Letzten Khurben,* Vol. 10, 1948

At the beginning of August 1944, after all the transports had departed from Lodz, about 70,000 Jews remained. My husband and I sought for possible ways to remain in the ghetto for a little longer. We knew very well that our children (Pesia, born on 8 March 1934, and Maishale, born on 1 April 1944) would certainly not survive if removed from Lodz. We then considered very seriously that the end may not be very far off. We thought that, despite the situation, we might still manage to save ourselves. We asked Podlaski, head of the workshop 'Leather and Saddles', to make us legal resident workers; that is, to live in and to receive food in the workplace. Because of our very young child, Mr Podlaski hired us so that we could remain for a little longer in Lodz. I and my husband worked for him in the workshop, as did several thousand other Jews. Soon after another 100 men together with their families were made legal workers. During the Aktion in August 1944, all the men whose names were called had to go to the assembly point at the ghetto jail on Tsharnietzkene Street. However, those who worked as legal workers did not have to go. Our workshop was encircled by a wooden fence. There [in the factory] we would receive food and we also slept there.

Aktions were carried out daily over a period of time. Jewish and German police used to go from house to house, gathering the people in trucks and taking them to the train at Radogast, a few kilometres from the town. The

Aktion lasted for three to four weeks. Jews in the ghetto numbered fewer and fewer, until there were only the legal ones left. They numbered a few thousand.

On 27 August 1944, posters appeared declaring that every Jew who was found anywhere in the ghetto on 28 August, with the exception of Tsharnietzkene Street, would be shot. The other prisoners were also affected by this decree. During the whole period of the Aktion we worked solely for the organisers of the Aktion. We made ladies' bags for their wives, leather bags for men. We still thought that we would be approved of by the murderers who might perhaps allow us to remain in Lodz.

Through our overseer, Israel Miller, we tried to influence the leaders of the Aktion by working for them. The Chief said that the order had come from Berlin. He could not change anything; he could help us only with a sealed letter. Miller was actually given such a letter from him. However, we did not know what was written in the letter. On 28 August 1944, we went by wagon to Radogast. We had the right to take our belongings with us, while others were not allowed to do so. In Radogast we saw the German who had given us the letter. While leaving Radogast, the 'legal' workers were treated better. As many Jews as possible were shoved into a wagon. They pushed from 30 to 60 people into a wagon. Despite the beatings, we all attempted to remain with Miller because of the letter.

We left at dawn on 29 August. In the evening we arrived at Auschwitz/Birkenau. We had to remain in the wagons all night. At dawn we were driven out of the wagons and saw exactly where we were. We were surrounded by many SS men as well as Jews in striped outfits. We heard shouts of: 'Everyone down. Leave everything!' The Jewish prisoners in stripes said to us, 'If you want to remain alive, get rid of your children!' I did not leave my children and I went together with them. While I was getting out of the wagon, I saw tens of SS men with Dr Mengele and Dr Fischer (I only found out later about their 'beloved' names [reputations) who directed the selection. Women, children and the weak – left; the rest – right. They judged simply by looking at us. Our foreman Miller, under a rain of blows which he received from both the SS and the Jewish prisoners, reached one of the main officers. Miller gave him the letter which he read, and then he led Miller to the head of the selection. He ordered that all 109 saddle workers should stand aside. But not all of the 109 wanted to do so; a number of them had already been 'selected', and they were not allowed to turn back. Even so, 109 Jews gathered together while other Jews replaced them. The 'saddle group' consisted of 25 men, 23 women and five children from the group: I remember husband and wife Zeleski with their two children (one of them was named Samek), Hershkowitz with a little girl, Mirka, and my husband and myself with our two children. We saw how more than half the transport was sent to the ovens; the smaller portion was sent to the baths. After the SS men were finished with the whole transport, they approached us. A woman prisoner had made a list of all of us, including the children. We told the SS that we had left our work tools in the wagons. They told us to go to the wagons to retrieve our work equipment.

Thereafter they took us to the baths. Before the shower, we were shaved and smeared with some sort of liquid. Our own clothes were not returned. We were given strange clothing to wear and led to camp 'Tz'. For two days we were all there together. The men and older boys were in Block Six, the women, girls and little children were in Block Three. Afterwards the men were sent to Camp 'A' and the women and children to the women's concentration camp (referred to as F.K.L.). It is hard to imagine how amazed the women in F.K.L. were when they saw me with a live four-month-old-child. The people there were unable to understand how we had managed to get through [the selection]. I told them about the situation. Everyone, old and young, cried. In the barrack there was a House Elder from Warsaw by the name of Rozia, about 30 years old; a mother, whose seven-year-old child had been taken from her. She did a lot for my child; brought whatever was possible, and cooked for the child (I was not allowed to use any stove). After being in F.K.L. for two days, I became ill; I had injured a foot in the groove of the plank-bed. I had to go to the 'hospital' as a patient. On the way I had to guard myself in case Dr Mengele saw me. I made contact with the female doctor, a Jewish woman from Hungary, who said that I needed to remain in the hospital. I told her that I could not do so because I had a baby. She was very compassionate towards me (I would agree to come in with the child, but not without). She made an effort to heal my foot without me entering the hospital. Every day, at half past two, when Dr Mengele was away at lunch, I would go to the doctor. It took three months for my foot to heal. The Block Elder did not report that I was ill because of the child; she would normally have reported sick persons together with their families. The Block Elder was a Jewish woman, Gizia, from Hungary.

In the middle of September 1944, after I had been in F.K.L. for two weeks, my Maishele became ill with flu. It was terribly cold in the barrack. A complication occurred when the child developed a lung infection. I could not go to any doctor (certain death!). For three weeks without relief the child had a temperature of 40 degrees. I thought that the child was already gone. In the camp there was a block for children of mixed marriages (mischlingen). The Germans still spared those children. There was a lady doctor with those children; she was also a Jewess from Hungary. Our child minder, a Jewish girl from Poland, went to that doctor and brought her to my Maishele. It was impossible to examine the child; it was terribly cold. She could only give him drops to strengthen his heart. His temperature began to fall and the child began to get a little better. But an abcess developed under his ear and from his ear it began to spread further. I didn't know what to do without a doctor, without medicines. However, the abcess slowly cleared up.

Our transport was left without tattoo numbers for a while longer. They used to tell us that, regardless, we were going to the ovens. Later we were tattooed. We were taken to a special section where young girls would do it. My number was A27664; my little son, B14897; my Pesale, A27663.

When we, three mothers with children, had been in the block for four weeks, the Block Elder came running – the mothers with children, move! We were going to the ovens. We started to shake terribly and to wail. The Block Elder took pity on my Pesale, a girl of 10 years. She said that the girl was already well developed, and in order to save her she alleged that she was 16 years old. The girl remained behind, and I and the little child in my arms went out to the selection, being sure that we were going into the ovens. As soon as we arrived at the 'Sauna' (the shower where the selection took place), a woman said to us: 'If you are asked whether you want to go with the children, you should not argue'. We answered that we ourselves knew what to do. Our lives should not be more valuable than the children's. Where the children go, we too would go. I regretted only one thing, that I had not taken the older child with me.

If I had only known then that we were all lost anyway [our end was near]. I stood, I saw the fire which burned from the people's bodies, and I believed that I too would soon go there. But they led us to the showers. One of the showers was occupied by the recently arrived Warsaw children. So they led us to a second shower. We stood for two hours just waiting until Dr Mengele arrived with his retinue and large dogs, and we could see that we were already lost. All the people who were there – 400 women – were standing naked for the selection. The female scribe shouted to us that we should undress and approach. We replied that we have time [using a rebellious tone]. The Recorder then said that we would be beaten. It made no difference to us; in any case we were going to our deaths. We, the mothers with children, had hidden ourselves behind a small wall of a storeroom. Dr

Mengele was really distracted and did not notice us. From our corner, we remained standing as we saw the whole group of the selected ones approach – who entered the gas chamber, who stood aside, who was to live.

The selection was over and people dressed themselves again. Dr Mengele and his retinue left. We cried bitterly and said to ourselves: perhaps our children are still worth something, perhaps my mother, my sisters and my brother interceded on my children's behalf.[44] I lost my whole family in Auschwitz, all of them perished, and we, the three mothers, were left alone. The others from the other blocks were taken away. The scribe knew that in relation to us she had nothing to wait for [there was no need to register them as they were spared death in the gas chamber].

We went out on our own and had no idea where to go. We did not dare to wander around the camp streets because there were always block spies. Among the prisoners only the Block Elders and those of equal status could move around. I said to the mothers: let's try to re-enter the block where we were before. We arrived there and everyone started weeping. They were unable to understand how we managed to get out of Dr Mengele's hands. We told them the whole story. The Block Elder said that she was afraid to allow us to enter because we were forbidden to be in the block; if we were caught there, she would be shot. We fell at her feet, wept, and asked her to take pity, not on us, but on the children. She turned to her friend and said: 'I see nothing, I know nothing, you do for the children whatever you can'. The Block Elder was a faithful Jewish daughter. On Rosh Hashanah [the Jewish New Year] and Yom Kippur [the Day of Atonement] she brought candles for all the Jewish women, lit two candles, and called on the oldest woman in the block to make a blessing over them. Whoever still had a little prayer book prayed individually sitting on the plank beds. There were a few women who would not eat [non-kosher] sausages, which they either sold or exchanged for something else to eat.

We were accepted back in the block and they set up a plank bed for us in the washroom, further away from the entrance. It was very cold there with broken windows and an open roof. Water poured onto our heads without cessation. The Block Elder and her helper did what they could for us. At night they sent comforters to cover the children, among them my child, because they knew that he was weak. I remained there with my child for nine weeks.

---

44  We can assume that she thought that her family might have interceded with God on behalf of the children.

In November 1944, people started to say that all the inmates of Camp F.K.L. would be sent to work, so we understood that no good awaited us. The Block Elder confirmed that everyone would be sent away to work. However, we, the mothers, who were saved at least once, had to face our death because no one with children would be sent to work. We felt that it was a great misfortune that such was our fate; we had only a few weeks to live, and now we had to go.

At that time Dr Mengele carried out selections in the block where we were, but the Block Elder hid the mothers and their children. As we were on the planks in the washroom, she told us to get under the planks quickly and to hold onto the little children, so that they should not be heard. The selection was over for that day. On the second day there was another one; on the third day a woman doctor accompanied Dr Mengele as his right-hand assistant (I don't remember her name). We hid ourselves each time.

In 1944 more and more transports left Auschwitz for work in Germany. For that reason, they began to liquidate our Camp F.K.L., so they came to our block. We soon saw that there was no more reason to get up early. One day the Block Elder came running, and screamed: 'Everyone out!' Everyone went to the transport. There were a few children, a few elderly women, all of whom had to get out. My 10-year-old daughter, who was supposedly 16 years old, also had to get out. But I knew that the girl would not escape Dr Mengele, and I wanted to go together with her and my small child. However, the Block Elder grabbed me and threw me back into the block. She said that the mothers with children should not go now because we would go to the ovens, so we had to wait until we were called. It took only a few minutes until everyone had left. Only the three mothers with the children remained. A few hours had passed before a small number of women, those who had passed the selection process, returned. They came to eat some soup and told us who had passed the selections and who had gone to the gas. My daughter had gone to the gas! Dr Mengele had approached her and asked how old she was. She replied – 16 years. He replied that she was not 16, she was too small. They sent her into the gas chamber together with all the people who had been chosen for death. I sat all day and a whole night in the block: I banged my head on the wall – I no longer had a daughter! How could I go out and see how the fire burns from my child; if only I had been with her!

Meanwhile the selected people waited until the transport was full to be gassed together. And in the meantime God helped. An order was issued: no more killing. The talk among us was that this was because America had made an offer to the Germans that for every Jew they would exchange three Germans. Whether that was true, I do not know. But I thought: how was I to be happy when I no longer had my child? The next morning a Russian woman came to me and said: 'Go outside quickly, your daughter is here'. I asked her if she was crazy. How was it possible? Twenty four hours had passed since she was sent to the gas. It was impossible! But the Russian woman replied: 'I am not crazy – go outside – you will see'. I put my little child down and I hurried outside. However, I was not allowed to go far. I crept along side paths, along the walls so that no one should see me, until I came to the block where the girl was. I saw her and also all the people who were chosen with her to be gassed. They all looked wild; completely naked, hungry, thirsty. Throughout the 24 hours they were given nothing. The girl was also stark naked, as God made her, and outside it was terribly cold and rainy. I was unable to recognise that this was my child. I quickly went back to my block where I told the Room Elder that my child had returned from the gas chamber and I described what she looked like. The Elder got hold of a dress, a pair of shoes and also something to eat, and took them to the so-called 'Dead Block'.[45] The room Elder told my daughter to get dressed and to eat everything which she had brought, so that she should look a little healthier, because she would still have to undergo three examinations by Dr Mengele, the woman doctor, and Dr Fisher to see if she was healthy: the room Elder had told my child to tell the truth about her age, because for her 10 years she was well developed. The room Elder told me that they would send my daughter to the Children's Block for Aryan children. After she had been in the 'Dead Block' for eight days the three doctors examined her and told her that she would be placed in another block. They located her in the Children's Block where all the surviving children were, even Jewish ones.

My daughter remained in that block for a few weeks. It was with great difficulty that I managed to see her, as one was not allowed to enter the courtyard. But if the child wanted to see me, and I her, she would take out the garbage pail in the morning, and together with a second child, they would carry it through the fields. My block was not far from the toilet and there we took the opportunity to see each other.

Meanwhile it turned out that my whole block was sent away to work in Germany. Of the three children who were with their mothers, two children

---

45 The block in which the Germans placed the inmates who had escaped the gas chamber.

were sent to the Children's Block (they were older than my little son) and the mothers were sent away. They wanted to send my little boy also to the Children's Block, but there they would not accept him because he was too young. That was my luck; I remained together with my child.

They put me in a block together with Russians and Ukrainians. I encountered great problems there. They could not bear to be with a Jew, and they demanded that I take the child to the Children's Block and that I go to work. The Room Elder from our block went to ask the Camp Elder, a Jewish woman with the name of Hilda (I did not know her family name) for a note that stated that they have to accept me in the other block. When I arrived at the block with the note, they were unable to do anything about it, and accepted me and my child.

Imagine what it was like for a Jewish woman with a small child to be among 150 Ukrainian women? I could not move around in the block and they did not allow me to use the stove even to cook something for the child. During the three weeks that I was there I was unable to prepare even a little warm water for the child. They gave me a plank bed to sleep on in a corner where huge rats ran around. [46]

Suddenly there was an outcry when we heard that we were to be sent away from this block. They sent us to the Gypsy Camp in Birkenau. However, there were no longer any Gypsies in the camp. There they sorted out everyone: Jews separate, Poles separate, every nationality separate – several thousand from many places. The children from the Children's Block were also brought here and placed in the same area as the women. The children were also sorted out according to their nationality. The children stood in separate groups. The Jewish children were placed in a block with the Jewish women. In this block there were several women with children brought from Pionki. There were about 160 children (the majority were Hungarian, but there were also Rumanian and Czechoslovakian children) and 10 women from a variety of places. I was again with my daughter!

I met a young girl from Lodz in this block, Mirele Hirshkowitz. Her mother had already died in the Lodz ghetto. She had come to Auschwitz together with her father. She had an aunt with the same surname as hers, and when she was separated from her father, she passed herself off as the aunt's daughter. However, the aunt was later transported and Mirele remained alone. I realised that, without help, the child (four years old)

---

46   Antisemitism was rife even in the death camps where prisoners of various ethnic groups were incarcerated together. Included were those who traditionally exhibited antisemitic behaviour.

would not survive. I kept her myself. I now had three children, despite the evil eye!

It was the end of November 1944, and we were allowed into the block at night. At four thirty in the morning we were taken out to the fields, kept until dark in the courtyard without food or anything to drink, and they counted us continually. For four or five days this continued. Inside the block, it was also cold as we lay on the hard planks. Small children caught cold and many were quite ill. Whoever was taken to the 'hospital' never returned. My little son developed a lung infection for a second time. A Jewish Hungarian woman writer had an aunt who was a doctor and worked in the 'hospital'. She brought the doctor to my sick son. I described what he had been through and asked for help. She brought medicinal drops. With God's help the child became well!

After a while my husband found out that I was in the Gypsy Camp. He was also in Birkenau, but I had no opportunity to let him know that we might manage to see each other. A week passed, then two. I ran regularly to the fence but I failed to meet him. On one occasion I met Mirele Hirshkowitz's father. He told me that he was together with my husband. Now the situation was that the two fathers knew that their children were there, but they were unable to find an opportunity to see them. They tried various means, and sought advice on how to get to see their children. Hirshkowitz started to look for 'protectzia' (influence) from the camp scribe (a Pole) who used to choose who was most suitable for work. He (Hirshkowitz) made a great effort to get work cleaning the room. He became a little more familiar with the scribe. He told him that his child was in the Women's Camp, and that also his colleague, Weiss, had a wife and two children there. He begged him, when he should have the opportunity, to register them for cleaning the barracks in the Women's Camp. They were sent to work there, and were led past our block. When I saw that the overseer was not there, and the Camp Head and the Camp Kapo did not notice anything, and our Block Elder was also not there, I grabbed the children and ran out of the block so that the fathers could see their children! They were afraid to stop, but they were happy that, at least while passing by, they saw their children. Later they were stopped from going to the Women's Camp for work, and they could no longer see the children. Their hearts were full of pain knowing that their children were there, and yet there was no possibility of seeing them.

In December 1944, an order was given that in a month's time the children would have to do without their mothers because they would be taken away, and the mothers would be sent to work in Germany. I became even more desperate; my life had become even uglier. My child had been saved so many times, and now I had to leave him alone! I knew, and had seen for myself, what they do to children in Birkenau. In F.K.L. the Room Elder certainly had a Jewish heart, but those in Birkenau did exactly the same as the SS. They beat the children and killed them. The small children were given a diet of better food, but not so with the older children. These children should have received three meals a day but they were given only one meal to eat. In all, 160 remained; more than half died at the hands of the perpetrators from hunger and cold. I knew very well that if I were to leave my children I would never see them again.

The next day, at four in the morning, I went out to the wire fence. Hershkowitz and my husband approached. I told them that there was an order to separate the children from their mothers during the following month when the mothers would be sent away. It was tragic for them too. They comforted me and told me not to cry and worry so much: we have a great God. In time He would help us, and perhaps within a month we would be redeemed [by being liberated]. An order was received indicating that we were to go for delousing. The delousing was a great torment. I had nowhere to hide myself with my child, so I had to go. It was cold and we sat there naked for 'only' 24 hours. The child became chilled; then we went back 'home'. By the morning my child had a temperature of forty degrees. The Yiddish Hungarian scribe went and brought her relative, the doctor. She examined the child and established that he was chilled and was teething. The following day I saw that my son's temperature had not gone down. On the second day I saw that the child was developing red spots. Measles! I felt that the world was crushing me, and I did not know what to do. I knew very well that if I were to tell them that my child had measles, they would take him to the hospital and I would never see him again. I also knew that the Block Elder and also the Room Elder and anyone else from the block would certainly kill me if they found out that the child has measles [sick prisoners were not tolerated because of fear of an epidemic so they were usually exterminated], and I did not report it to anyone. It made no difference to me. I took hold of myself and thought: what will be, will be. Before I would lose my child in the hospital I would want to be killed by the Block Elder. I would know that I had done everything that I could for my child.

Four days after the doctor had examined the child, she came again on a Sunday and wanted to examine him. As soon as I heard that she was there, I thought about my misfortune; she would see that the child had measles.

The world was crushing me! I did not know what to do, but at least I looked for advice. I, with my child, hid behind the bunks. The Room Elder came to the block several times looking for me, and shouted loudly: 'Weiss!' I did not emerge. The Room Elder approached my daughter, and asked where I was. She answered that she did not know. The doctor left, so I emerged. It was then shortly before the *appel* [time for the roll call], about four o'clock, and I had to go out. The Room Elder entered and asked, 'Where were you? The doctor was here and wanted to examine the child'. I replied, 'I was outdoors, in the field, in the fresh air with my child'. The Room Elder shouted out, 'When the child is so seriously ill, you should not go out'. I answered, 'It does no harm, a bit of fresh air is quite healthy'. It was quite obvious to me that my child was very ill, it was already three days since he had opened his eyes, but I had to say that it does no harm, and that the child was a bit better. I was afraid of one thing – his throat; if the measles should go to his throat! Every evening I did what I could for my child: I laid compresses on him and tried other women's medications. A few days passed and the child started to improve. I noticed that one could no longer see the spots. This was a relief for me. I started to give the child some food, but he was unable to take it. As soon as he swallowed something it would come up again.

I approached the scribe and asked her if it was possible for the doctor to come as the child kept on vomiting. He had become terribly dehydrated; I felt as if there were nothing to be done for him. The doctor arrived, examined him, and said that she did not know what would become of him. The child was too dehydrated. She prescribed drops and tablets to stop the vomiting. After a few days the vomiting stopped, but then the child developed abscesses in the mouth, and for whole days and nights liquid dribbled from his mouth, from two to three litres per day. As if this weren't enough he kept his eyes closed all the time, never opening them. I looked for an eye-doctor (a Jew from Lodz, a Dutch woman whose husband was also a Lodz doctor). I don't know what her fate was, but I had seen her in Auschwitz until 18 January 1945. I found out in which hospital she worked, so I went to her and asked for her help: 'You are also from Lodz, help me to save my child'. She began to treat the child's eyes. She came to the block every day to bandage him. It took two weeks for the eyes to heal. A nurse (a convert from Hungary) came every day to paint the abcesses in order to dry them out.

The eyes were healed, the abscesses gone, and then talk started that we were all to be sent away. Where to? No one knew. It was said that the Russians were getting closer. Fresh worries. Where to? Every day we heard these stories. What? When? Meanwhile Mirele Hershkowitz became ill with a lung infection. I tried to save the child. No days, no nights. [unclear what she means] Every day, every hour, it seemed that we would be sent away. I had another worry: what should I do with her? Suddenly my child received his portion of suffering too; he became seriously ill again. The doctor came, examined him, and established that it was a lung infection. For the third time! She constantly urged me to take the child to the hospital; perhaps they would be able to save him there. According to all the talk we were to be sent away, so I was afraid to send the child to the hospital. I asked her to do whatever she could to save the boy. Her answer: the boy needs an injection which she did not have; perhaps there might be some in the men's camp?

At dawn I went to the fence, called my husband, and told him about everything that our child needed. Through 'protektzia' [influence] he attempted to obtain the injection. He bought it with bread and gave it to me. My son looked so bad that the doctor said that she did not know if it would help. At least she gave him the injections, and after the fourth one, the child became a little better and started to open his little eyes.

On 18 January 1945 while they were still ill, an order was issued to the effect that we were all to be sent away. At two o'clock at night I had to take my sick child, and also the sick Mirele, to dress them and to go to the field outside. We were counted every minute to see that no one had escaped or hidden away. They searched for guns in the blocks. They found some arms belonging to Russians, so five men were shot, and the tumult became even worse. Because of this we had to stand until midday. At midday things became a little easier. They stopped guarding us so closely. They said that first they would send all the men away and the women would follow. Having sent all the men away, they again turned to the women, again shouting: 'Everyone out!' People started moving towards the gate. Children, as well as elderly women and the sick had to go back.

As soon as I heard that, I said to my daughter, 'Pesale, come back here'. I was afraid that they would take her away. I asked the people who had gone back, why they had done so? They answered that at the gate they were collecting the children and sick to transport them. We returned to the block where we had been. The majority were gone. Russians and Ukrainians who had hidden themselves were the ones to remain.

One night, a loud alarm was heard. An air-raid. We all thought that we would be killed by the bombs. The night ended and the alarm stopped. The following day the Camp Kommandant (a German, who had come here only recently, whose name I do not know; before him it was Rudolph Hoss) called everyone out and said to us: 'We are leaving now; whoever wants to work should leave the children and go with us, because in any case we will not be able to withstand an assault here'. No one wanted to do it [leave]. We thought: 'We are fortunate enough in getting rid of him. Whatever happens to us here, we will at least be together with our children.'

That was on Friday morning, 19 January 1945. We had no water; before leaving the Germans had destroyed everything. We remained without any guards. They closed all the gates so that we would not be able to escape. Then they set Birkenau alight. There they had kept all the best that they had looted from the prisoners.

There were a few wagon loads of butter which they did not manage to take away. We carried the children and went outdoors to look for a way out in case we had to escape. We were afraid that they might set fire to the camp on all sides. A few Russian men (civilians who had been brought from the Russian districts) who had hidden themselves remained. The fire in Birkenau burned for three days and we thought that we were already free. The men started to loot the kitchens and the cellars; they found a lot of food. It was said that the Soviets were very close by. Whether they would let us live or not we did not know.

On Sunday 21 January 1945 in the afternoon, an SS man arrived and began to create order. A new Block Elder, a new Room Elder, again the counting, again *appel*. We thought that they were coming back again. This lasted for two days; thereafter we did not see any Germans. We did not see them on Tuesday, Wednesday, or Thursday until midday. Every minute there were air raids. The talk was that the Russians were 30 kilometres from Auschwitz. Who knows whether we will survive? Every minute people were killed by the bombs.

On thursday afternoon a number of women who also had children approached me and said: 'Come, let us go to the Men's Block which is empty. Over there, there are always rooms where the Block Elders used to live and where there is an oven. There we can heat the food so that the children can have something warm to eat.' We went there, collected wood, coal and something to eat. It became a little more hospitable. Suddenly, four SS men entered and shouted: 'All Jews step out!' We believed that they were going to shoot us. We had to get out as we were and leave; the sick from the hospital also had to do the same. They lined us up, and searched for anyone who might have hidden anything. We started to walk. The sick who were unable to walk were immediately shot. We were led to a bridge. On the bridge they started to play all sorts of tricks on us (we had to lie down, stand up, run). We were sure that here on the bridge they would finish us off. Suddenly a car arrived, an SS man got out, and called the four away. They spoke for a while and then got into the car and drove off. We didn't know what to do; to go, to stay, where to? Dark night. We were afraid to go back so we went further. The road was full of the military, big guns, machinery. We went where our eyes led us. We noticed stacks of wood, perhaps two or three metres high. Behind the wood, prisoners lay hidden (women, men). Miller, a woman with a child (from Lodz, and now she lives in Leipheim in the American Zone), said to me: 'Mrs Weiss, perhaps we should also hide?' I said: 'No, I will go where the others go'. We were about 400 souls (the majority were women, a few men, and a few children).

In the distance we saw a large gate and all around there were barracks. We didn't know what they were and we were afraid to enter. We sat down in the snow, rested for a while, and said: 'What difference does it make? Let's take the risk and go inside.' We went into one of the barracks and saw that it was impossible even to sit down; it was a horse stable. Shivering from fear and cold we moved on. In the distance we saw a man's face: we remained standing. He approached us and said that we should not be afraid, he was also a Jew. He spoke German well. We continued and came across another Jew who said to us: 'Go further and you will come across a house where a lot of Jews have gathered. Over there is the sick bay of Auschwitz.' On the way we passed many Jews going in the opposite direction. We entered a block. We were given something to wear, a cover to put over ourselves. When they saw a small child they could not do enough for him; they brought whatever they had for the child so that it would lack nothing. This was on Thursday night.

We sat for all of Friday; we heard that help was very close. We saw no Germans at all. On Friday night a Jew (a doctor from Hungary) came in with another few Jews and said that we should not sleep, and that we should be ready because the town of Auschwitz was on fire from bombs. The barracks were being shelled. It was possible that because of the air raid we might have to flee from our location. It was quiet until five in the morning. We saw how the walls of the barracks trembled from the bombs. They had started to shell the barracks. We realised that it was no good, but no one had any helpful suggestions. What could we have done? In the block in which we were sitting the window panes fell out. Glass splinters fell on the tables but luckily they did not harm any of us. At seven thirty in the morning it became quiet. People started to appear. They said that we would soon be helped. The Russians were only 500 metres from Auschwitz. At 11 in the morning the children ran out of the barrack and returned with a shout: 'We have help, the Russians are here!' We did not believe it. We started to run to see if this was really so. We went out and saw the Russians! We hugged and kissed them.

I did not know where my husband was at the time. On 20 January, together with a group of 10,000 men and women, he had been sent to Germany. There he landed up in Dachau and was freed only on 30 April. Then he started to search for me and the children. He first found us in September 1945, in Lodz, where I and the children had been since the beginning of March. After more wandering about we finally settled in Stuttgart. Mirele also found her father and is now with him in Seeshaupt near Weilheim (Upper Bavaria).

I and my children tore ourselves out of the hands of the devil. What the state of my child's health will be after so much illness, God only knows!

# MEMORIES OF THE GHETTO OF STANISLAVOV

Eyewitness Account by Lusia Gerber

Collected by the Historical Commission of Berlin-Mariendorf.
Published by the Munich Historical Commission in the Journal Series
*Fun Letzten Khurben*, Vol. 8, 1948

More or less a week after the Germans entered Stanislavov (Eastern Galicia) they issued an order to all the Jewish 'intelligentsia' [professional and generally well educated people] demanding that they appear before the Gestapo for work places. Anyone who did not heed the order would be shot. Out of great fear, all the doctors, professors, pharmacists, engineers, and the district rabbis, Bertish and Rabbi Horovitch, responded. As soon as they crossed the threshold of the Gestapo headquarters blood began to flow like a river. On the second day they were led to the forest, Pavelcze, 14 kilometres behind the town, where they were forced to dig pits. They ended their lives in these graves. This happened on 2 August 1941, and from this date onward the terrible fate of the Jews began. Hard labour from morning to late at night. We received 400 grams of bread to last us for a week. Many people collapsed at work from weakness and some died on the spot.

On 12 October 1941, all the Jews were driven from their homes and were made to assemble in a large square in the middle of the town. Everyone had to bring gold, money and other valuable items. They were told that they were being taken to a camp. Later many Jews were arranged in columns; then the Germans began to drive them forward. This procession was pathetic, with the elderly holding tiny children by the hand and people carrying bundles of clothes. The Jews continued quietly until they reached Batori Street. Here for the first time the Jews saw where they were being taken, and as they approached the cemetery they began screaming and crying. The cries could be heard over the whole town. Large pits had already been prepared in the cemetery for the innocent victims. The Gestapo Chief, Kruger, was already waiting for his 'babies' with a smile. He immediately collected all their valuables, and the Aktion started at 11 o'clock during the day.

Every Jew was forced to undress completely. Parents had to undress their children. All the surrounding area was pierced by the sounds of crying and shrieking and the sounds of repentance and begging God, because no one wished to die such a dreadful death. But the blood-suckers paid little attention to all of this; they fired their machine-guns without cessation. There were also Poles among the murderers. The Aktion ended at one o'clock in the morning. On that day 1,200 adults and 400 children perished.

In August 1941, the Germans created the ghetto. At the same time they formed the Judenrat and Jewish Police Force. Goldstein, who was known in the town as a reputable person and the owner of a mill, was nominated as head of the Judenrat. Jews were brought from every corner of the town and crowded into the ghetto, two or three families in one room. We worked at various forms of labour all winter. At the same time people were horribly punished. Throughout winter large numbers of Jews succumbed to hunger and cold.

Two days before Pesach [Passover] they began the second Aktion against the Jews. This was on 31 March 1942. I remember the exact date because that day was carved into my brain. In that Aktion I lost my greatest treasure, my beloved child, Stella, who was only five years old. I also lost my father, my sister and youngest brother in this Aktion. A terrible fear overwhelmed the Jews as they were forced out of all parts of the ghetto. We felt that these were our last moments. Jews hid themselves in cellars and concealed themselves wherever there was even a 'mousehole'. I hid myself in the cellar of my house; at that time my little daughter was with my sister in the house from which she was taken away, together with my whole family. The Germans continued to search ceaselessly. They set alight houses which were full of Jews and they threw small children from upper floor windows. At the Jewish orphanage, the Germans threw the children into sacks and then flung them into the river. That evening was especially horrible. Cold, it rained and snowed, and the ghetto was burning all over. The Aktion lasted until 12 at night. The following day, when the corpses of the Jews were collected, there were 600 of them, and 4,000

Jewish survivors were transported by train to Belzec where they were incinerated in the crematoria.

There was not a single quiet day following the second Aktion. They brought Jews from the neighbouring towns into Stanislavov. People were brought here from Kalish, Helitch, Burshtin, Nodvorna, Lahyf and other places. Daily, people were chased to the cemetery to their death, old Jews and the young like roses in bloom. They cried and screamed to God. But it did not help.

On 10 May 1942, there began a new registration – 'ABZ'. Every Jew had to personally register himself at the Judenrat where a special commission of Gestapo personnel – Kruger, Brandt, Kovalski and Shot – were in attendance. The Jews who were identified by the letter 'A' were allocated work; the Jews with the letter 'B' were separated from the others and placed in different streets of the ghetto; and whoever received the letters 'TZ' was sent within the week to the camp next to Rudolf's mill in Holitcze Street. After two days the whole group was transported in wagons to Belzec where they were cremated.

The Jews from the surrounding towns who were brought to Stanislavov were sent straight to the camp. The camp was situated in the ghetto in Holitcze Street, in Rudolf's mill, and was enclosed by a wire fence. On one occasion a transport was brought from my birthplace, Vanislav, near Kalish. I saw my friends in one of the newly arrived transports. By some miracle I managed to enter the camp. At that moment I saw some gruesome scenes. Jews wandered around hungry, in tatters and very fearful. My friends surrounded me and began to shout loudly asking me for help. I myself was helpless. To my sorrow I knew what awaited them. By the following day the camp was quiet. Only the empty buildings remained. I asked one of the policemen where everyone was. He answered that they were already in the cemetery.

During winter the Gestapo personnel were too sluggish to kill Jews outdoors. They would often come to the ghetto in the evenings to 'hunt'. On each occasion the Jewish police had to place about 200 Jews in a special room. Most of the time the Gestapo officer, Kruger, would sit in the middle of the room and he would create a fine entertainment for himself. Around him naked men and women danced, and they had to act as various characters and perform tricks. The well-known Rabbi of Burstin was in one of the groups. The Germans photographed him showing the rabbi dancing in the nude with women. After this entertainment everyone had to line up in a row while waiting for death, because that was when the shooting would take place. In the morning the Jewish police would take the martyrs to their resting place.

In July 1942, a Ukrainian policeman complained to the Gestapo that a Jew had hit him. The Germans now had a reason to begin another Aktion. They immediately issued an order to the Judenrat who were to provide the Gestapo with 1,000 Jews within three days. The Judenrat did not comply with the order.

Early on a Shabbat [Sabbath] morning the Germans and the Ukrainians blockaded the ghetto, then entered quickly with bloodhounds and started to gather Jewish men, searching for them in their hiding places. On that day they gathered about 3,000 men, including the Judenrat and the Jewish police. They were forced to dig trenches in Belveder Street. During the night the Germans and the Ukrainians assembled the women and children, and on the following day at five in the morning they started the Aktion. They hanged Goldstein the Chairman of the Judenrat, taken from the first row, and after him the members of the Judenrat, and also the Jewish police. They were left hanging on the electricity poles in Belveder Street so that the Poles and the Ukrainians should see them. All the others were shot. The Germans felt that it was a waste of a bullet for a child, so they threw the living children into the graves. The shrieks and the cries of the unfortunate people were monstrous. The Germans and the Ukrainians, though, took great pleasure from this. They repeated many times: 'You are calling on God for help? Where is your God? You don't have a God!' Later they filled in the graves. From the graves could be heard how the unfortunate ones screamed out: 'Shoot us, we are still alive!' Even an hour later the earth from the grave was still moving. In this scandalous way they murdered our brothers and sisters.

The Gestapo officer, Shot, was a frequent casual visitor to the ghetto. Every day, he would select for himself the most beautiful woman, take her to his home, rape her and shoot her on his bed.

The ghetto was continually being decreased in size. Jews lived in cellars, garrets and in the street. Starvation was rife. Every day, 20 to 30 people perished from hunger.

Central Historical Commission, File No. 847

# THE FORTRESS OF DEATH
# (IN THE NINTH FORT OF KOVNO)

By Michal Gelbtrunk

Collected by the Munich Historical Commission.
Published by the Munich Historical Commission in the Journal Series
*Fun Letzten Khurben*, Vol. No. 10, 1948

On 26 October 1943, we, a group of six people, left Kovno ghetto with the aim of joining the partisans. According to the partisan members we should have gone to Augustov to form a partisan unit there. But a number of Lithuanians knew about our group and we were denounced by them. Behind Godlove, 13 kilometres from Kovno, we were pursued by police. After a long struggle, in which the neighbouring Lithuanians took part attacking us with thick wooden sticks and beating us to the poinbt of unconciousness, one of us, Katz, dropped dead and a second person, Meir Zalinger, was wounded. A Lithuanian doctor from the police hospital was called. He established that the wounded man had received a dangerous shot in the stomach and, in light of this, he wrote up a method for treating him. But he gave no medical aid to him. The Lithuanian police refused to end his terrible suffering with another shot. It was a pity to waste a bullet for a Jew, they said. We were forced by the police to bury yet another man alive.

Gestapo personnel arrived. They interrogated us and tortured us terribly in order to find out where we had come from. None of us revealed anything and we said nothing about our being from Kovno ghetto. We were locked up in the Kovno Yellow prison [the large Kovno prison]. We remained there for more than four weeks.

# The Fortress of Death (in the Ninth Fort of Kovno)

On 28 November a large guard of the Security Unit took us to the Ninth Fort. There we were attached to a kommando which worked at digging up the corpses of Jews in the mass graves and burning them. The kommando consisted of 58 Jews, among them 10 Jewish Red Army prisoners who were captured early in the war. They remained in the fort from among thousands of prisoners who were poisoned or buried alive. Later another 15 Jewish Red Army soldiers of higher rank were added to the group. As Russians they remained alive for longer; they lived in a military prisoners' camp until they were denounced as Jews. In the kommando there were also Jews from Kovno ghetto. There were also converts in the kommando. A youth from Telzh, who had hidden himself for a long time in the forest until he landed up in here, was also with us. In the fort he was called 'forest-person'.

The work of burning the dead took place under an extensive guard of Security Service men. In the morning, while sending us out to work, they would place chains on our feet. This made the work even harder. The Security Kommando 'comforted' us saying that our end would be exactly like that of our brothers with whom we were busy. The victims lay in long trenches, each one 25 metres long. The hardest work was done by the 'cultivators'. They had to lift the corpses out. This was not at all easy work because the corpses were entwined and twisted with each other. According to what was said by the first 10 captives who witnessed the executions in this fort, the majority of the murdered Jews were hurled into the trenches while half-alive, not completely dead after being shot. The victims moved for a long time in their agony. There was not much earth covering them, and for a long time screams of pain and choking calls for help emerged from the graves. While pulling out the corpses we actually saw how their hands were pressed against their mouths, like those asphyxiated from lack of air. The same captives told us that more than once, on the day following an Aktion, children who had been thrown onto the top level of the mass graves crawled out of the trenches in the seventh tier. The Security Kommando would immediately order that they should be driven 'into the holes again'.

The Kovno Jews were treated with special guile and trickery at the executions. The Jews from other lands were executed in their clothes. The murderers were also not so mean with bullets and the dead would fall right into the trenches. However, the Kovno Jews were ordered to undress, remaining only in their underwear. The young women were naked. Before they were killed the Lithuanians would amuse themselves and rape them.

On the 17 or 18 December 1943, at about four o'clock in the afternoon, a car drove into our workplace. All of us, the workers, were chased away from there. From a distance we saw that four people were thrown out of the car. They cried and screamed loudly. We heard shots and desperate cries from the wounded. The Germans themselves threw them into the fire. We did not know who the victims were. In the evening one of the prisoners received a short coat from a German. The German who handed it to him said at the same time: 'Here you have a gift from the present guests'. A little later we searched the garment and found papers from the lecturer, Dr Chaim Nachman Shapira, the son of the Kovno rabbi.

The following morning, when we had to attend to the fire, we noticed a half corpse which had fallen from the pyre. We recognised the face of the master lecturer. Lying there was also the corpse of his son. The four who were murdered were Lecturer Shapira, his wife, child and mother, the old Kovno Rabbi's wife.

Thoughts of suicide were rife among a number of us. We were unable to take part in the horrible work. The ones who stopped us from doing so told us about the plans of the Brigadier, a Jewish Soviet Second Lieutenant, and of Ch. Moshe, both of whom aimed to escape from the fort. In the event that escape does not work out for everyone, at least it will succeed for a few. This is what they hoped. The thought would flare up in our imagination; such a thing would be our greatest achievement. First, such a terrible secret, which the Germans would want to conceal, would be revealed for all!

Under the most difficult conditions we went to work to break through an iron door in one of the walls of the Ninth Fort. It took more than four weeks. Only eight people knew about this. For the others it was a deep secret. We were afraid of failure. Among the eight there were five from Kovno ghetto and three Jewish Soviet military men.

We would use up tens of knives a night sawing through the iron door. The dead came to our help because we found knives in their clothes. Finally, on 24 December, the opening in the wall was ready. In the evening we gathered together the active ones and gave them the fantastic news, that on the following evening we would free ourselves from the Ninth Fort. The people were divided into groups with the active ones chosen as group leaders.

On December 25 we got through, sustained by the image of the freedom awaiting us. On an ordinary day, without doubt the watching eyes of the Security Kommando were a danger for us, but it was the first day of Christmas. We did not work and, in honour of the gentile holiday, we were given a lot of 'schnapps'. However, no-one tasted even a drop of this. Everyone understood that we must be completely sober and worry-free conspirators, ready for what would take place that evening. Everyone was terribly tense.

On 25 December 1943, at 10 o'clock in the evening, we started our breakout. The escape from the fort did not happen easily. We had to crawl through a tunnel and climb over a high wall. We all got through successfully and ran out into the free fields. A few turned towards Kovno ghetto, and a number went to the forest.

# 24

# RESISTANCE MOVEMENT IN THE GHETTO OF KOVNO

By Rochie Ben Eliezer

Collected by the Munich Historical Commission.
Published by the Munich Historical Commission in the Journal Series
*Fun Letzten Khurben*, Vol. 10, 1948

As soon as the Kovno Jews moved into the ghetto, an 'initiative-group' was organised with the goal of creating a resistance movement. Those who belonged to the group were: Chaim Yellin (a young Jewish writer), Elia Maisel, Pesach Gordon, Leah Neimark, Yasher Glazer (Director of the Kovno Jewish Youth-Theater), Rachel Antipotski, Rochi Berman, Alte Borochowitz and Moshe Sherman.

The group's meetings took place in a house down from Krikshtshu-keitshia, not far from the Lithuanian children's home. The group's first task was to draw people into the resistance movement and to acquire 'cold and hot arms' [arms ranging from knives to guns]. The group attracted people who helped to keep up the spirits of the youth and to draw them into the struggle. Within the circles of the Resistance Movement people were stirred up by memories of our literary classics. Those who encouraged this were the journalist Reuven Tsorpas, the teacher Fania Tsorpas, and Shmuel Rozental. Artistes from the Kovno Jewish theatre also participated in the festivities [celebrating Jewish culture]: Rachel Antupitski, Rochelle Berger, Sonia Erdi, Mania Karnowski-Mesenblum, Liuba Bar-Kupewitz and Rochie Berman.

After the great Aktion a number of friends from the Resistance Movement were taken away. Chaim Yellin became head of the Resistance Movement which comprised 180 active members. We obtained for ourselves a radio set so that we could hear the news from the various fronts, and generally to be able to orient ourselves to the situation [i.e. the state of the war].

The Resistance Movement linked up with the leaders of the ghetto police, Yudel Zupawitz (Police Chief), Ika Greenberg, Moshe Levine, Yaacov Godinski and so on. On a personal level people belonged to different political parties; for example, Grinberg belonged to Hashomer Hatzair and Moshe Levine to Betar. As time passed the police personnel also joined the Resistance Movement and helped us a great deal. Our movement also linked up with two members of the Judenrat, Doctor Elkes and Hirsch Levine. Levine gave us great help financially. From time to time he would tax the ghetto speculators for large sums of money. And with this money we would buy guns. These two members of the Judenrat helped in equipping us with clothing for the partisans, boots and so on. In accordance with their orders the ghetto workshops manufactured various goods for the movement, and also gave us military items which were brought to the workshop for repairs. Slowly people from the Work Kommando were also drawn into the Resistance Movement, among them the engineer Shimon Ratner who later became one of our active members and one of the leaders. Under pressure from the Movement, individuals from the ghetto police also came to our aid. Certain Jewish policemen at the gate, Chaim Alexandrowitz, Yosef Duzhnitski, Yankel Verbovski and Sasha Perkel, would help our people to pass through and, most importantly, to bring in guns and to smuggle people out to the forest.

At the end of the summer of 1943, news began to reach us about Red partisan groups in the forests of Rudnitzki, Keidan and Augustov. In autumn 1943, the Resistance Movement sent people to those places in order to make contact with the partisans. Those who went to Keidan were: Borodovka (19 years old) and Lipkowitz (18 years old); and to the Rudnitzki forest Bezalel Joffe (23 years old), Israel Milner (20 years old), and Moshe Mariamfeler (18 years old). About 35 men were sent to the Augustov forest. There were young people in this group from different places. On the way [to the forest] the members who went to Keidan and Rudnitzki met up with White Lithuanian partisans who wanted to detain them. A struggle ensued during which our people lost their lives.

The Augustov group was detained by Lithuainians nine kilometres from Kovno, near Godleve. A great struggle ensued. A number of our people fell immediately and the remainder were transported to the Ninth Fort.[47]

Through the Polish woman Mania – we called her Leshtzinska ('mother of the Jewish partisans'; a widow with three children, who lived not far from the ghetto, in Rogutshia No. 14) – we received more reliable and trustworthy news: that in the Rudnitzki forest there were genuine partisan units under the leadership of Heinrich (Genia) Ziman, former teacher at the Shalom Aleichem High School. So Chaim Yellin, himself the leader of our Resistance Movement, went to the aforementioned place [the Rudnitzki forest]. After 10 days he returned, having travelled about 360 kilometres through forests. He brought concrete information; he also had an order to recruit the young people from the ghetto who were capable of joining in the struggle. Yellin's information took us to a new phase in the Movement. We started working in a feverishly active way. Yellin had also brought letters to the non-Jewish Underground Movement in Kovno about being helpful to us. The non-Jewish Red underground movement was by then already well organised and established. The people from that movement made cars, uniforms and documents available to us.

In the middle of November 1943, we were already able to send out the first group of 11 people to the Rudnitzki forest. They travelled there in a truck and arrived safely.

Both boys and girls were accepted into the Resistance Movement whatever their political orientation. In the first instance we saw to it that we invited only people who were personally acquainted with the active members of the Movement. When we received favourable reports about them (trustworthy, well-grounded, able to keep secrets), they would then be accepted and become active, and we would begin their military training. Our sole aim was to oppose the enemy with force.

One of our main concerns was to acquire guns. With the help of the Work Kommando who were employed in the gun stores, we succeeded in placing our people with them and also with the Fifth Fort, the Medical-Collection unit, the Staff Battalion, and Fortification Artillery. During the period of November 1943, until January 1944, we received 22 rifles, 3 light machine guns, 42 mortar shells, 20 hand grenades, 15 parabellum

---

47 See 'The Fortress of Death' testimony by M. Gelbtrunk in this book. The Ninth Fort was part of a fortress constructed in Kaunas (Kovno) in the nineteenth century. After the occupation of Lithuania by Nazi Germany, the fort was used as a place of execution for Jews, captured Soviets, and others.

revolvers, and two crates of bullets. A number of these arms still had to be repaired. This was done in the ghetto factories by Faivel Sidrer and Zion Zun. Mottele Brik, who was an expert in making hand grips for revolvers, worked for us in the factory. An assortment of clothing, boots and other necessary items was also prepared in the workshops for members of the Movement who were leaving for the forest. The tailoring work was done under the supervision of Noah Freisinger. The military preparations, physical and theoretical, were conducted by members Ika Grinberg and Yerachmiel Berman. The practical exercises took place in a house opposite the ghetto workshops, in a bunker which was built there specially for this purpose. The exercises were conducted after work from about six o'clock in the evening until 10 at night.

Medical lectures were also presented in the house of Dr Rosa Golach. The lecturers were the doctors: Rosa Golach, Moshe Berman, Benjamin Zacharin, Zvi Elkes and Leib Feldshtein.

From November 1943, until 29 March 1944, on the morning after the children Aktion in the ghetto, the Movement succeeded in moving 280 members to the Rudnitzki forest glade, 200 of them being men. They all arrived safely.

From various sources we would often receive reliable information about our own informers in the ghetto. With this in mind, a special commission was formed which consisted of members of the Resistance Movement as well as trustworthy leaders in the ghetto. The members of the Resistance Movement who were part of the Commission were: Chaim Yellin, Chaim David Ratner, Pesach Gordon and Shimon Ratner; and from the ghetto they were Ika Grinberg and Moshe Levine.

When they first started functioning, the Movement began to receive information from their people who were employed in various Work Kommandos, and also from their [Lithuanian] 'Saugumo'[48]

In the summer of 1942 we were handed a letter, together with a list of the leaders of the Resistance Movement in the ghetto, which a certain person had delivered to the Lithuanian Saugumo. This person was also a member of the Resistance Movement. Before the matter was taken any further by Saugumo, an investigator who was one of our contacts sent us the original letter. The guilty person in the ghetto had to appear before an

---

48  The Lithuanian Security Police (LSP), also known as Saugumas (Lithuanian: Saugumo policija), was a local police force that operated in Nazi-occupied Lithuania from 1941 to 1944.

enquiry immediately and it was revealed that he was a provocateur. This person could not escape from us and he was liquidated.

One of the issues in autumn with which the special Commission had to deal was the case of the inhabitant Paine. The young man Paine, a person of about 25 or 26, was arrested in the town for having dealings with Lithuanians. However, he was released and returned to the ghetto. He constantly shadowed the leaders of the Resistance Movement. Later, he approached one of the leaders of the Movement, asking to be sent to a partisan group. The Movement had already received information about Paine. One of their reliable people (a non-Jew) maintained in a coded letter that Paine was released from prison on condition that he would inform on the Resistance Movement. The Commission checked on him through the Jewish police and also began to do some research. It emerged that Paine had actually undertaken to spy for the Gestapo and to reveal details about the Resistance Movement. Paine never again saw freedom, and from the following day he was no longer among the living.

At that time (the end of 1943), the organisation [the Resistance Movement] began to draw in the young traders from the ghetto who daily used pliers to cut through the barbed wire of the ghetto fence and to bring in goods through these 'gaps'. According to Dr Elkes, the Partisans formerly from the Judenrat in the ghetto, and also those still in the ghetto, were in constant danger because of these developments, and many other people might also suffer. In accordance with the advice of the Judenrat committee, they should be drawn into the Movement and, as in the past, they should be sent to join the Resistance units in the forest. Additionally, and most importantly, these people were daring and would be of great benefit to the struggle. The leadership of the Movement selected five people from among the group of merchants. They were a shrewd and experienced group. Two weeks later, drills and other preparations, and also theoretical discussions about the goals and aims of the Jewish partisans took place, and each one of the traders received a revolver from the Movement.

Two days later an armed robbery took place in the ghetto. People with guns forced their way into the business of the ghetto inhabitant, Feivish [he had been placed in Paine's business as an employee], and demanded money from him for the arms fund of the Resistance Movement. They shot Feivish. Hearing his cries, the neighbours from the adjoining room, the printer Lazer Antopinski and his wife, came running. The robbers shot them dead. With a huge effort the ghetto doctors kept Feivish alive for 24 hours. Feivish managed to describe how the attack took place and who the murderers were. They were the five people from the traders' group. The ghetto police arrested them with great difficulty, because they resisted with firearms. After a night of interrogation they confessed. At the hearing it emerged that they had recently robbed the ghetto warehouse too, and taken sewing machines, again in the name of the Movement. After a meeting with the Judenrat all five were sentenced to death. Thus the ghetto was cleansed of its own murderers.

After the transport of 29 March 1944, it was decided that all the active members of the resistance must leave the ghetto during the next few days. The active ones together with the leaders numbered 150 members. Initially, with the help of the Work Kommando in the sock factory, 'Silva', guns were transported out of the ghetto. To this end, Nina Finkelshtein, the daughter of the late advocate and Deputy of the Polish Parliament, Ezer Finkelshtein, worked energetically to aid them. The Kommando 'Silva' was led by Moshe Konichovski who was the foreman in the factory. Konichovski placed the guns in a prearranged place in the town [after they had been spirited out of the factory].

One night at the beginning of April our people left through the ghetto fence. They were led into the empty section of the former ghetto. One of our meeting places was there at Fuodzhin Street, 16, which was under the supervision of a particular Russian woman, Mania Peters. Chaim Yellin, the Commander of the Movement, meanwhile worked in the town organising the transport for the group. But the Lithuanian Political Police, Saugumo, tracked him down. On 6 April, when Yellin went to the laundry, 'Trinkolit' in Daukanto Street, where he used to meet a Lithuanian agent, a different Lithuanian agent suddenly appeared and ordered him to put his hands up! In each hand, Yellin clasped cocked revolvers which had been put into his coat pockets earlier. Through his pockets, he immediately shot the agent and killed him on the spot. Nearby neighbours began to chase after Yellin because of the sound of the gunshots. While escaping, he came across two military men, a German Major and a Lithuanian Captain, who wanted to detain him. In the same way, through his coat pockets Chaim shot them. He was being chased and was under fire, and while still running he used up all his bullets. Chaim Yellin was later found by the Germans in the cellar of a cafe, 'Monika'. He had cut the veins of his neck and hands using broken glass. However, the Gestapo revived him and began to question him. They tortured him for two days but they got nothing out of him. Then the Gestapo took him, half alive, to the Ninth Fort and there they burned him.

After the loss of the Commander, Chaim Yellin, the second in command, Yerachmiel Berman, took over his work, assisted by Dima Halperin. An order was issued that those people hidden in the old sector of the ghetto should return to the ghetto. Except for a few fellows who had been sent to look for new possibilities for transport, all the rest returned to the ghetto.

On 14 April a group of 12 men were sent to the Rudnikski forest and had to travel by foot. Our friend, Abba Diskant, led them out of the ghetto to the Kovno Shoshay Hill, to a predetermined point near the town of Moravia; from there the group was taken over by a non-Jewish liaison person who brought the entire group safely to the forest thicket.

On the Sabbath, 15 April, at eight in the evening, 12 people from the Resistance Movement, drove out in a truck covered by a tarpaulin. In addition to the Commander, Yerachmiel Berman, who led the group, the others were: the engineer Shimon Ratner, Menashe Supozcnik, Saul Finkel, Riva Uryash, Meir and Moshe Marshak, Yosef Shapira, Tzion Froy, Lieba Schwartz, Abba Diskant, Abraham Maneiski. While they were crossing over the Slabodski bridge, a black vehicle in Janover Street blocked the way, not far from the merchant synagogue. The people in the group recognised the police vehicle and immediately understood that this was a betrayal by the Lithuanian agent. Right away Berman shot him through the small window and hit him in the head. After that shot, a hail of bullets rained down on the group from two additional trucks which were already standing by. With great force Berman cut through the tarpaulin cover on the truck using his dagger, and gave the group an order to jump down! Berman was the first to jump and after him a few more [of those who were still hidden] squeezed themselves under the vehicle and then disappeared into the nearby houses. The hail of bullets aimed at the vehicle was continuous. Berman lay under the truck and shouted out an order to fire! Unfortunately, his order could not be followed. The remaining eight people in the truck had already been killed by the hail of bullets.

Noticing that the Jews were quiet, the Gestapo Kommandant, Willy (a German from Sanz who was awarded the position of Punishment Master; he used to lash the poor people with a whip), together with two aides began to move towards the car. From under the car Berman, noticing the three approaching, shot a few rounds of bullets from his two automatic revolvers. All three of the Gestapo men were killed on the spot. Then Berman, under a hail of bullets quickly ran to the blacksmith's forge. Fortunately the bullets hit him only in the lapels of his leather coat which were flapping about in the wind. He ran through the yard of the forge to the Wilga River. With great difficulty he succeeded in reaching the raftsmen's shelter at the edge of the river. By threatening the peasant in the shelter with a revolver, Berman persuaded him to take him across the river to the Slabodka side. Step by step throughout the night he slowly reached Ragutshia Street, 14, home of Mania Leshtzinska. From there he went over to the ghetto. Within a few days the three other survivors of the group returned to the ghetto: Riva Uryash, Abba Diskant and Meir Marshak.

The two sisters, Ira and Liola Berman (the daughters of the owner of the 'Beror' soap factory) who lived in Godlove Street with false papers, often came into the ghetto. At the end of April 1944, they told us that there was a possibility of setting up a Partisan base near Kovno, in the Kozlev forest. According to what they said there were already Red parachutists there. After a short consultation the first five people were sent out under the leadership of Ira Berman. They arrived safely. On 4 May Ira Berman returned, and took back with her another group of six men, among them the leader of the remainder of the members of the Resistance organisation in the ghetto, Yerachmiel Berman. While crossing over Veiverei Street, the highway which cut through the forest, the group encountered Gestapo men dressed in civilian clothes inside a vehicle. They rapidly fired. After a short battle we lost our dedicated comrade Ira Berman. With great difficulty we successfully entered deeper into the forest and escaped from the enemy.

The first and second groups to arrive in the forest joined with the two Red parachutists. Gradually, 10 local trustworthy Lithuanians also joined them. Two weeks later, by chance we met with 12 Soviet soldiers who had escaped from German imprisonment. They were all armed and joined us, as did Jews who had escaped from the nearby tarp-camp in Koslev forest. The Jews in the forest together numbered 27. Later, one of us, Mottel Katz, returned to the ghetto on a mission and was unable to return to the group. We Jews now numbered 26. All the groups in the forest united into one Resistance unit which took upon itself the task of hindering German traffic in the district. Daily we shot at the passing military vehicles along the big highway (Leningrad, Dvinsk, Kovno, Mariamfal, Konigsberg) and the military trains on the nearby line (Minsk, Vilna, Kovno, Konigsberg, Berlin). One day we derailed a long transport train on its way to Konigsberg. We killed about 500 German soldiers. We also disrupted all of the export from the forest through the second railway line (Koslev-Rude, Shostankove, Alite). Advised by our trusted people we got rid of a lot of the Lithuanians who had participated in the slaughter of Jews in the nearby towns and villages.

On a beautiful summer's day, a separate incident brought a great triumph to our unit. On 10 June we received information from our trustworthy men in the town that in a nearby village, Salamabuda, there were three stationary cars filled with Germans and Lithuanians dressed as civilians. At the time various military functionaries from the higher echelons had started to retreat. In response to an order from the Unit Commander, Yanka (as Yerachmiel Berman called himself in the unit), four persons clad in German gendarme uniforms came to him. The Commander himself was dressed as an officer. All the other partisans, dressed as civilians, gathered not far from the village near Rand forest as cover. The gendarme group, in an organised manner, conducted a raid on the village, supposedly looking for deserters running from the German army. The group suddenly surrounded the house where the 'guests' were, entered with cocked automatic guns, and gave the order: 'hands up!' The Germans and the Lithuanians were disarmed immediately. After the partisan Commander had looked through German documents, he recognised a man from Pulkove, Matulevitshius, an officer from the former Lithuanian army and later Chief of the German Saugumos. Matulevitshius, in the summer of 1941, had participated in the shooting of Jews in the Kovno Seventh Fort. From the additional documents found on people, it became clear that they had participated in the Aktion against the Jews, as well as in Estonia and Latvia. Without any further investigation the five were taken to the courtyard and shot. Their cars were set alight.

At the end of July 1944, when the Russian front came closer, we linked up with the regular Red Army. Our group was made part of a special unit which had the task of cleaning out the local area of Germans and Fascist Lithuanians. At the end of August, our 17 surviving comrades from the group were transferred to Kovno. Here, we were dismissed from the army. Of the 26 Jews in the Koslev-Rude forest only two survived: Liola Berman and Yerachmiel Berman.

# PART TWO

# THE CHILDREN'S NARRATIVES IN
## *FUN LETZTEN KHURBEN*

Eight children's testimonies were published in the Journal *Fun Letzten Khurben*. Both Israel Kaplan and Moshe Feigenbaum[49] were convinced that children's testimonies had particular historical and social significance. The Central Historical Commission prepared guidelines for the 'zammlers'[50] who were sent out to gather children's testimonies. This was done in order to keep the testimonies as true to the child's narrative as possible. Referring to Israel Kaplan and Moshe Feigenbaum, Boaz Cohen stated: 'In a way, these early survivor-historians, with their ethnographic work and the targeting of children and other groups, were years ahead of their time'.[51]

Child survivors, both orphans and those who were fortunate enough to be reunited with family, demonstrated a particularly acute need for rehabilitation after their horrendous suffering during the Holocaust. In Jewish tradition children are valued and loved, not only as individuals, but as the symbol of the future of the Jewish people. During the Holocaust, parents made desperate efforts to save the lives of their children by any means and, taking huge risks, hid them with gentiles and, sometimes, even managed to preserve their lives in the camps. In desperation some parents threw their children out of the window of the cattle wagon which was taking them to their deaths, in the hope that some benevolent person might rescue the child and take care of it. At times children were totally dependent on their own initiative and ingenuity, cunning and singlemindedness, learning how to survive at all costs. Jewish children in Nazi occupied Europe were denied the opportunity to have any schooling during the war years. Thus the children's testimonies presented here vary in the quality of their accounts. 'Those who had survived the camps felt a need to tell what they had seen and did so, "quietly, without emotion, with a kind of cynicism that chilled

---

49   Moshe Feigenbaum was elected to the position of Chairman of the Central Liberated Jews of Germany. He was also the first editor (albeit for a short while) of the Journal *FLK*, before Israel Kaplan became the permanent editor.
50   Collectors.
51   B. Cohen, 'Bound to Remember – Bound to Remind: Holocaust Survivors and the Genesis of Holocaust Research', in J.D. Steinert and I. Weber-Newth (eds), *Beyond Camps and Forced Labour: Current International Conference*, London, 29–31 January 2003, pp. 290–300.

their audience'".⁵² The sheer horror of what they had been through reverberates in the testimonies. At the end of World War II international organisations such as the JOINT and UNRRA, the Ort schools, as well as others, recognised the need to re-educate and rehabilitate the surviving children. Schools and educational facilities were arranged in the DP camps and also in orphanages. Teachers were sent from the Yishuv [the Jewish population] in Palestine to create widely encompassing curricula in these schools, where Jewish volunteers from Palestine did the majority of the teaching. During a Bible class in the Landsberg DP camp, the children were studying the life of Moses and the teacher wanted to know if his mother was justified in abandoning him to a stranger, the Egyptian princess: 'Was that how a real mother would act?' she asked the children.⁵³ Their experiences during the Holocaust had taught them about a reality different from that which we might consider as normal: 'of course, agreed the children, that's how a real mother would act'. They bolstered their view by citing examples of how some mothers had even thrown their children out of trains, and one young boy stated: 'Some of us in this class were given by our mothers to Poles. That's how we escaped.'⁵⁴

The Historical Commissions, particularly in the American Zone, collected hundreds of children's testimonies, many of them recorded soon after the Allied victory and the overthrow of the Nazi regime.

According to the opinion of Israel Kaplan, editor of *Fun Letzten Khurben*, 'dates and facts are not important. The event is unimportant, the main issue is the child's attitude, his approach, and what happened. How the events affected him, the psychological and educational aspects'.⁵⁵

What do these testimonies convey to us about the child's physical and psychological condition? What sort of world view did they develop during and after their enormous suffering? How did their loss of innocence and their incarceration in the insane world of the camps affect them? Their need for constant vigilance in a tumultuous world, and the desire for self-preservation, taught them that maintaining their silence was often the only way to survive, as they were well aware that any sort of sound while they

---

52   Zeev W. Mankowitz, *Life between Memory and Hope: The Survivors of the Holocaust in Occupied Germany*. Cambridge University Press, 2002, p. 153.
53   A. Konigseder and Juliane Wetzel, 'Displaced Persons, 1945–1950: The Social and Cultural Perspective', in *Post-War Europe: Refugees, Exile and Resettlement, 1945–1950* (trans. J.A. Broadwin) p. 4.
54   Ibid.
55   Boaz Cohen, 'The Children's Voice: Postwar Collection of Testimonies From Child Survivors of the Holocaust'. *Holocaust and Genocide Studies*, 21, No. 1, 2007, p. 11.

were in hiding might betray them to the enemy. Constant danger and painful bereavement left them severely traumatised. Children had been placed with Christian families, in orphanages, or in convents, where they were told that they had a new identity, and must learn to assimilate in a completely strange culture, and possibly with a new language. Their relationship with the gentile world changed completely. They encountered gentiles who took great risks to save a Jewish child, but they also encountered gentiles who were filled with hate and suspicion and fear, and would willingly have betrayed them.

The children's testimonies which appear in this work were selected for publication by Israel Kaplan. It was his belief that the voice of the child was extremely significant in the documentation of the Holocaust, and he made every effort to preserve the testimony in its original form. It is not known on what basis Israel Kaplan selected the children's testimonies for publication. However, he did add a note to the testimonies about the need for some editing, even if it were minimal.

A child's view of the world under the Nazi regime is encapsulated by the words of six-year-old Mirele and her sister, 12-year-old Chayele, in the Bialystok ghetto. They worked out a way to understand the new reality in which they lived:

'Papa,' the six-year-old Mirele says to her father, 'Why are you so afraid, you have work, the Germans won't touch you. They take away only small children who are not yet able to work.' Twelve-year-old Chayele stands in front of the mirror on tiptoe to see if perhaps she is big enough to be accepted in a factory and to receive a work permit just like an adult.[56]

In the children's testimonies published in *Fun Letzten Khurben* there appear certain general characteristics. They are all written in a very direct manner, without a focus on emotion, and are by and large unembellished. Death and cruelty were constants in the lives of child survivors, and they were witnesses to the deaths of hundreds of people, in the transports, in the ghettos, and in the camps.

---

56  See 'The Last Road for Twelve Hundred Bialystok Children', *Fun Letzten Khurben*, Vol. 7, 1948, p. 74.

# 1

# MY EXPERIENCES DURING THE WAR

By Josef Shuster

From the Series of Children's Work
published by the Munich Historical Commission
in the Journal Series *Fun Letzten Khurben*, Vol. 7, 1948

I was born in Kovno on 19 February 1936. We lived there before the war. Now we live in Munich in Zultzbacher Street. When the Germans entered Kovno, we immediately felt that something bad was about to happen. Jews were forbidden to buy anything in the shops. For buying a little bit of bread they arrested and shot you. They caught people and sent them to the 7th Fort and shot them. The ghetto was encircled by barbed wire, and German and Jewish guards were put in place. In the ghetto there was a Jewish police force, a Committee with Dr Elkes as President, and a Jewish Elder Liptzer. Kommandos were formed and every morning they went to work accompanied by German soldiers, and returned late in the evening. In the ghetto we were always in a state of fear, and this increased when a car arrived with a German coming to meet the Committee. As soon as the ghetto was closed the first Aktion took place, and more than 500 people were killed. After this the big Aktion took place and more than 10,000 Jews lost their lives. The Jews were gathered together in a certain place in the ghetto, and they were lined up according to their work kommandos. My parents and I stood in the unit where my father worked. When selecting the Jews, a German told us to go to the left (the bad side). The moment the German said that, my mother said to the German, 'My husband is a master builder'. When the German heard this, he looked at us, then said 'Ach – then here', and sent us to the right. Those who were sent to the left were taken to the 9th Fort and shot there.

About two years later the Estonian Aktion took place. We lay hidden all day in the cellar. In the middle of the day, when we came out in order to eat, Germans entered to take us away with them. My mother immediately fainted because of her weak heart. A neighbour of ours, taking note of what had happened, went to a policeman whom he knew and the policeman came and said that he would wait until we had packed and he would take us with him. The German left and we again concealed ourselves. We lay in our hiding place until late at night when the Germans left the ghetto. Then we went home again.

After the Aktion my mother and I left the ghetto. From the start my parents wanted to send me out alone, but I didn't want to go because I was afraid of remaining without a father and mother, although my mother would threaten that the Germans would come and take me away. I would not go alone and I answered: 'Whatever happens to you, will happen to me', and for this reason my mother went with me. In the evening, when it was properly dark, my mother and I went to the ghetto gate from which we were to leave. Not far from the gate my yellow patches were removed, and then a wide shawl was wrapped around my neck to cover the places where the patches had been so that I should not be recognised. At the gate waiting for us were the Chief of Police, Zupovitch, and a few Jewish policemen who were supposed to help us get out of the ghetto. When we arrived at the gate we had to wait for a little while. At the moment that a kommando arrived and blocked the Germans' view, Zupovitch took us by the hand and led us out of the ghetto. At the back of the ghetto our former servant waited for us, and we travelled with her seven kilometres behind the town. The road was very bad and muddy. While we were on our way we fell into the mud several times until we arrived at the house of a Christian who hid us for three months. My father joined us two weeks later.

In the room at the Christian's place there was a double wall. Behind it was a small room which was our hiding place. It was always dark in the hiding place. There were two layers of planks on which one could only lie or sit. The entrance was under a bed where there was a small door exactly like that of a dog's kennel. Entering the hiding place could be done only by crawling on one's stomach. The owner of the house had a little white dog, a very pretty one, a poodle with the name of Bobik. The poodle was so spoilt by them that it would eat only sweets and ice cream. The Christians were always petting him, kissing and playing with him. I was very envious of him because he was free and could run around outside.

At first while we were hidden, the Christian man treated us quite well, but later when searches began for escaped prisoners-of-war, the Christian began to be afraid and demanded that we leave. We had no choice, so our former servant travelled 80 kilometres further and found a place for us in Visokidvor, at the home of a Christian acquaintance of my grandfather. She made an arrangement with the Christian that she would come on such and such a day to pick us up. At the same time, a raid took place on the house where we were hidden. German and Lithuanian policemen arrived. They searched the whole house but, miraculously, they did not find us. A few days later the Christian lady came and took away my parents. A week later she came again and took me with her.

When I met my parents again, I also met an aunt of mine there. They had already created a hiding place. The Christian man treated us very well. We were with him for five months. In the new hiding place we were often able to lie there peacefully, but we could not breathe a word. At one time I had a cold, and at the moment when I wanted to cough, strange people came into the room, and I wasn't allowed to cough. [To hide the sound] My mother wrapped me in an eiderdown where I could cough a little. It happened that sometimes we could not emerge from hiding for several days. The greatest trouble happened in May. The village was far from a church and the local farmers would come to our Christian to say their Easter prayers. They would come early in the evening and leave late at night. They would be in the room next to us the whole time. During quiet times we would go into the room where my father would teach me to read and to do arithmetic.

The Christian had a little daughter of six years old who was very clever, and she always protected us well. The Christian owned a very vicious dog which the neighbours feared greatly. One day when the owners were out in the fields, we came out of our hiding place and sat in the room. The six-year-old girl was sitting on the porch keeping watch to see if anyone arrived. Suddenly another Christian arrived and wanted to enter the house. When she saw this she called out: 'Don't go in, the dog is inside the house, wait, I will take him out'. She ran in to tell us to hide. Then she went out again and laughed heartily. 'It's a lie, I tricked you.' In the evening, the Christian came and described how the little girl had tricked him.

One day the peasant's wife went to the village, and came back full of joy to tell us that the Russians were almost there. We could not believe this, but a few days later we persuaded ourselves that it was true. The Russians had arrived in the village. We came out of the hiding place and went to the village. During the first few days after leaving our hiding place it was difficult for me to walk. Later we left the village and went to Kovno.

Central Historical Commission, File No. 1800

# 2

# MY EXPERIENCES DURING THE WAR

By Ella Griliches

From the Series of Children's Work
published by the Munich Historical Commission
in the Journal Series *Fun Letzen Khurben*, Vol. 9, 1948

I was born on 8 July 1933 in Kovno. My father was a leather worker. In Kovno he worked in a tobacco factory, 'Ziv', which belonged to our family.

At the age of four I began to attend kindergarten in the real school. When I finished the first grade in preparatory school, the Russians arrived in Kovno and then I entered a Lithuanian school. After about one year, the Germans arrived. They murdered Jews in the streets; we were not allowed to walk on the pavements. We were told to wear a yellow patch. A month or two later the Jews were expelled from their houses and were sent to the ghetto. A few days later the Germans came into the ghetto and looted goods in the homes, and demanded that silver, gold, money and other things must be surrendered. The Germans entered our house and took watches and other valuable items.

During the great Aktion we had to stand outdoors for a whole day. At midday we were selected. We were fortunately sent to the good side. My father worked in the Committee, and my mother in a work kommando. At one time she worked in delousing – a week on night shift and a week on day shift.

I remember that one day we hid in the attic. The Ukrainians caught the Jews in order to send them to Estonia.

Once, during a winter night, my mother and my father took me to the gate. A car stood there and the Jewish policemen ordered us to push the car. While they were pushing the car, I and my mother left the ghetto. There a Christian boy was waiting for me, and he led me to his home in a street near the cathedral. I remained there for two days. While I was at the Christian home my mother came and took me to the Kovno Christian Children's Home. I was there for two or three days. I was presented as a Russian child because I had a good command of Russian. After this a farmer came and took me to a children's home in a village, Tamoshave, near Ukshta-Dvarim. There I worked together with all the children, scraping potatoes and working in the field. The children did not know that I was a Jewish child. But the adults there knew that I was a Jewish child. There were other Jewish girls there, younger than me. I recognised this from their faces. They did not know that I was a Jewish child, and this was not spoken about.

When the Russians arrived I still remained in the orphanage. My mother and father had been sent to lines [of people] when the Jews were taken from the ghetto to the train. When the Russians also came to Kovno, my aunt asked a Jewish acquaintance, Levin, who lived near the orphanage, to pick me up. His sisters came to pick me up. I lived with them for three weeks; then they took me to Kovno.

When the war ended, Jews came to Kovno from the camps. From them I found out that my father had died in Dachau and my mother died in the camp, Stutthof. My brother survived in Dachau. My aunt took me to my uncle, Solly Ziv, in Munich. I met my brother in Munich, and about a year later he went to Eretz Israel.

# 3

# MY EXPERIENCES DURING THE WAR

By Fania Olitzki

From the Series of Children's Work
published by the Munich Historical Commission
in the Journal Series *Fun Letzten Khurben*, Vol. 8, 1948

I was born on 1 February 1932 in Kovno. My parents owned a tobacco business and were also partners in the tobacco factory 'Ziv'. Up to the outbreak of war I had completed two classes in the Volkschule. When the Germans entered Kovno I lived with only my mother. The Jews dared not appear in the street; and my mother would hide me in our house at Lukshio Street, number 4. In the ghetto my mother would go to work and I would remain alone at home, and I would wait until my mother would return and bring something to eat. In the ghetto I would also hide myself from the Germans.

During the Estonian Aktion my mother was very ill and lay in bed. The people dragged themselves and their baggage to the ordained meeting place. The place was nearby the Department of Work. When the people were counted it was revealed that some were missing, so they went out and continually captured more people. At that moment I hid myself in a stable. Hearing a shot, I left the stable because I had left my mother alone. Right then the Aktion ended. They had captured the required number of people.

I went to the ORT school every morning. One day, at the end of March 1944, I went to school. Everyone from the ghetto was at work, either in the town with the kommandos or at the aerodrome, or in the factories. Suddenly, SS vehicles were driven in and they encircled the whole ghetto.

In school I heard that children and the elderly were being taken away. At that moment I jumped out of the window and ran home. My mother was away at work, but our neighbours were at our home. One hour passed, then two hours, and a Ukrainian entered and he said that I must accompany him. As much as I begged him to leave me, it did not help. Then one of our neighbours, Broyer, offered him a gold 10 rouble piece, but the Ukrainian did not want to leave me. Then Broyer showed him my mother's wrist watch which was a very beautiful one and looked like a bracelet. This did appeal to him. He took the gold and the watch, but he said that he had to take me with him. The Ukrainian took me to Krikshtshiokaytshiv Street, Number 91. Black vehicles with tinted windows were there, and music was playing so that the screams would not be heard. When the Ukrainian brought me to the vehicle, it drove away. A new lot of children arrived, and at that moment the Ukrainian gave me a wink to signal that I should run away. This is how I remained alive after the Children's Aktion.

A decree was announced in July 1944, that everyone must leave the ghetto and come to the assembly place where we would begin a march. We were in a bunker. There were a lot of people in the bunker; there was no air to breathe. There were children in the hiding place who were restless. There was a moment when a father wanted to choke a child. We lived with the hope that the Russians would soon arrive. It was impossible to remain in the bunker, and on the ninth day Kommandant Geke and his SS men discovered us and ordered us to get out. As they were driving us out, the ghetto was in flames, people were lying wounded, or murdered.

From this place they took away the children, myself among them. My mother gave the guard gold, and in a little while he brought me back to my mother, and then they lined us up to go to the train. They took us to Stutthof, 35 kilometres from Danzig. At night the men were taken away for delousing. The women were taken the following day. They took our money from us, removed our clothing and dressed us in camp clothes. They chased us to the barracks. After rollcall we were given coffee and a little piece of bread with margarine. On the first night we slept on the floor. Early in the morning we heard a bell, then we were chased into the courtyard. It was still dark and in addition very cold. We stood on our feet until 10 or 11 o'clock in the morning. They kept on counting us and finally we received a little bowl of soup. It was a happy moment when we could go back into our barrack, Number Five, and stretch out our frozen feet. At two o'clock during the day, the same scenario took place, also until six in the evening.

After we arrived in Stutthof there was a very large selection. All the women with small children were placed aside and they were sent to Auschwitz. When my mother saw that they were also taking women with older children, she winked at me and we slipped away between the barracks until we came to the morgue where the dead lay. My mother told me to lie down amongst the corpses, and she tore off a piece from her shirt and covered my face, and around me and on top of me she threw a mound of corpses. She told me not to move, and in case she did not return, I should not dare to climb out. I lay like this for 24 hours. When it became quieter in the camp, my mother returned and took me outside. The following day a German woman overseer noticed that a piece of cloth had been torn off my mother's shirt; so she started shouting that my mother was spoiling state-owned goods. For this, my mother had to stand for five hours with her hands held high.

We did not go to work. The day passed with rollcalls. Whenever a transport of Jews arrived, we were driven out of the barracks, lined up with the new arrivals, and then they would begin a selection. Most of the transports arrived at night. The alarm woke us even in the middle of the night, and we were driven out to the rollcall. We would stand until seven in the morning. Then they would give us a little bit of coffee and chase us back into the barrack. We would sleep, but it was crowded and filthy and very noisy. At about 12 o'clock a whistle was blown and we knew that a selection would take place. There was great panic. I was taken many times but my mother would always save me. My mother received many beatings for her attempts to pull me out. My mother knew about every corner around the crematoria in Stutthof itself. It was not just once that, in the last moments before the gassing, that she pulled me out.

Later, when I was working in the hospital, I and all the other people there did not have to attend the *appel*. I have to thank the lady doctor Kaplan-Malk for my being taken to work in the hospital.

The bombing raids started. Then they would charge the wire fence with a high electric voltage so that no one would be able to escape. We had to lie in the barracks. The kapos and the Jewish overseers would hide themselves in the bunkers. It was three o'clock in the day when a bomb fell onto our hospital. There were many dead. I was also in the barrack but I was in a different corner. In the camp, where the men had been, many bombs fell and we heard the sound only from the distance. We did not know what actually happened there. One day the Kommandant gave an order for us to leave the camp. Whoever was able to walk should go, and whoever was not would remain in the camp. The lager [camp]would soon be destroyed, he said. There was great panic and in the tumult mothers left their own children who were weak. I was also very weak but my mother would not leave me and dragged me with her for the whole journey. My mother's feet were very swollen and she was very weak because she was recovering from typhus.

On 24 April 1945, we were led out of Stutthof and taken to a field. It was after a big downpour and we were told to lie in the mud and to go to sleep. Early in the morning we were put on a ship. We sailed all day. Then, under terrible conditions, we arrived at a harbour. A bombing raid started and we were all chased into a forest. We sat under a baking sun until evening. Later we were chased to another place. After this we were driven onto another ship. We sailed for nine days. I saw only the heavens and water. People were packed together. We were three children in all. Every morning many dead were thrown into the sea. During the whole time we were given food only once. On day nine the SS personnel left us and fled. We remained alone at sea. There were Norwegian prisoners on the ship with us. The ship was small and old and now without a crew it had begun to sink. The Norwegians took over the running of the ship and helped us to save ourselves. Finally we saw land. Two Norwegians sprang into the water and they brought two small boats from the shore and began to transfer people. Those that landed were hungry. Nearby there was a village so people went to the houses to ask for bread. Germans in the village announced that Jews were running around in the village. So the SS arrived with machine guns and started to shoot at the ship. People began to run away like flies. Then they gave an order that everyone had to jump into the water. Those who chose to remain on the ship would be shot. Whoever could jump into the water did so, and whoever was unable to do so met his death. There were about 400 victims. My mother jumped down and stood up to her middle in the water. She begged me to also jump. And I did it. Then they lined us up in rows and led us to Neustadt. As we arrived an aerial attack began. Even so the guards said that they were taking us to our death. But at that moment the British arrived. It was 3 May at about two thirty in the afternoon.

Central Historical Commission, File No. 1890

# 4

# MY EXPERIENCES DURING THE WAR

By Arieh Milch

From the Series of Children's Work Collected by the Trades School in Aschau. Published by the Munich Historical Commission in the Journal Series *Fun Letzten Khurben*, Vol. 3, 1946

These are the names of my parents: my father, Abraham, my mother Etel, surname Lerer. I was born in the town of Pidhaisi in the Tarnopol Oblast of Western Ukraine on 25 June 1932. The outbreak of World War II prevented me from completing more than three classes, two in Ukrainian and one in Yiddish. Then in 1939 the Russians came to us, so we moved to the town of Mikolince. We lived there until the Germans came. The Germans came to us on 4 July 1941, and on 8 July 1941 the Germans killed my mother. After the death of my mother we lived with a good friend for a short time and then we returned to our town. When we arrived we discovered that the Germans had already formed a Judenrat which was to be the organisation linking them and the Jews. The people of the town forced father to become part of the Judenrat. They formed a Jewish police force which was called the Security Service. They were used by the Germans, more than once, as convenient tools to carry out various gruesome acts against the Jews. During the period of so-called 'lapankes' [abductions] the largest group of participants were the Ukrainian police and the Volks Deutschen (Poles). The men were in danger. People built hiding places. On the morning of the Day of Atonement [Yom Kippur], on 21 September 1942, the Gestapo and SS men came to us and carried out a pogrom. At the last moment I looked through the front window of our house and I saw an SS man with his rifle on his shoulder guarding a group of people. On the sides of the people there were two SS men with revolvers in their hands. I immediately went into our bunker. The pogrom lasted a whole day during which 1,500 people were murdered. We were choking in our bunker all day without water and without air. In the evening we left the bunker. The town was deserted; the people had been taken away to Belzec [extermination camp]. Life carried on but with this difference – orphaned children remained. On 30 October 1942, the second pogrom took place in our town. On this day also 1,500 Jews were killed. My father was among those killed. After this pogrom we stayed with our uncle.

After the second pogrom the Germans gathered together people from the area and formed a ghetto in our town. In the ghetto conditions were terrible. Ten people lived in a small room. Typhus spread and my brother became ill. The whole ghetto was overcome by frantic fear.[57] Night after night people would stand at their windows to see if the German murderers were coming again.

On 17 April 1943, at night, I left the ghetto together with my brother and uncle and went to hide with a gentile. Initially it was good for us there, but later it got worse. The gentile brought us newspapers. We read that the Red Army was advancing. We began to have hope again. Early on 6 June 1943, the gentile came to us and said that the ghetto was being besieged. The last annihilation pogrom was then carried out. The Germans assembled the people, took them behind the town, and shot them. To the remaining people who were in hiding, they announced that they should emerge and that they could take with them only the most necessary possessions, and that they would be transferred to the Tarnopol ghetto.[58] When they went out to the back of the town, Gestapo men (who were hiding) sprang out from among the crops. There graves had already been prepared and the people were all shot. The town became 'Judenfrei' [free of Jews]. The houses were ransacked and then destroyed. We shed tears but again began to live with hope. The Red Army was advancing. They conquered town after town. Their units were already fighting in Tarnopol, 70 kilometres from us. The gentile wanted to inform the German murderers about us. But the Reds

---

57  During epidemics the Germans would destroy the whole ghetto.
58  In order to deceive the Jews in hiding, the Gestapo, after the big Aktions, would announce that there would be no more Aktions; those who would appear of their own free will would be sent away to work. See *Fun Letzten Khurben*, No. 2, 'Nazi Word of Honour'.

were already in our town so he let us live. At last the bright hour arrived. The Soviet advance troops were in our town. It was on 28 March 1944. After 52 weeks of being locked in a cellar, for the first time we left the dark grave and breathed the air into our thirsty lungs, which made us feel drunk with its freshness, and indicated to us that we were free at last. We were rewarded for this with being named the few surviving orphans from the Polish Jewish Community.

Central Historical Commission, No. 159/301

# 5

# MY EXPERIENCES DURING THE WAR

By Yaakov Levin

From the Series of Children's Work
Collected by the Munich Historical Commission.
Published by the Munich Historical Commission
in the Journal Series *Fun Letzten Khurben*, Vol. 5, 1947

## Kovno Ghetto – Auschwitz – March to the Tyrol

I was born on 19.2.1932 in Kovno. My parents owned a factory and a knitwear business. For three years I studied in a Hebrew school and thereafter in a Yiddish school, until the Germans entered our town in 1941. They divided Slobodke, a suburb of Kovno, into several areas, and formed a ghetto. Everyone had to move into the ghetto. The ghetto was surrounded by barbed wire; Lithuanians and Germans guarded it. The ghetto was divided into two sections (a small ghetto and a large ghetto) because there was a highway in the centre. They built a wooden bridge to link the two parts.

In the small ghetto we were allocated a room measuring 10 square metres, to accommodate four people. One day the Germans came and carried out a search. They took away the better furniture, crockery, gold and so forth. In addition they shot a number of Jews. They then distributed 'Yarden passes' to all tradesmen (Yarden was the Kommandant of the ghetto at that time). Thereafter they liquidated the small ghetto.[59]

---

59    1 October 1941.

The liquidation took place in the following way: in the morning they ordered all the Jews in the small ghetto to assemble in the marketplace. From our house we passed by a hospital which housed the Jewish sick. At the hospital Jews were digging graves and Germans guarded them with machine guns. We thought that they were going to shoot us there, but the Germans chased us to the marketplace. There were already Germans with machine guns and rifles at the marketplace. We were placed in groups, and in family units; each group had to pass by a German control point. Those who possessed Yarden-passes were sent to the large ghetto. Those who did not have Yarden-passes were gathered together and told that they would be taken to dig potatoes. While crossing the bridge we saw that the hospital was burning. Later we were told that all those Jews who were assembled together were shot in the 9th Fort.

Some time later there was again an Aktion in which 12,000 men were taken away.[60] The young and healthy were sent to the right, back to the ghetto. The old, the weak and the children were sent to the left. My father and brother were young and healthy, so we returned to the ghetto. Those people who were sent to the left were shot in the 9th Fort. Workshops were formed in the ghetto. My parents and brother were taken to work in the factories. I was being taught in a Trades School to become a joiner. Early one morning my mother woke me, grabbed me and we ran to the workshop where my father worked. As we were leaving the house a car arrived. In the car sat the Jewish Elder, Liftzer, together with a German who told him to announce through a public hailer: 'All Jews must remain in their houses, and those who do not do so will be shot'. We ran again. There was panic in the streets; everyone was running to and fro. We ran until we came to the factory. We were allowed into a bunker. There were many people in the bunker. We lay there for two days in two rooms in which there were 180 people, without water, without food and without air. We went out on the third day, and we learned that there had been a children's Aktion in which they took away many children and the elderly.[61] Within a short time the ghetto was evacuated.[62] We once again hid in the bunker. My parents and I entered the bunker; but my brother was unable to join us because he had to work. It was suffocating and a very tight fit. It was uncomfortably hot and everyone had to remove their clothes. We lay there for 24 hours until

---

60  The 'Big Aktion' in Kovno, 28 October 1941.
61  This was the Aktion against children, the aged and the sick, 21–28 March 1941.
62  8–14 July 1944.

the Germans discovered us. They entered the cellar and began to shout: 'Everyone out!' But no one responded. So they threw a hand grenade inside and the Jew Shulman was lightly wounded. Everyone began to shout: 'We are coming out!' My mother opened a side exit, but the Germans were standing there too. They led us out, naked, because in the bunker it was so hot and dark that no one could find their clothes. I went out in bathing trunks. My mother gave me a long coat. They lined us up in twos. We thought that they were going to shoot us, and a little girl of six or seven years of age started to beg the German: 'Dear Sir, don't shoot me, my two sisters were shot yesterday'. The German started to look closely at her and said: 'Why do you think I will shoot you?' And he told her to carry on. They took us to a place where all the Jews from the ghetto were lying. We lay there for a day and a night. At dawn they began to lead us to the railway line. Many attempted to run away, but they were immediately shot. We walked for a few hours until we arrived at the railway. There they divided us up and placed us in wagons, 80 to a wagon. They gave us bread and locked us in the wagon. In a few minutes we began to travel. Another group left with a second transport. We travelled for two days until we arrived at a station, Tiegenhof (near Stutthof). There they separated the women from the men. The women were placed in a smaller train and sent to the camp Stutthof. The men were again locked in the wagons. Suddenly the second transport arrived where I met my brother. The women were sent off to the camp and the men were sent over to our group. In the afternoon we travelled further. We travelled for three days until we arrived at Landsberg Am Lech [in south-western Bavaria, Germany]. They unloaded us from the wagons and sent us to Camp 1. They confined us and took away our possessions. They put us in a cell, 20 men to each cell. We had to get up at six o'clock in the morning every day for the *appel* (rollcall). One day, during the *appel*, all the children were registered. On the following day, 131 children were separated from the adults and loaded onto a truck. A number remained because there was no room in the vehicle. We travelled for an hour until we arrived in Dachau camp.

    When we arrived in Dachau we were completely soaked by rain. So they took us to the heating room of the baths so that we should dry out. We thought that they wanted to burn us; so we started to shout that we wanted to get out, we didn't want to warm ourselves. After we had showered we were placed in a block where we were kept locked up for 10 days.

    One morning we were sent to the railway station. We were loaded onto three freight wagons. There were two soldiers in every wagon. At some of the stations we were allowed out of the wagons, and we noticed that placards were stuck onto the wagons, where the word 'Auschwitz' was written. We were given a loaf of bread to share between three men. At one of the stations a railway official told us that we were being sent to be burned. During the rest of the journey panic engulfed us. In our wagon we attempted to persuade the soldiers not to notice should we would begin to jump out of the little window of the wagon. Only two of the fellows had jumped out, because we noticed how one of them, after jumping out, was left lying by the railway line. After seeing this, an older man did not allow any more of us to jump.[63]

In the middle of the night we arrived at Auschwitz where we were placed in a guarded barrack. In the morning we were taken to the shower. After we had showered, we were given civilian clothes. On the shoulder and on the sides of the trousers there were striped patches.

We were given some soup to eat. After we had eaten we were sent to a quarantine camp. In that camp we were given a loaf of bread to share among four people and a little soup made from turnips. We slept on three hard planks. The narrowness of the planks was terrible. We lay pressed together like herrings in a barrel.

A few days after our arrival at Auschwitz an epidemic of measles and scarlet fever broke out among us. All of those from our barrack were transferred to a second barrack where we were kept locked in. The sick were isolated in another barrack. During the 'Days of Awe' (Yamim Noraim),[64] everyone in our barrack was told to get out and to go to the *appel-platz* where Dr Til carried out a 'selection'. He said that the 'cripples' amongst the older people must be registered. Children up to the age of 13 were also registered. After rollcall we returned to our barrack. Half an hour later all the registered people in our barrack were removed. We also saw that the sick from the isolation ward were taken out of their barrack. Altogether about 80 children, dressed only in shirts, and barefoot, were taken out of the camp. It was said that they were being taken to be burned. We really did not see them again.

After a short while another selection took place amongst the children. Those children who were a metre and a half tall were taken out of the barrack. Those shorter than this height were left in the barrack. Dr Mengele

---

63    See *Fun Letzten Khurben*, No. 4, p. 80.
64    Ten days between Rosh Hashanah and Yom Kippur, a period of introspection for Jews when they should ask forgiveness for any harm which they may have caused.

carried out the selection. In the meantime a military man appeared; he spoke to the doctor about something and the selection was interrupted. Nothing happened to anyone. After the selection we were allowed out of the barracks and we were taken to unload potatoes from the wagons. A few weeks later we were transferred to a work camp in Auschwitz proper, in Block 29. There we worked at various jobs.

In the children's block, 29, we were not badly treated and we also had enough to eat. A German Block Elder was our overseer. He was a political prisoner. We wore the same clothes and underwear that we had received when we arrived in the camp. We were often taken to the showers.

In winter, at the end of 1944, the Russian Front moved closer. The Germans started to evacuate people from the camp. The whole camp left by foot. The children marched in front. When we had covered 50 kilometres we, the children, started to shout that we were tired and could not continue any further. We were taken along the highway through villages to Althammer camp,[65] which was situated at the back of a village. In the camp we came across about 100 Jews who were building the camp. We were there for about two weeks. Every night we could hear the shooting from the Front and we also saw the fires. The food situation was very bad. The German guards soon left and armed German civilians moved around the camp.

When we once invaded the soldiers' kitchen which had already been abandoned by them, the German civilians saw this. Using the telephone they contacted the SS men from the main town. They came to the camp fully armed. They conducted rollcall, counted the people, and early the following morning they took us out. In the afternoon we arrived at a railway station where they loaded us into freight wagons. We were 90 children and they pushed us into one wagon.

On the same day Russian aeroplanes attacked our train with machine guns. There were eight dead in our wagon. Amongst these dead friends there was one Lithuanian, Chaim Arke, 14 years old. The other dead were from Poland. A boy, Shagan, from Kovno was wounded in the head. The military personnel were the first to give aid to the wounded. The Wehrmacht took Shagan away from us. I do not know what happened to him. There was only one killed in the other wagons. Our wagon suffered the most from the attack because it was near the engine which the

---

65   In September 1944, Althammer labour camp was established by the Germans as a sub-camp of Auschwitz. It was located in the town of Stara Kuznia and the first group of Jewish prisoners were transferred from Auschwitz to Althammer in Sptember 1944.

aeroplanes targeted. Military transport stood not far from us. The attack on them was much worse and there were many dead soldiers.

We travelled for a long time on the train. We arrived in Mauthausen camp on a rainy day. After we were showered, we were led into a barrack and we were left without anything to do. Food was very meagre. Later all the Jews from the Mauthausen main camp were transferred to the tent camp[66] where we came across Hungarian Jews who had previously worked at the Front digging trenches. In this camp, a boy of 14 or 15, from Aschmene ghetto, died.

The Americans were approaching Mauthausen. Only the Jews were being evacuated and we were sent by foot along the road which led to the city of Wels in [upper] Austria. On the way, during the first night we slept near a Wehrmacht camp. On the second night, near an SS camp in an open field. During the day we bypassed Wels, and at night we slept in an open field. We eventually stopped in a forest camp, three kilometres from Wels, and we remained there for two weeks. We were terribly hungry and filthy and full of lice. Hundreds of people died, mostly Hungarian Jews. However, one day we were given food by the Red Cross.

On a day in May we heard isolated shots. In the evening an American Jeep with several American soldiers arrived, but they left immediately after. Right away Jews invaded the food warehouses. There we encountered German soldiers who had been helping themselves to food. They then wanted to get out of the warehouse [where the food was kept]. However, at the same time the Jews tore at the doors in order to enter, and they blocked the exit for the soldiers' escape. The German soldiers began beating the Jews with rifle-butts. The Jews then grabbed their rifles and the Germans fled. The Hungarian Jews then expropriated the guns, and shot into the air throughout the night. We took over the whole warehouse of food.

That night we slept in the camp. However, in the early hours of the morning we left for Wels. On the way we went to houses where we asked the Germans [civilians] for food which they gave us. We spent one night in Wels. All the prisoners there were Jews. The following day the Americans gathered all the prisoners and took them in vehicles to the Camp

---

66   East-northeast of the main camp was the so-called tent camp, which consisted of 14 large tents with a total inner surface of 6,200 square yards. The camp authorities erected it in the autumn of 1944 to accommodate large groups of prisoners evacuated from concentration camps and forced-labour camps in the East. In the winter of 1945, the overwhelming majority of inmates in the so-called tent camp were Hungarian and Polish Jews.

Herrsching aerodrome. There we waited for a long time, but eventually they took us to a town near Linz. There we met many Jews. Soldiers from the Jewish Brigade arrived in the town and began taking us to Israel [i.e. the British Mandate of Palestine prior to May 1948]. I too went with them, but while travelling through Salzburg I suddenly saw my older brother who already knew that I was alive and had come to look for me. He told me that our father and he worked together in a flax warehouse in Munich. He and I travelled to join our father.

A few months later, our mother, who barely a year before this was separated from us in Stutthof camp, joined us in Munich.

Central Historical Commission, No. 948/1047

# 6

# MY EXPERIENCES DURING THE WAR

By Genia Shurtz

From the Series of Children's Work
Collected by the Munich Historical Commission.
Published by the Munich Historical Commission
in the Journal Series *Fun Letzten Khurben*, Vol. 10, 1948

I, Genia Shurtz, was born in the town of Podhaitze[67] in 1932. In 1941, when I was nine years old, the Germans arrived in our town. They did not conduct themselves too badly for the first few days. The Ukrainians, however, organised a police force and treated the Jews shockingly; they dragged all and sundry among the Jews to do the most strenuous work; they beat and killed and just laughed. But this did not last for long; within a week the Germans themselves took over.

Our suffering was indescribable. I remember one day when I was walking with my brother, they took him from me. I did not know where to, and I screamed out after him to run away. He listened to me and he escaped. The Germans shot at him. He hid himself in a stable. They asked me in which direction he had run, and I pointed in the opposite direction to the one he had chosen. One of them saw that I had deceived him, so he hit me in the face with his whip and I bled profusely. I will always remember this, the way in which my blood spurted from my face onto the wall.

---

67  Podhaitze (Podhajce, Podhaitsy) was located in the Polish province of Tarnopol.

But that was not the worst. After two weeks of hard labour and in fear, the Jews were instructed by the Germans to establish a police force which then carried out each order that they received from the Gestapo. As a reward the Gestapo promised them that they would remain alive and nothing would happen to them. It was terrible for us to be caught by our own Jews in order to be sent to labour camps and so on. In this way a year passed by.

After one year an order was given that all the Jews should assemble in one street which was then called the ghetto. It was dreadfully cramped with 10 people living in one room. Many people died from a typhus outbreak. The Germans would come to inspect the ghetto and would shoot anyone who was sick in his bed. I was very frightened because we had a number of sick people with us, among them my mother and father. When I saw how my mother became weak from hunger, I sneaked out of the ghetto in order to buy something. I had already bought some food when, on the way back, I recognised my former Ukrainian school friends. They beat me until they drew blood. I did not let go of the bread because I knew that I could save my mother with it. I arrived home all bloody and gave my mother a bite to eat.

Our house was inside the ghetto area. We owned a mill. My father made a plan for a bunker. After two weeks of hard work by all the 50 people who lived together with us, the bunker was ready. The bunker frequently saved the men from being taken captive and sent to the camps. Our bunker was not only the best in the town but in the whole district. The Germans dug up the whole house more than once. They were obsessed with finding the bunker, but they did not succeed. Also our Jewish police whose lives were dependent on finding the bunker, did not manage to do so. They promised that they would not take the men to the camps, if we would only tell them the whereabouts of the bunker. But we said nothing, because whatever they told us were lies. We went through a very bad period until Yom Kippur. Prayers were taking place at our home. That day I went out into the street where I waited for my friend who was coming over to me. I saw her from a distance, but she started running home. When I looked I saw that she lay there, shot. I heard the screaming of mothers who were searching for their children. I immediately ran into my home and said: 'Run to the bunker!' They ceased praying right away and ran into the bunker. That night and all the next day we heard shouts and the sound of vehicles. In the morning we went out into the street; blood had flowed in the whole ghetto. Four thousand Jews were taken to Belzec. This was the first pogrom in our town.

From that day on we stood guard day and night. We guarded the bunker for two months. I and another girl used to stand in the attic from where we saw that the whole ghetto was lit by floodlights. We understood that they were preparing for a pogrom. We quickly woke everyone from their beds. Everyone ran in their nightwear. My grandfather, who could no longer bear to look, said to me: 'I will not go into the bunker, I don't want to live any longer'. I begged him to go. But at that moment the Germans began to bang on the door. I ran down but he remained. In the bunker a child who had sat on my knee was being stifled; it cried, so someone put a rag into its mouth. After 24 hours the Aktion came to an end, and I saw that the child was dead. I almost went crazy from fright. However, I got used to this too.

During the second Aktion 2,000 Jews were shot in a trench behind the town.

After some time the third Aktion took place. All of us again stayed together. After the Aktion we came out and it was completely different from the time after the last Aktion. The ghetto was surrounded by 'kubaner' [they were Russian prisoners who helped to kill the Jews]. An order was issued immediately that after 24 hours there should not be even one Jew remaining in the ghetto. We asked the 'kubaner' where we could go. They replied: 'It is not our concern, and if a Jew is found in the ghetto after 24 hours, he will be shot'. We saw that they wanted to shoot everyone.

About 600 people remained in the ghetto. Everyone ran about wildly, each one saw death in front of him. We counted the hours till death. People tried to bribe the guards but it did not succeed. Even when we did bribe the guards we saw that they drew knives with which to stab us. So we saw that there was no other way but to wait for death. Waiting for death is the worst time in life. People lost their sanity. My friends ran wildly in the street. Blood just flowed. People poisoned themselves. And whoever did not have some poison was the most unlucky. Very few people remained. People poisoned themselves, committed suicide, and stabbed themselves. We did not have any poison; we said goodbye and cried about having to end our lives. I remember the will to live in the children who parted from me was so powerful that we tore at the walls and could not imagine that in a little while we would have to go to our death.

I remember the discussion amongst the children. One said: 'It is so beautiful outside, but not for us'. The second one said that he wanted to be free just once in his life, and to eat until he was full and then to die. Another said, who knows if there is a second world and whether we would meet again? We agreed that as soon as they began to shoot us we should immediately think about meeting in the next world. This is how we talked the whole night through until the morning.

In the morning Germans came into the ghetto and issued an order that at 11 o'clock that morning all the Jews must gather in the assembly place and they would be taken to a ghetto where there were still Jews. We were momentarily happy in the hope that perhaps we would be freed. We were unable to go to the assembly place because my mother had broken a foot. She said to us, 'Children let's go into our bunker and stay there until we die, because in another ghetto we will still not remain alive'. We agreed with her, and the whole household also affirmed that they would stay in the bunker. We had only two hours grace. We started to bake round crackers in the kitchen. We had water in the bunker because there was a well in there. We immediately went down. We took everything possible to eat and the best things were spread out on the paved surface of the bunker.

About one hour later we heard a lot of shooting; the Germans had shot all the Jews whom they had deceived.

We remained that way in the bunker for two weeks. We were suffocating because we had little air. But later it became worse when the food and the water ran out. The pain was indescribable. Each one was almost dead. We tore at the walls and people cursed one another. Two young boys and my brother went out of the bunker. They quickly returned and said that there was not a single person in the ghetto, but the ghetto was still surrounded; they [the Germans] were guarding their provisions. Initially, they [the boys] brought down food, various bits and pieces which they had collected from the whole ghetto. And so we survived for another few days in the bunker.

When it seemed safe we all went outside to look for something to eat. We found flour and other dry goods which we decided to cook. When we had finished cooking, Germans arrived and began to bang on the door. In a flash we got into the bunker. They searched and searched but did not succeed in finding us.

One day my brother left the bunker and a German came across him. My brother did not run away from him because he wanted to say to the German that he should take us to be shot. The German wondered how we had managed to survive for such a long time, and he said that if we had held out for such a long time, he was not going to expose us. He told us to wait in the bunker until he returned and he would take us out of the bunker, and out of the ghetto. We waited for another two days. One night at 12 o'clock he returned and told us to divide ourselves into two groups, and to come to the ghetto fence, and at a signal from him, we should jump over the fence. We gave him a lot of money, gold and diamonds which he had not demanded. The first group went out and got through successfully. Our turn came. I remember that when we left the house, I was the first one and the whole group followed after me. In the meantime Germans arrived and we separated ourselves from the group. I started to run and they chased after me. I did not even look back for my parents, I just ran. I felt as if I was about to be caught but they soon stopped chasing me. I looked around and saw that they were now chasing the group and not me. I fell down and fainted. I came round when I felt a hard blow from a German. I thought that I was being captured. But the German thought that I was dead so he left me alone. I stood up and ran until I left the ghetto. I stopped and rested in a ruined Jewish home and there I met my father who had also succeeded in running away from the group. I was very happy that I was not alone. We started to run blindly. We sat down in a small forest and then I was reminded that we were without my mother and my brother. I did not want to go any further, I cried because I had run without them. A child's feeling for its mother arose in me. While sitting and crying we heard the sound of shooting and I started to scream: 'Mama they are shooting you!' and continued to shout, 'Mama!' I remember the terrible moment, but then I heard a voice from far away: 'Genia' (that is my name). I was so happy, like a person who has lost a mother and then she rises from the grave. From weakness I was unable to stand. So my father left me and followed the voice. It was in that way we all came together again. I could not believe that I still had a mother and a brother because I really could not take it all in. It could only be a miracle or a dream. They told us how they were saved. The Germans chased them so they returned to the bunker and they sat there hopelessly. But the German who had led us out returned to them and again led them out of the ghetto. My mother did not know where we were, but her heart drew her in the direction where we had gone. Everybody had gone into a small forest where there were already Jews who had obtained guns to use against the Germans. I will leave them [i.e. I will not tell their story] as I first want to finish telling about our experience.

We went into a field and remained there until nightfall. It rained heavily and we had to remain quiet in the grain field. We remained like that until dark. Later we decided to go to a gentile acquaintance. The gentile was previously a stranger to us. But he had seen us through the fence in the ghetto and he took a liking to us and said that if we should ever be in a hopeless situation, we should come to him, not all of us, only two. But after such experiences we decided not to part again, either we all live or we die together. We started to walk. Our clothes were wet from the rain. We struggled on for 10 kilometres until we arrived at the gentile's home. He took us up to an attic and gave us food and drink. The gentile was a young man, 24 years old. We were afraid of him but we had no choice. We gave him all our gold, money and possessions in the hope that he would keep us until the liberation. He dug a bunker in the stable. The bunker was so small that we had to sit one on top of another, but the only consolation was that we were together.

During the first few days he fed us, but later he said that two of us should remain, but two should leave. We got dressed and wanted to leave together. He looked at us and then did not let us go. However, he stopped feeding us. We started to experience hard times. It was hot, we were hungry and thirsty. The gentile had decided to starve us until we would die. Our suffering was indescribable. Once a day we received a tiny pot of food, no bread, no water, no change of clothes. As we became filthier the dirt began to affect us. This is how we lived for five months. We did not have any light. I remember that I found a small mirror. I looked in the mirror and and I began to cry and shout that this was not a human image. We could no longer bear this. I became sick and was no longer able to stand. On a frosty day my father and brother went out without the gentile knowing, and brought back food from other gentiles. One day I left a little piece of bread in the pot and my mother returned the pot to the gentile with the bread in it. When he saw the bread, he understood where we had obtained it. Furious, he started to choke my father. For us there was nothing to lose, and my mother ran up to him and started fighting with him. He loosened his grip and we started to shout at him to let us go, that he was worse than Hitler, that he wanted to get rid of us by death from starvation. From then on he improved a little. However, I was already sick and we looked like skeletons. We made an agreement that if one of us should die, then after liberation we would take revenge on the gentile and not let him live.

Nevertheless, after 10 difficult months of hunger, cold, thirst, dirt and sickness, the day came. On 28 March 1944, the gentile came in with the good news that the Russians had entered our town. We could not even rejoice immediately because we looked like ghosts from the other world. In this ravaged condition, they carried me for 10 kilometres into the town. I could no longer stand. To the present day, I have a 'memento' to remind me of the German murderers. When we entered the town we came across only individual Jews. From the people in our bunker only a young girl, our cousin, had survived. All the others were killed by Germans, Ukrainians and Poles. She was the only one left out of 600 people who were murdered by the Ukrainians. She crawled out of the grave [in which she had been buried alive] and remained alive. One could write a book about how she managed to remain alive. You can go grey from hearing how she survived.

The Russians soon retreated, and we followed them. We returned to our town, Podhaitze, in 1945. There was only one thing we could do to take some revenge: we erected a memorial on the grave of our innocent people.

I am now free in a camp in the American Zone, but the painful times are not yet over. The Jew still has to suffer. Unfortunately I do not have much education. I am now completing the sixth class in the Hebrew school. My goal and that of my parents and brother is to go to Eretz Israel to give our lives to our country.

Bad-Zalzschlirf, June 1948

# ADDENDUM

# Select Information Pertaining to the Testimonies

## Mielec

Mielic is a city in South Eastern Poland which had a flourishing economy prior to World War II. In 1936 a state-owned factory making aircraft chassis and also armaments was established. This single industrial enterprise was the backbone of Mielec's thriving economy. However, after the outbreak of World War II, the factory was occupied by the German invaders and was in their hands from 9 September 1939 to 6 August 1944. The Nazis increased the production of aircraft and armaments during the war producing bomber and fighter planes which were of prime importance to the Nazi war effort. The factories were staffed by slave labour, initially Jews from Mielec, but with the increase of airplane and armaments production, additional prisoners were brought from numerous other labour camps. They consisted of Jews from other regions, prisoners of war and political prisoners.

In 1942 most of the Jewish labourers were transported to death camps, but at the same time, hangars became the site of the mass murder of hundreds of Jews who were buried there. The Germans continued to benefit from the factory until 1944.

## Ninth Fort

In the 19th century, the Kaunus fortress in Lithuania was constructed as a stronghold against any enemy. It consisted of eight fortresses, with the 9th fort being added later. When the Soviet forces occupied Lithuania in 1940–1941, the 9th fort was used as a prison and as a way-station for prisoners being transported to gulags. It came to be known as the Fortress of Death. After the occupation of Lithuania by Nazi Germany in 1941, the 9th fort was used as a place of mass execution for Jews, and captured Soviet soldiers. The prisoners who were kept as slave labour were chained together at night to prevent any attempts at escape. At least 10,000 Jews were taken from Kovno ghetto and transported to the 9th Fort where they were massacred. Jewish slave labourers had to dig mass graves into which the dead and half dead were thrown. With the approach of the Soviets in 1944, the remaining Jews were forced by the Germans to exhume and and burn the buried corpses. This was an attempt by the Germans to obliterate all signs of the crimes which had taken place there. In 1944 the Germans liquidated the ghetto.

In October 1943, a Russian Jewish prisoner was brought to the fort, and he immediately started to plan an escape. He gathered together a band of men who agreed to take part in the plan which was to dig a tunnel beneath the subterannean structures of the fort. They carried the earth from their tunnelling in their pockets and later threw it in the killing pits. The prisoners copied a key to one of the underground storerooms which led to a tunnel which they extended. The daring plan was carried out despite many vicissitudes and the prisoners escaped on the 25 December 1943. This event was regarded as one of the most remarkable in the history of wartime mass escapes.

## Dubno – Hermann Friedrich Graebe

The testimony by Moishe Weisberg, "Life and Death of the Jews in Dubno", had a sequel after the end of the war when a labour contractor, a German civilian engineer by the name of Hermann Friedrich Graebe, gave two interviews to Allied investigators in Wiesbaden, Germany, about the liquidation of the ghetto in Dubno in October, 1942, and mass killings in Rovno in the same year. During the war, Graebe was in charge of very large engineering projects in the Ukraine for the Solingen Building Group, which erected buildings, bridges and railways for the German Army, using slave labour from ghettos in Rovno and Dubno. He tried to save as many of his workers as possible in Rovno, raising the ire of SS Sturmbannfuehrer Dr Puetz who commanded the Rovno Security Section. He put his own life in danger as he tried different schemes to prevent his Jewish slave labourers from being transported and then being slaughtered. He gave two testimonies on the 10th of November, 1945 at the Nuremberg Trials, about his experience when he witnessed both Aktions, but the most detailed and chilling was his description of the events of the 5th October 1942 when Einsatzgruppen, supported by Ukrainian guards and militia, herded ghetto Jews out of town and executed them with machine guns. He described at length the day of the murders and the appearance of the victims, but his brief narration of the killings by a single executioner was especially chilling:

"I looked for the man who did the shooting. He was an SS man who sat at the edge of the narrow end of the pit, his feet dangling into the pit. He had a tommy gun on his knees and he was smoking a cigarette." Graebe added: "I was surprised that I was not ordered away, but I saw that there were 2 or 3 postmen in uniform nearby."

Hermann Graebe was one of the very few German witnesses to atrocities to give testimonies to the Allies after the war. Because of his moral courage, he was placed on a death list created by SS survivors and had to be sent to America for his safety. In 1985, Douglas Huneke published his story, *The Moses of Rovno*. Graebe was acknowledged by Yad Vashem in Israel as one of the Righteous Among the Nations, an honorific given to non-Jews who saved Jews during the Holocaust despite putting themselves and their families in great danger.

## Dubno

Axel Freiherr von dem Bussche-Streithorst was not known to Hermann Graebe and yet his story is inextricably linked to the horrific massacre in Dubno. Born in 1919, von dem Bussche was nearly 2 metres tall, blond and blue-eyed, the ideal Nazi image of the Ubermensche. He came from a background of minor German nobility and joined the army in 1937 at the age of 18, the 9th Prussian Infantry Regiment, an elite unit whose motto was "justice, duty, self-esteem, courage".

In October, 1942, his regiment was ordered to provide assistance to the SS Einsatzgruppen which massacred the Jews of Dubno. After witnessing the horror of the Dubno catastrophe, von dem Bussche said that this event turned him against the personal oath of obedience which all soldiers swore to Hitler, contradicting as it did the motto of his regiment. He decided on a suicide mission to kill the Fuhrer. Chosen to model a new army uniform because of his fine physical appearance, von dem Bussche had to model the new uniform for Hitler whose approval was required. He planned to carry two hand grenades in the jacket pockets and to detonate them when he was near the Fuhrer. Two attempts were planned, but neither eventuated because, before they could take place, von dem Bussche was severely wounded in Russia where his leg had to be amputated. After the war Axel von dem Bussche became a diplomat in the West German government.

## White Russians

The term 'White Russian' refers to one of the factions that took part in the Russian Civil War, 1918–1922; this was a multi-party war which took place immediately after the Russian Revolution of 1917. Many different factions wished to determine the political future of Russia. The two largest combatant groups were the Red Army, fighting for the Bolsheviks, and the White Army, which favoured the cause of Czar Nicholas II. The White army was virulently anti-semitic as a natural outcome of the Czar's policy towards Jews.

During World War II anti-Jewish propaganda influenced sectors of the Soviet population, especially in the Ukraine, Byelorussia and the Baltic states. These states collaborated with the Germans in massacring Jews during the German occupation of these countries. However, the White Army was divided in its loyalties, with some forces fighting against the Allies and others fighting the Nazi forces.

## Joseph Schleifstein

Joseph Schleifstein, at the age of four, was the youngest person to have survived Buchenwald concentration camp. He is pictured on the cover, sitting on the running board of an UNRRA (United Nations Relief and Rehabilitation Administration) truck shortly after the liberation of the camp by American troops.

Joseph was born in 1941 in the Jewish ghetto of Sandomierz, Poland, during the German occupation. His parents, Israel and Esther, kept him hidden from the SS guards in a cellar; had he been detected, he would have been taken to his death in one of the Kinder (Children) transports. He and his father were sent to Buchenwald in January, 1943 while his mother was taken to Bergen-Belsen concentration camp. When they arrived in Buchenwald, his father managed to hide two and a half year old Joseph in a sack which contained Israel's leather crafting tools and some clothes. The little boy was told not to make a sound, and was covered up by the contents of the bag.

For some time, Joseph's presence in the camp went unnoticed by the German guards, and he was cared for by his father and two Communist prisoners, Antonin Kalina and his deputy Gustav Schiller. They saved many other children as well by placing them in Block 66, which became a children's block. Kalina, as a political prisoner, had certain privileges and was thus able to provide relatively good care for the boys.

Eventually the Germans became aware of Joseph but, fortunately, they took a liking to him, and treated him like a camp mascot, giving him little tasks to carry out.

On 12 April, 1945 Joseph and his father were liberated by the American army. Clothes for child survivors were in short supply, so UNRRA made little uniforms out of cut-down German ones. In the picture of Joseph sitting on the running board of the UNRRA truck he is wearing one of these outfits.

Eventually Joseph and Israel were reunited with Esther, and they later emigrated to the United States.

Joseph's story was the inspiration for Benigni's film, *Life is Beautiful*.

# BIBLIOGRAPHY

## Primary Sources

### Journals
Fun Letzten Khurben (From the Last Catastrophe), editions: 1 August 1946, 2 September 1946, 3 October 1946, 4 March 1947, 5 May 1947, 6 August 1947, 7 May 1948, 8 June 1948, 9 September 1948, 10 December 1948.

### Memoirs
Dror, Tamar. *A Green Parrot*. Sydney: Kitia Altman through Book House at Wild & Woolley, 1999.
Eilati, Shalom. *Crossing the River*. Translated by Vern Lenz. Tuscaloosa: University of Alabama Press, 2008.
Schwarz, Leo W. *The Redeemers: A Saga of the Years 1945–1952*. New York: Farrar, Strauss and Young, 1953.

## Secondary Sources
Abzug, Robert H. *Inside the Vicious Heart*. New York: Oxford University Press, 1987.
Aleksiun, Natalia. *Every Jew Witnessed History. Every Jew Ought to Write It Down. The Central Jewish Historical Commission in Poland, 1944–1947. Polin* Vol. 20, Liverpool University Press. (2007).
Bauer, Yehuda and Rotenstreich, Nathan (eds). *The Holocaust as Historical Experience*. New York: Holmes & Meier Publishers, Inc., 1981.
Bauer, Yehuda. *Flight and Rescue: Brichah*. Edited by Moshe Davis, Contemporary Jewish Civilization. New York: Random House, 1970.
Bauer, Yehuda. *The Jewish Emergence from Powerlessness*. Toronto: University of Toronto Press, 1979.
Bauer, Yehuda. *Out of the Ashes*. Oxford: Pergamon Press, 1989.
Baumel, Judith Tydor. 'The Politics of Spiritual Rehabilitation in the D Camps.' *Simon Wiesental Center Annual*, No. 6 (1989).
Berenbaum, Michael. *Witness to the Holocaust*. New York: HarperCollins Publishers Inc., 1997.
Berkowitz, Michael and Patt, Avinoam J. (eds). *'We Are Here': New Approaches to Jewish Displaced Persons in Postwar Germany*. Detroit: Wayne State University Press, 2010.
Brenner, Michael. *After the Holocaust*. Princeton: Princeton University Press. 1999.
Brenner, Michael. 'Displaced Persons and the Desire for a Jewish National Homeland'. In *Post-War Europe Refugees, Exile and Resettlement (1945–1950)*, edited by Dan Stone. Gale Digital Collection, 2007.
Cesarani, David. *Final Solution: The Fate of the Jews 1933–49*. London:Pan Macmillan, 2016.
Cohen, Boaz. *Bound to Remember – Bound to Remind: Holocaust Survivors and the Genesis of Holocaust Research*.International Conference; Beyond Camps and Forced Labour: Current international Research on Survivors of Nazi Persecution, 2003, London. Published by Secolo, Germany, 2005.

# Bibliography

Cohen, Boaz. 'Children's Holocaust: Children's Survivor Testimonies Published in *Fun Letzten Hurban*, Munich Historical Commission *1946*,' *Documentation and Education: Children's Holocaust Testimony Project of Bar-Ilan University*.

Cohen, Boaz. 'The Children's Voice: Postwar Collection of Testimonies from Child Survivors of the Holocaust.' *Holocaust and Genocide Studies*, 21, No. 1 (2007): 73–95.

Dawidowicz, Lucy. *From That Place and Time 1938–1947*. New York: W.W. Norton & Company, 1989.

Dawidowicz, Lucy. *The War against the Jews 1933–1945*. Tenth Anniversary Edition. New York: Penguin Books, 1975.

Dean, Carolyn J. *The Fragility of Empathy after the Holocaust*. Ithaca: Cornell University Press, 2004.

Gilbert, Martin. *The Boys: Triumph over Adversity*. London: HarperCollins, 1986.

Gilbert, Martin. *The Holocaust*. London: HarperCollins, 1987.

Gilbert, Martin. *The Holocaust: The Jewish Tragedy*. London: HarperCollins, 1986.

Gringauz, Samuel. 'Jewish Destiny as the DPs See It.' *Commentary*, 4, No. 6 (1947): 501–9.

Grobman, Alex. 'American Jewish Chaplains and the *Shearit Hapletah*: April–June 1945.' In *Simon Wiesental Center Annual*, edited by Henry Friedlander, Yisrael Gutman, Alex Grobman, Daniel Landes, Sybil Milton, Gerald Margolis, 89–111. Chappaqua: Rossel Books, 1984.

Grobman, Alex. *Rekindling the Flame: American Jewish Chaplains and the Survivors of European Jewry*. Detroit: Wayne State University Press, 1993.

Hartmann, Geoffrey. *The Longest Shadow: In the Aftermath of the Holocaust*. Bloomington: University of Indiana Press, 1997.

Hertzberg, Arthur. 'The First Encounter: Survivors and Americans in the Late 1940s.' In *Monna and Otto Weinmann Lecture Series*, edited by United States Holocaust Research Institute, United States, 1996.

Hilliard, Robert L. *Surviving the Americans: The Continued Struggle of the Jews after Liberation*. New York: Seven Stories Press, 1997.

Hilton, Laura June. 'Prisoners of Peace: Rebuilding Community, Identity and Nationality in Displaced Persons Camps in Germany, 1945–1952.' PhD thesis, Ohio State University, 2001.

Hoffman, Eva. *After Such Knowledge*. New York: Public Affairs, 2004.

Jokusch, Laura. '"Collect and Record. Help to Write the History of the Latest Destruction." Jewish Historical Commissions in Europe, 1943–1953.' Dissertation, New York University, 2007.

Jokusch, Laura. 'A Folk Monument to Our Destruction and Heroism: Jewish Historical Commissions in the Displaced Persons Camps of Germany, Austria and Italy.' In *'We Are Here': New Approaches to Jewish Displaced Persons in Postwar Germany*, edited by Avinoam J. Patt and Michael Berkowitz. Detroit: Wayne State University Press, 2010, pp. 31–73.

Klausner, Abraham J. *A Letter to My Children*. San Francisco: Holocaust Center of Northern California, 2002.

Klein, Kerwin Lee. 'On the Emergence of Memory in Historical Discourse.' *Representations*, 69, Winter (2000): 127–50.

Klemperer, Victor. *I Shall Bear Witness*. London: Weidenfeld and Nicolson, 1999.

Kochavi, Arieh. 'The Politics of Displaced Persons in Post-War Europe, 1945–1950.' *Post-War Europe: Refugees, Exile and Resettlement, 1945–1950* (2007), http:/www.tlemea.com/postwareurope/essay6.asp.

Kolinsky, Eva. *After the Holocaust*. London: Pimlico, 2004.

Konigseder, Angelika and Wetzel, Juliane. 'Displaced Persons, 1945–1950: The Social and Cultural Perspective.' In *Post-War Europe Refugees, Exile and Resettlement 1945–1950*, edited by Dan Stone. Gale Digital Collection, 2007.

Konigseder, Angelika and Wetzel, Juliane. *Waiting for Hope: Jewish Displaced Persons in Post-World War II Germany*. Translated by John A. Broadwin. Evanston: Northwestern University Press, 2001.

Kuznitz, Cecile Esther. 'Yivo.' In *The Yivo Encyclopaedia of Jews in Eastern Europe*. Yale University Press, 2008.

LaCapra, Dominick. 'History and Memory: In the Shadow of the Holocaust.' In *In the Shadow of the Holocaust*. New York: Cornell University Press, 1999, pp. 8–42.

LaCapra, Dominick. *Representing the Holocaust: History, Theory, Trauma*. Ithaca: Cornell University Press, 1994.

Langer, Lawrence A. *Holocaust Testimonies: The Ruins of Memory*. New Haven: Yale University, 1991.

Lipstadt, Deborah. *Beyond Belief*. New York: Macmillan, 1986.

Mankowitz, Zeev. 'The Affirmation of Life in She'erit Hapleita.' *Holocaust and Genocide Studies*, 5 (1990): 13–21.

Mankowitz, Zeev W. *Life between Memory and Hope*. Cambridge: Cambridge University Press, 2002.

Myers, Margaret L. 'Jewish Displaced Persons. Reconstructing Individual and Community in the US Zone of Occupied Germany.' *Leo Baeck Institute Year Book*, (1997): 303–24.

Ouzan, Francoise. 'Rebuilding Jewish Identities in Displaced Persons Camps in Germany 1945–1957.' *Bulletin du Centre de recherche francais de Jerusalem*, 14, Spring (2004): 98–111.

Pinson, Koppel S. 'Jewish Life in Liberated Germany: A Study of the Jewish DPs'. *Jewish Social Studies*, 9, No. 2 (April 1947): 101–26.

Portelli, Alessandro. 'The Peculiarities of Oral History.' *History Workshop Journal*, 12 (1981): 96–107.

Proceedings of the Sixth Yad Vashem International Historical Conference. *She'erit Hapletah*. Jerusalem: Yad Vashem, 1985.

Roskies, David G. (ed.). *The Literature of Destruction: Jewish Responses to Catastrophe*. New York: The Jewish Publication Society, 1989.

Sachar, Abram L. *The Redemption of the Unwanted*. New York: St Martin's/Marek, 1983.

Wajnryb, Ruth. *The Silence: How Tragedy Shapes Talk*. Crows Nest: Allen & Unwin, 2001.

Waxman, Zoe Vania. *Writing the Holocaust*. Oxford: Oxford University Press, 2006.

Wiesel, Elie. *Night*. Translated by Stella Rodway. New York: Hill and Wang, 1960.

Wyman, Mark. *Europe's Displaced Persons, 1945–1951*. Cranbury: Associated University Presses Inc., 1989.

Yablonka, Hanna. *Survivors of the Holocaust*. Translated by Ora Cummings. New York: New York University Press, 1999.

Yerushalmi, Yosef Hayim. *Zakhor*, The Samuel and Althea Stroum Lectures in Jewish Studies. Seattle: University of Washington Press, 1982.

Young, James E. *Writing and Rewriting the Holocaust*. Edited by Alvin Rosenfeld. Jewish Literature and Culture. Bloomington: Indiana University Press, 1988.

Zeitlin, Froma. 'New Soundings in Holocaust Literature: A Surplus of Memory.' In *Catastrophe and Meaning: The Holocaust and the Twentieth Century*. Edited by Moishe Postone and Eric Santner. Chicago, 2003, pp. 121, 173–208.

Lightning Source UK Ltd.
Milton Keynes UK
UKHW010619020420
361224UK00002B/25